FROM
BEAR ROCK
MOUNTAIN

THE LIFE AND TIMES OF A DENE
RESIDENTIAL SCHOOL SURVIVOR

Antoine Mountain

BRINDLE
AND GLASS

An imprint of TouchWood Editions
TOUCHWOODEDITIONS.COM

Brindle & Glass
An imprint of TouchWood Editions
TouchWoodEditions.com

The information in this book is true and complete to the best of the author's
knowledge. All recommendations are made without guarantee on the part of the
author or the publisher.

Edited by Rhonda Khronyk, Claire Philipson, and Warren Layberry
Book design by Colin Parks
Cover photograph © Nathalie Heiberg-Harrison
Photos by Antoine Mountain unless otherwise specified.

CATALOGUING DATA AVAILABLE FROM LIBRARY AND ARCHIVES CANADA
ISBN 9781927366806 (hardcover)
ISBN 9781927366813 (epub)
ISBN 9781927366882 (paperback)

TouchWood Editions gratefully acknowledges that the land on which we live
and work is within the traditional territories of the Lekwungen (Esquimalt and
Songhees), Malahat, Pacheedaht, Scia'new, T'Sou-ke and W̱SÁNEĆ (Pauquachin,
Tsartlip, Tsawout, Tseycum) peoples.

We acknowledge the financial support of the Government of Canada through
the Canada Book Fund and the Canada Council for the Arts, and of the province
of British Columbia through the British Columbia Arts Council and the Book
Publishing Tax Credit.

Printed and bound in Canada
23 22 21 20   2 3 4 5

To my sons, Michel Luke Fieh Bah Mountain and
Victor Lorne K'enah Hinderewih Mountain.

And to my ehseh—mahsi.

"If you have a dream, you must do something each day to make it come true. Once this vision comes true no one can take it away from you, for you alone worked to make it come true."

—PETER MOUNTAIN SR.

CONTENTS

FOREWORD

Antoine Mountain has been a storyteller since I first met him about forty years ago. He has always had an aura of timelessness about him. When he tells a story, he weaves it from yesterday into today, reverberating from the past to the present to the future, and this is what he has done in *From Bear Rock Mountain*. In writing his autobiography, Antoine has had to rediscover who he is as a First Nations person, and in doing this he has revisited the history of the First Nations peoples of the Americas, which he views through the lens of his own experience. This book is not a straight chronological narrative but follows the itinerant ramblings of his mind, much as a storyteller would relate multiple relevant strands of a story and then tie them back to the main story. Antoine allows himself to follow a stream of consciousness as the threads of each tale lead back to the main point and inform our understanding of his life and viewpoint.

Antoine's book is filled with musings, personal anecdotes, and memories reminding me of the book *Memories, Dreams, Reflections*, in which Carl Gustav Jung reviews his own life with insights gained.

Antoine's story is very personal and takes the reader along on his journey, almost as a confidante. He shares personal anecdotes and details in an intimate manner; he also relates his experiences to both his cultural teachings and directly to specific places, rooting his personal anecdotes to the land. He speaks of his travels with his elders and shares their wisdom with the reader. Bear Rock Mountain is truly a sacred real place, neither imaginary nor legendary, and when he speaks of the Dene hero Yamoria, he, too, is rooted in that land.

We begin to understand his residential school experiences and how they affected him in later life—how he recognized and fought his particular personal demons, which were a direct result of his experience of colonialist Canadian government policies and practices. He sees this as cultural genocide and relates it to the holocaust against the Jewish people of Europe during the Second World War.

Antoine also tells of his experiences at art school in Florence, Italy. There he saw the pinnacle of Western culture, yet he still remains true to himself. He is an artist who learned from Western culture, finding relevance in technique and methodology, and yet continues to express his culture through his art in ways that move us and help us to understand his experiences.

Antoine's voice is the genuine voice of a Dene man, artist, painter, and writer who is rooted to his land and his culture, who has experienced the worst that the Canadian government could do to him, and who views himself as a survivor of a cultural genocide. Antoine is an authentic knowledgeable carrier of his culture, and we are fortunate that, in telling his story, he has decided to share this much of it with us.

Diane Pugen
Associate Professor
Ontario College of Art and Design (OCAD) University
Toronto, Canada

One recurring dream...
The parrots of South America
can eat twenty-seven different poisons
toxic foods
    and then clay
    to digest the toxins
and still live

Like us Indians
in residential schools.

§

When I awaken...
From Bear Rock Mountain
reappears
both modern-day and ancient
drumbeats
to fend off
ignorance
and defeat.

Day by day.

Being Dene

"As I walked out the door toward the gate that would
lead to my freedom, I knew if I didn't leave my bitterness and hatred behind, I'd still be in prison."

—NELSON MANDELA
(QUOTED IN *Living History* BY HILLARY CLINTON)

"He (God) owes me answers to many questions."

— HOLOCAUST SURVIVOR AT AUSCHWITZ, 1985
(QUOTED IN *Explaining Hitler* BY RON ROSENBAUM)

When I first sought the advice of one of my editors, Bruce Valpy
at the *News/North* newspaper in the Northwest Territories, in
the spring of 2014 about writing my memoir, he mentioned that I
should keep my audience—to whom these writings are directed—
in mind because this would serve as a useful guide.

Up to then I had been writing A. Mountain View, my regular
column in *News/North*, for almost a decade. It did give me the
discipline for writing, yes, but more along the lines of commen-
tary—social, cultural, and otherwise—nothing of the soul-jarring
content I dared myself to face in writing a memoir, digging up them
ol' bones. Were they just best left buried someplace?

Yet again, I had been seriously thinking that I wanted to
dedicate something of my true Dene self to the children of future

generations, that they should know from a survivor's point of view what exactly took place at residential schools, both in Canada and in the United States. And more, what those schools intended, and ultimately failed, to accomplish: the cultural genocide of Indigenous Peoples. With all of that potential gravity in mind, I also wanted to avoid an outright political condemnation of the times we all went through, our collective history.

How can anyone blame the pages of time having turned, however written? Like it or not, this is a part of our rich communal uniqueness: First Nations and Euro-American. When I began to dig deeper into the ruins and lessons from other places and experiences, I could not help but think of this quote:

Yes, I thought about this. But nobody did anything. (I was) fifteen years old and had people with grown-up experience all around and nobody was doing anything. People change under some conditions. People asked me, "What did you learn?" and I think I'm only sure of one thing – nobody knows themselves.

The nice person on the street, you ask him, "Where is North Street?" and he goes with you half a block and shows you, and is nice and kind. That same person in a different situation could be the worst sadist.

Nobody knows themselves. All of us could be good people or bad people in these different situations.

Sometimes when somebody is really nice to me, I find myself thinking, "How will he be in *Sobibór?*"[1]

—POLISH JEWISH PRISONER TOIVI BLATT,
ON THE NAZI DEATH CAMPS

Although I am a survivor of the horrors of residential schools, I do not write this memoir as a victim. Though victims we were, seeing as how we innocents had no say in the matter. Given the extent of the internal damage left by residential schools, it is simply not possible for one person to be able to come to a place of such healing that it is possible to do something like write a memoir all by themself.

A good part of my healing journey began with learning about the reality of colonization and how I've experienced its effects first-hand. And much of this happened when I became involved in the Indian Brotherhood, which became known as the Dene Nation. I eventually began going to visit our southern Dineh relatives in Arizona in the early 1990s, and I continue to do so to this day. Theirs is a kind of stubborn resilience born of great suffering. As both the Dene and the Dineh know, part of any thriving future involves working with your country as it is and going from there while still holding on to your own ways.

So, no victim I.
Far from it.
Having survived a shipwreck
any ground becomes new land
every day a gift from Creator.

And neither do I write
as a Good Indian
saying pretty things all Mola
want to hear
to assuage their collective guilt.

One person who understood what I was trying to do more than most was the late Edwin Kalousuk, a fellow residential school survivor. Until his untimely death about a year after I began work on this book, Edwin gave me his unqualified help whenever I felt my wounded life to be just too much. Along with an immediate pronouncement for *From Bear Rock Mountain* ("It's already a bestseller, bro!"), he gave me all the right kinds of valuable information—hints on publishing and even the book launch—two days before his sudden passing on June 25, 2015. When I said a special prayer for him, I noted an eagle flying, and I saw a big heart in the burning braid of sweetgrass I held in his honour and memory.

§§§

With its programs, the Canadian government set out to undertake the outright cultural genocide of Indigenous Peoples. But it failed to take into account our strength, which is more than evident in the face of all that has happened since the first European ships touched ground on our Great Turtle Island. Those who hold outdated colonialist notions continue to try to reference a self-serving history written in such a way that avoids the treacherous waters of historical fact. As a survivor of this colonialist attempt at cultural assimilation, I would, for the most part, agree with Vera Laska, a Czechoslovakian freedom fighter for wartime resistance to Nazi Germany, who said: "Only by reaching out a helping hand and by actively opposing wrongdoing, do we earn the right to be called human."[2]

Keep in mind, too, the common belief among all Indigenous Peoples that laughter is good medicine. Remember, long after the White man is gone, we of the First Nations will still be here in our beloved lands.

§§§

The Inuit say, "Never in anger," for when good judgment is cast aside, we leave ourselves open to any and all kinds of hurt.

Rather
    and far better
to use not the anger itself
but the energy it takes.
Harness it
like a team of good dogs
who do your bidding
with you
    and no one else
in control.

One way I began to leave bitterness behind was in a class at the Ontario College of Art and Design (now OCAD University) with Peter Mah, who suggested we do a drawing a day. Now it's been forty years and counting. I simply started doing the same, drawing first thing every morning as an exercise in feeding my spirit and to improve my drawing skills over the years. Recently, I've started posting them on Facebook.

Post-Traumatic Stress Disorder (PTSD), a medical condition shared by soldiers and their families and survivors of residential schools and their families, is an insidious illness that seeps into your system, slowly collecting deep within your being. It can take years to be coaxed out, usually with the help of professionals, either in the medical field or, my own personal choice, Indigenous ways of knowing, including ceremonies.

It is very likely that other survivors are the only ones who can truly appreciate how hard it is to simply go back to an innocent person's darkest blind spots, to know that making a daily effort for several long years is a monumental task. There is always that familiar tightening of the stomach and a kind of PTSD trigger to work through, no matter what. Needless to say, it leaves you hopeless for anything that resembles a normal life beyond.

For many other survivors, though, passing time without reaching out for help can be fatal. And, in the words of my grandfather Peter Mountain Sr., "Before we know it, it's all over." For too many, especially those who took their own life or otherwise died before their rightful time, this kind of a memory was just a dream too removed from the shame, our only fare, and they weren't able to ask for help.

> Through it all, though
> Bear Rock Mountain remains
> as legend
> at the very heart
> of our Northern Dene Nation

For all of it, these are the simple words of my life and times, an artist born on the land in my native *Denendeh* (Dene Nation) to the digital world we now inhabit.

Only being Dene remains.

PART I

Another Lost Generation

1949 – 69

CHAPTER 1

How Muskrat Created the World

No one can tell our old-time stories like an elder can.

When I was in Tulita in 2012 for my final summer of Sahtú in the Arts, an arts co-op program initiated by the Northwest Territories government, I spent a good deal of my time with elder Maurice Mendo. Since we are both Mountain Dene and closely related, we shared a common sense of humour, and we were close. I broached the idea of creating a mural for the new swimming pool in town, with a story involving our animal relatives. We eventually settled on "How Muskrat Created the World," the Dene creation story. Maurice was a born storyteller, but he had an added talent—he knew the traditional way of acting out all the parts of the story, including some absolutely lifelike imitations of the foibles and noble deeds of *D'se* (Muskrat). As he told it:

> All the animals were marooned on a large wooden raft, adrift on a flooded sea, trying to figure out a way to put the world they knew back together. The only way to do so would be to send their best diver down to the bottom of the ocean and come back with even a bit of dirt, so they could rebuild the world.
>
> Loon volunteered, but it was decided even she could not do this impossible feat. Instead, Otter took his

dive and was gone for some time. When he did come back up, he had failed.

Next to go was Beaver, known for his way of dropping right straight down, sinking like a heavy boulder. Even he came back with naught to accomplish the task of creating the world anew.

Finally, Muskrat piped up and was brave enough to volunteer to make his descent to the bottom. At this, all the animals laughed, saying that if even their best swimmers could not come back with the earth then what chance did this measly creature have of success?

While all of this was being debated, Muskrat simply disappeared with a sharp splash like a small stone falling from on high and was gone ... it seemed for all of eternity. There was nothing the rest could do but to wait for his return.

Which he finally did, miraculously popping back out of the surface of the sea and landing back on the raft. His poor lifeless body lay there barely gasping for air.

But when the rest of the Animal Nation checked his paws closely, there in a tight grip was just a bit of ground, maybe enough to create the land they needed so.

They worked and laboured to make the world as they had loved it before. Wolf was sent forth to run and howl every now and again, so they would know the size of Mother Earth.

When they were satisfied, they all turned and gave thanks to the mighty Muskrat for remaking this world we now live in.

Dogsled Nursery

In the present day of Internet and cell phones, it is hard for anyone to imagine a time any different.

As many of my generation, I was born on the land. A look at the calendar says the day was a Tuesday in November in 1949, although a change in time one week or the next probably meant as much as the wind blowing through them Arctic winter wilds. The place was called *Dugha Indin*, roughly translated as "Among the islands, down the *Duhogah* (Mackenzie) River, just below Grandview." This is about fifty kilometres (30 miles) north of the Arctic Circle. There are only a few places in the world as far north as this place that are habitable by humans, and those are in Norway, Finland, and Russia.

When I asked my mum about it, she said, "We were travelling at the time, a long way from *Radelie Koe* [Fort Good Hope], and we stopped for only one day." When she was told that the ladies of today take months off for maternity leave, my mother just laughed and said there was no such thing then. At the time, our ancient Dene traditions were very much alive, and there was a rather sad and sobering note to my coming into this world. Life was hard physically, and my parents must have thought I would not be able to survive because my mother had tuberculosis when I was born. I was mistakenly led to believe by a close relative I was left out in the cold to simply die. I learned, too, that one of my sisters was left behind when it came time for winter trapping, so I had no reason to question what turned out to be smalltown northern gossip gone bad. I was also told that it was my maternal grandmother, NoCh'o (Marie-Adele Mountain), who convinced the rest of them to bring me on back in, all cold, blue, and nearly frozen. Truth was I was so tough as a baby my mom could leave me in a swing outside whilst she went about her camp chores. She called it a "blessing."

> And though the hand
> that cast the dice
> may be steady and true,
> the distance of time
> chance and showing
> makes us all
> > one way or another
> uncertain clouds passing
> paused
> on a breathless day
> called fate.

I also later learned that because my parents were not married, my dad was given the choice of joining the army, going to jail, or marrying my mum. The Royal Canadian Mounted Police was the only legal authority in the North at the time, and very likely forced the decision on my father. Although my parents made every effort, they became parents when they were both very young, and I always felt responsible for cutting their youth short. My father was eighteen and my mum only sixteen when I was born.

> That kind of very basic loss
> > from a time even before
> > conscious thought
> creates a hunger
> for something out there
> that simply does not
> exist.

A constant reckoning
with a dream
come too soon
out of skies
suddenly darkened
with no more need
for the light.

My supposed near-abandonment goes a long way in explaining my life out in the cold, as it were, never really feeling connected to anything in particular. To this day, I can withstand extreme cold temperatures and still prefer to sleep with a window open, even on the coldest nights. I've also always had a problem with intimacy, getting close to people emotionally. As an artist, I feel things very strongly, and I am passionate with all I do, but I have always preferred to keep others at a distance.

At least one of my siblings has a similar early childhood experience, creating a wedge between parent and child. Each of us has our own stories to tell.

My sister Judy and I, especially, were taught in the old way to never talk back to any elder and not to even touch something that was not yours. Judy, who was born three years after me, was the closest of my seven siblings. Bella, Betty, and Lucy were born in the late fifties. Robert, Stella, and Fred John were all born in the sixties. In a small community with only several hundred people, every adult was thought of as an extended parent, so they had every right to tell you right from wrong. For all of these reasons and more, I have always thought of myself, even now, as a part of a different, forgotten time.

For someone
who's always been
more spirit than mere human,

it all makes a
strange kind of magic,
doesn't it?

My paternal grandmother, Elizabeth, was already getting on in years when I was born, but Judy and I spent our earliest years in her company. Grandma Elizabeth was born in 1888, two years before the end of the Indian Wars with the infamous Wounded Knee Massacre on the Pine Ridge Lakota Reservation far to the south. Through her stories, we had a direct link to the old Indian days. When my grandfather Michel passed away in the late fifties, it must have been very hard on her. We did know she missed him so. Yet life along the Duhogah River was the best. Granny always began her life lessons by talking about the Dene concept of *gohsheneh*: to do things carefully, lovingly, and right the first time.

Portable Fort
We even had our own Little Chicago!

I was born downriver from the present site of Radelie Koe, near one of its former sites. Historical records show that Radelie Koe has been situated in five different locations, depending on where the Hudson's Bay Company (HBC) thought best for access to our People (the Dene), the Gwich'in, and the Inuvialuit farther toward the Arctic Coast.

The first site, built in 1806, was at the famous Sans Sault Rapids. Then, in 1811, the fort moved farther downriver to Manitou Island, just across from its present site. In 1823, it was situated much farther down the Duhogah at Thunder River, very likely for the Gwich'in and Inuvialuit who lived that way. Finally, about 1825, Radelie Koe settled back to Manitou Island, and then moved one last time just across the river, a little over thirty kilometres (20 miles) south of the Arctic Circle.

Our ancestral homelands just happened to be in one of the world's prime countries for sable, marten, and other valuable furs. At a critical time in its formation, the HBC traded for up to three-quarters of its take from this northern district of our rich lands.

The HBC, which was jokingly called "Here Before Christ," was just one of the trading companies associated with our first contacts with Europeans. In Dene tradition, with people living so far apart for most of the year, there was no overriding chief, as such. When trading companies came in pursuit of fur, they would pick one spokesperson, very likely a prominent hunter, to deal with. This system of having one chief was designated upon the arrival of the *Mola* (White people), likely to make it easier to get a signature on a treaty.

One notable spot along our Duhogah River was a rough and rowdy camping spot for would-be miners on their way farther west. It was dubbed Little Chicago during the Yukon Gold Rush of 1898 and right on into the 1930s.

Hyslop and Nagle built a trading post in 1900 on the present site of Radelie Koe. The post was sold to the North West Company in 1912 and finally to the HBC in 1938. Like the American West, many of the first communities in the North have the word Fort in them, probably to keep the wild Indians out, except when they should have money, of course. Radelie Koe was no exception.

People in the area lived on the land until the 1950s or so. Then the Mola quickly grabbed up all the prominent jobs at the Hudson's Bay, missions, police, and nursing stations. This may have been fine with our People anyway, since we had learned to camp more in the sheltered valleys, to cut down wood for fires, and to get out of the wind. At temperatures of −34°C to −40°C in winter, this made a lot of sense.

When I was yet a lad, Radelie Koe was home to a few hundred souls. The seasons still had a lot to do with where people lived. Winters found many out on the land, trapping and fishing. People only came into town at certain times: for Christmas, Easter, and summer, when life was more relaxed. Even then, we would go out to the fishing camp.

Everything beyond the town was "outside," usually in reference to the South. Mail only arrived by bush plane, so you often had to wait several months for a parcel to arrive from Eaton's or Simpsons-Sears. All of the store supplies came in by barge in summer. Thus, life was one of a regular pattern, which helped shape us as proud and independent Dene and Métis.

Our Old Log Home

It may well have been my grandfather on my dad's side who built the two-storey log house, about seven square metres, that we lived in above *Ohndah Dek'ieh Leline* (Jackfish Creek), which runs along the southeastern side of old Radelie Koe. We also had a very similar house across from the Esso oil company town of Norman Wells, some 160 kilometres north on the Duhogah River.

Up until I was seven, my paternal grandfather, Michel Barnaby, husband of Elizabeth, was with us. I remember him being a very gentle person who watched as I played with toys he made for me. From what my uncle Thomas Manuel tells me, he died in February of 1957 at Canoe Lake, 160 kilometres north. "He had a good dog team, and they took him back to town," Uncle said. Another person I remember from that time was Albert Lafferty, a venerated elder.

My grandmother Elizabeth was one of the most constant people in my life and my sister Judy's. As with most of my immediate family, she did not speak English, except for the words "Lie," "Talk!"—which she would loudly exclaim when excited. Having gotten on in years, she spent a good deal of her time in bed on the ground floor. She always had her big metal cup of tea on a wooden chair by her side and one of those Big Ben wind-up clocks, the constant ticking keeping her company.

Most of the elders at the time chewed Copenhagen "snuff," chewing tobacco, so we always had to empty and change the liner for her *siewh'a'* (an empty lard can for spitting). Ol' granny took great delight in me and Judy, and every once in a while, she would break out in song, and we would dance in front of her, just kinda hopping, to her glee.

I recall my grandmother being a very wise person who would give advice to people. They were often lined up waiting to speak with her.

We didn't get to see much of my father, or even Mum. My father spent most of his time working as a guide in tourist lodges around *Sahtú* (a region including five communities in the Great Bear Lake region) and would come home every so often. There was a lot of tuberculosis then, and Mum was out for treatment for a number of years at the Aklavik Roman Catholic Mission in the Delta, farther up the Duhogah River. So our little family in town consisted of my grandmother Elizabeth, one of my dad's sisters, Auntie Marie, myself, and my sister Judy. We had other siblings, too. The Oudzi family in *Kabami Tue* (Colville Lake) adopted Bella. Two other sisters, Betty and Lucy Ann, lived with Mum there when she was not ill. My brother Robert was not yet adopted, and my brother Fred John was not yet born.

Auntie Marie was so serene, with a good sense of humour. Nothing seemed to get to her; she had the patience of a true Mountain Dene. As with the young ladies, she was independent and capable and went out with the dog team every time we needed firewood and to check her snares and loche hooks. At least one full square container of fish was brought in from the nets twice a day, so all of the women and girls were kept busy cutting it up to make dry fish.

The dogs, including our favourite, Ol' Buffalo, were tied up around the *dahk'o* (a warehouse built on stilts to keep the mice out). Animals were never allowed indoors, but there was an exception: an elderly widowed lady, Maggie Fisher, who had been married to a Mola and lived some houses toward the church and the Point, had cats.

Because our family had no constant male provider in this hunting community, as my father was often out guiding for fishing lodges, we were very poor and often ate only the basics, with maybe a loche from the hooks on the river. People shared everything, so when someone shot a moose, it was an occasion to feast. There were also rabbits in the willows nearby.

I remember cold winter mornings in the house on Ohndah Dek'ieh Leline. From out of a deep sleep in warm eiderdown blankets, I would hear the muffled voice of my grandmother Elizabeth calling for me to wake up and build the morning fire. "Adzareh [short version of my Dene name], *Rehinht'lah!* (Wake up!) *Gonihtl'ah!* (Start the fire!)" It was so cold I would have to hear this several times before I made a move.

Once up, I was not allowed back in bed, although I probably did a time or two, it being so cold. Because we lived so far north, our Dene life was based on discipline and respect. You learned early to only have to be told something once and to do it. Any adult had your interest at heart, and besides, doing things right the first time just made life easier.

The walk to the stove was the hardest part of winter mornings, the wooden floor chilling my body to the bone, with blasts of breath visible in the dim light from the east-facing window on the creek side. We had one of those old 45-gallon oil barrels made into a country woodstove, with a door in front cut and shaped with an axe. Our elders were experts at making all kinds of things out of found metal, even the brakes for the dogsleds, which were an ingenious contraption to slow and stop the harnessed dogs. They were even fitted with a hinge, making it possible for them to rest on the sledboard and not drag on the ground.

We would never allow the fire in the stove to go out completely, for we had to keep the water on the stove from freezing when it was −22°C outside. Birch is the best kind of wood to put on the night before. Being harder and denser than other woods, it will often as not leave coals after burning all night. The wood shavings prepared the night before were a work of art in themselves—as was most of what we did as traditional Dene, although we did not think of it that way. The wood shavings were expertly cut from pre-split logs and would sit there all curled up and ready to be carefully arranged in the middle of two larger blocks, with the narrower ones to be put on top.

In our extended family, it was actually my godmother, Henrietta Kelly, who taught me the proper way to start a fire. She explained it as "building a small house," with the two main facing walls in an opened wedge, and to "make sure there is enough air in between to make the flames go." These kinds of practical everyday lessons stay with you for life and always come in handy.

We had those old Lucifer matches, the "strike anywhere" type. To show off to friends, we would light them on our teeth or even on some hapless fellow's pants! Some guys would even make a sort of gun out of wooden clothespins with the matches as the ignitable "bullets" that caught fire when they hit the intended target, including someone else's head.

But, once touched with a Lucifer match, the whole set-up of kindling, smaller sticks, and the wooden frame caught up in a great flash of light, with sparks flying hither and yon. Soon, even the tea kettle and pots of water left on top of the ol' barrel stove were fairly dancing to the merry morning fire tune!

My grandmother always wanted her tea first thing in the morning, so I made sure to get the large black pot of it going. The old folks liked their tea strong and would often just leave their second cup sitting for a while and drink it cold.

So there I sat, bum on the still-cold, grey-painted floor, pulling on my woolen duffels and mukluks for the day ahead, the light from the stove the only thing visible in the early blue northern morning. To this day, people often comment on my marked preference for different shades of blue in my paintings.

Most of what we did was out of necessity, so we never thought much about the beauty of the way we lived. Wood, especially in winter, took a lot of hard work to get from the forest to the fireplace, so it had to be used wisely.

We were very humble folk, eating very simply, so often a pot of porridge and fried bannock was our breakfast.

The only source of light in most log homes in town was the gas lamp, the red or green Coleman kind, with the cloth mesh mantle filled with gas that would burn with a comforting hiss in the bush tents or log houses in the community.

Most mornings, my sister Judy and I would take off for the government day school way over on the other side of town, with a stop at Billy McNeely's store if we had any money. He used to have those Superman hard candy bars for ten cents and a can of pop for a quarter. If there was no school, we would hitch our huge dog Ol' Buffalo up to a sled and go racing around town like a couple of fools.

To this day, I much prefer sleeping as I did then, with the cool air fanning my dreams of life on the land.

Household Chores

That Swede saw would just go ziiiiing!

Once up and out of bed, we set about our normal day as a family. By the time the gas lamp was lit, we could also see by the dim morning light before the sun actually rose at about ten in the morning. By then the ol' woodstove would be blazing and making a racket with all of the pots on it to melt water from the ice in the porch.

Judy and I would always have to be reminded to "wash behind your neck." While Grandma had her tea, the rest of us sat down at the table nearby for porridge and bannock.

Our job as children only included making sure we had plenty of wood cut and stacked on the tar-papered porch in front of our log home. This was a time long before any such thing as chainsaws. We only had them old red Swede saws, the serrated long blade kept very sharp.

Auntie Marie went out every few days to haul in the spruce logs, which burned the best. We used poplar too, but that was harder on the axe for splitting. To saw the logs, we put the dried log on a sawhorse, a simple contraption made of two-by-four boards with bracing on the side. Once that Swede saw got going good, you could actually make it sing, a high, sweet *ziiiing* that both cutters tried to keep going, with an extra helper to replace the cut logs with new ones. Thus, I learned early to handle a saw and axe.

Wood, as all else in nature, can be read like a book. Each piece already has everything in it to tell you about it, the knots being where the tough spots are and the grain clearly showing you where to strike your axe.

When the wood was ready to bring in, we made a game of who could take the most and tallest pile of split logs into the porch without having it all fall over. At times we would be barely moving along one tiny step at a time, but we were determined from the start to prove ourselves to an adult world.

It was a very tight-knit community, so whenever someone needed anything done, there was usually a volunteer, especially for the elderly. We would gladly do a job of hard physical work for a single piece of hard candy or a cup of tea.

Children were taught to be courteous, so when we went to someone else's home, we would simply stand there until asked what we wanted. "Akureh Neahnet'ih?" was a way of asking if you were there to just visit or if you needed something.

The adults did all of the harder jobs, but once in a while we would be asked to haul ice from the huge chunks along the Duhogah River, which ran south to north along our town of Radelie Koe.

Summer or winter, Judy always wanted to be close to me. I often had to rescue her, when, for instance, she fell in the big springtime puddles of water!

K'ohoyieh

Very few of my earliest years were spent in town.

Summers would find us at different fish camps along the Duhogah River. These all had traditional names, such as *K'ohoyieh* (Under the Clouds) and *Warih Duhgun* (Rafter Poles Taken Down). Both camps were up the river a little ways and within sight of Radelie Koe. Farther up were Albert's Cabin, on the eastern side of the Ramparts, and *Farahezen* (Black Rock Rim Around). Another, down the river, was *Ohk'ie Fiehk'la* (Birds in Rock Crevice).

The one we spent the most time at, though, was *K'afohun* (Willow Point), past *Ohgosho* (Big Eddy) and the bowl-like waterfalls said in legend to be a giant, Wihst'edihdel, relieving himself.

All of these places would have several families camped together, the number of people depending on the amount of fish at the eddy or pool of still water where they could be caught.

All camp activity centred around gill nets set along the river, only the carved wooden *daleleh* (floats) and a large wooden stump at the far end of camp were visible. These nets would be checked twice a day to ensure a catch of fresh fish. "Drowned" fish, fish that died in the net and decomposed, served as dog food.

Dogs were tied in the willows out of the sun, but would still have a time of it, with the hot July sun and swarms of mosquitoes and bulldog flies attracted by the hanging fish.

There were no larger motorboats at the time, only 5.5-metre freighter canoes with eight- or nine-horsepower outboard motors, which could be heard for miles, echoing off cliff walls of the Ramparts. In camp, though, because of the short distance, people just checked the nets with homemade ratting canoes.

The fish were moved from the nets and stored in big, square, galvanized metal tubs, the tails of some of the huge conies sticking out several feet.

After the nets were brought in, the women were kept busy for several hours, slicing up the catch so that the heads and tails were in one pile and the bodies of the mainly white fish were all flat and in rectangular pieces in another. It made for easier drying in the twenty-four-hour midnight sun.

In our traditional Dene world, chores were clearly gender defined, and I was not expected to handle the catch except to go out and help at the nets and hauling when needed. Except for our few chores, we children had the time of our lives. We spent most of our days swimming in the water and playing along the shores. We even built our own little willow-hut village.

Wood was not hard to find in the camps, as it came lazily floating down the Duhogah River when the water was higher. For tools, all we ever used was a length of long strong twine with a rock tied on the end. When we saw a big log we wanted, we simply tossed the rock over the end and pulled it all back in.

We spent a fair bit of our time in the long hours of the season of the midnight sun, a day lasting six weeks or so, looking for a good length of poplar, with its softer core, to carve our own boats, which we sometimes even painted. We saved tin covers from Copenhagen snuff cans to serve as rudders, which would make that low "brrrrr-gh…brrrrr" sound we much prized.

If we wanted the drier kind of wood, without so many saw-damaging pebbles in it, for making fires, we had to hike up a narrow path to the top of the cliffs at the Ramparts and go inland. There were blueberry patches on up there, too, in the month of August.

One part of these summer months we really looked forward to was when the *alla sho* (barges) came by. The deckhands would wave to us and toss oranges and apples into the river for us. The fresh oranges would squirt right into our eyes as we peeled them! Those McIntosh apples were so tasty. I've actually never had one as good as they were, ever.

The Old Ways

We often talk about wanting to go back to our old Dene ways, not really knowing what they were all about. Of course, we lived in an idyll of sorts out in our fish camps in the summer, but we also had our challenges. People tend to romanticize the old days, but we lived very poor, and we worked hard and kept busy. The reality is that we were isolated, and there was not much access to outside help.

For the most part, being so isolated from the rest of the world, we were a pretty superstitious lot. As children, and for our own protection, we heard a lot about the Rarei'eh, bushmen who were lost, wild White men just waiting to get their hands on a Dene child who wandered too far from the group of tents.

With changing times, other parts of our lives benefited from the Mola, especially nearby in town with the police and the nursing stations.

Unfortunately, wife beating was one sad feature of Dene life. It did change over time, as youth returning from residential schools felt that it was essentially wrong and could not continue.

And camp life made for the presence of lice, which was a daily bother to the people involved in healthcare. Eventually tuberculosis became a part of medical history, but not before claiming many of our people.

Very likely it is the spiritual connection—our people felt so close to nature—that drew people to the camps. And as our elders often said, "You don't have to go far to find food and whatever else you need." They often spoke of the land as a kind of bank, from which we could take whatever was there.

Ahso Vitaline's World

Growing up in the fish camps along the Duhogah, I recall elders like *Ahso* (Grandmother) Vitaline. I never heard any one of them complain. Rather, we were always told to try to be cheerful, especially when travelling, for someone "might be having a bad day, so be careful what you say." These kinds of teachings were woven into everything that went on in camp life.

Often, there would be an elder singing a song with a drum. This sound echoed off the steep cliffs of the Ramparts along the river.

At that time, before town life began for my Dene people, all the food we ate came from the land, so we were seldom sick. This all changed when the Imperial Oil company began to build islands to drill from right on the river at Norman Wells. The fish were no longer firm, their flesh became mushy.

Other and more ominous changes are now a part of Northern life—or should I say death? Since the tar sands have been in operation, hundreds of miles to the south in Alberta, more and more of our people are dying of cancer, something we never even knew of before.

Going out hunting with an elder, the late Joe Martin, taught me that the further you go back in time with a First Nations person, the more aware you have to be of how you must view the future; and the closer you are to nature, the more spiritual and meaningful the experience.

My question for the future is: will we ever again have a day when an elderly woman can just feel a part of life by cutting up a fish to dry in the hot sun?

For the time being, and over half a century after living there at the fish camp, I am doing my painterly best to keep these images alive.

In the Mountains

My grandparents on my mother's side, Peter Sr. and Marie-Adele Mountain, are from the Sheetao T'ineh, the Mountain Dene. Grandfather Peter came from the Mayo region in Yukon, and we still have some relatives there. His wife, Marie-Adele, was closely related to the Tobacs. One curious fact is that, although my grand-parents were quite elderly, I had uncles who were younger than me. Life there in the 1950s must have been the last of the moose-hide boat days, when we would harvest moose and then go down the river and spend the summers in the fish camps.

I recall the dog team ride up to my grandparents' was one glorious affair with the stars visible and the clear sounds of the dog bells, those big round and shiny *loogoolu*, echoing off the trees and rock faces.

That high up, though, sometimes we had to walk, and that made for treacherous going. When we came to a fast-moving stream, we had to cut down a big tree for a bridge that everyone had to go over, gear and all.

Once camp was set up, there was no other place quite like the mountains to live in, with that feeling of being apart and in a separate and divine world. Everyday concerns as we knew them simply did not take on such importance.

I first saw a traditional teepee there, covered in spruce bark, I believe. It would be quite a number of years before I would see another, in, of all places, our first home about thirty thousand years ago: Siberian Russia!

Those years were also my very first recollections of having tried my hand at any kind of art. Of course, there were no such things as paper and pencil in a traditional Dene camp. My sketch-pad was a simple block of spruce with a smooth enough surface, and I used pieces of coals from the fire to make my artwork. It was always a little sad for me to have to see my brilliant first works of art go into the fire! But no one said anything, and that was that.

Camp life was always busy, with everyone having a set of chores to do. My mum in particular always told us, "If you see something that needs to be done, just do it. Don't ask anyone, just do the job."

In that way, we learned very early to do things for ourselves that would be of use to others. There were some things you really had to watch out for, though. Some of those chores had their risks, like knives, axes, and gathering water.

The streams in that high country run much faster than down below, and I was almost swept away when I put my pail in too fast to get our drinking water. There was the roar of the rapids as they swept past our camping spot, but it becomes so much a part of daily life that you tend to forget the danger. As a young boy, your mind tends to wander to other things ... *What's happening with the guy(s) with the guns? Maybe they've spotted a moose or woodland caribou or are shooting at some jolly ducks.* Then, wham, you feel the sharp tug all the way up to your arm sockets, and you grab for the curved metal handle of the water bucket and almost topple right into the churning ice-cold mass headfirst before finally being able to regain control.

That sudden shock quickly took me out of my silent reverie, let me tell you! You wouldn't want anyone to know you almost lost your life, so you'd just go back, put the water in its place by the fire, and go on with your day. Such is camp life.

Of course, being one with an artistic spirit, I was often taken away just by the deep and rich colours in this country. I was outside, as usual, very early one morning to catch that certain shade of enriched blue in the willows and trees. I had a piece of bannock, a kind of country bread fried in a large black cast-iron frying pan, which I held behind me as I gazed at these wonderful hues playing in the snow-laden bush with the dawn just breaking over the higher peaks. When bannock was still frozen, it was so good to just gnaw on outside in the cold.

But a loose dog came along and snatched my bread! So I learned to eat my food right away and not walk around with it. Then, in places like those blue willows, I could just give in to the hypnotic power of the land.

I didn't really know what that power was then, and to this day hope I never do, but gazing at the way the snow and early morning pink dawn played against the snowy branches, I just let my eyes go unfocused. This is a kind of self-hypnosis, allowing for a super-vision of sorts, where even the most minute of sounds drops off and fades far away from our cold mountain abode with none but the morning star or a wishing moon, a new moon you can make a wish on, as a guide.

I was taken to a warm, glowing haven filled with images that slowly transformed themselves in pure imagination. I even learned to name this place—The Near Room—but not until much later in life. Some call it a vision. I didn't know what to call it. But I did know, even then, there is a place connected with it. Our camp, being so far from anywhere, gave me the notion that it was everywhere at once.

Meanwhile, back in camp, we were making moosehide boats. It took up to fifteen green untanned moosehides to make a boat. With a spruce tree frame, a boat was big enough to carry a number of families. There would be about thirty people aboard, braving the roaring, splashing waves rushing past the boat! It was the only way to get out of there in the springtime. Those times took me all the way back to my family's Mountain Dene roots.

As you can well imagine, it was a lot of work making those boats, especially for the girls and women who did the double and folded-over stitching to make the craft waterproof. When the boat was ready, it was indeed one glorious and adventurous ride all the way down the roaring streams to the Duhogah, far below, with a hodgepodge mass of dogs cowering in the bottom and we children squealing for joy! It was dangerous, with sharp rocks on all sides ready to rip the entire craft to pieces and drown all within. I lost uncles on these boat rides.

With all of this tragedy only the thickness of the sewn moosehide away, our elders had to make sure we stopped along the way to make offerings to the Spirits of the Mountains for our safe passage over the waters they dwelt in.

After this big adventure, life along the Big River, the Duhogah, settled to a slower pace.

Life with Ahso/Granny

From a time before Wounded Knee.

The warm summer days went by in a continuous, lazy way. Once in a while, you would hear the echo of a small motor coming from town, people travelling to and from their own camps farther along, stopping on a moose-hunting trip or just visiting.

Whenever my cousins, the Masuzumi boys, came to visit, they always brought extra clothes for me. We were money poor, but never lacked for any food—in summer, anyways—nor love.

When we were ready for bed, Grandma would often take her old smoking pipe out. It was my job to fill it up from a tobacco tin. After it was lit, we closed up the mosquito net and solemnly passed her pipe back and forth between we three, completely filling up that net with smoke so we couldn't see anything!

She always told us stories, too, some going all the way back to a time Dene storyteller George Blondin later called "When the World was new." These were legends that never quite reached their end before we fell asleep. When given the chance, we'd pick our favourites, ones she called "The way people are."

She began one story by telling us of the trips she would take into town for supplies. "There is always some kind soul at the Point to meet me when I land. This person takes me to the store where I get what we need. I don't even care that I have dirt on my face and willow twigs sticking out of my hair. On the way there, I see these women, all white with some kind of face cream on their faces so you can no longer call them Dene. They have their hair all curled up and lipstick from ear to ear, not even knowing how to use them things the right way. Judy, I never want to see you like that, and not you either, Antoine! When you use makeup, people can no longer tell who you are." Simply because we were so young at the time, we never did forget her wise words.

Granny would always warn me, "*Suwehohinleni nest'abareh ehshuhe wohsi* [If you don't listen, I will poke your ears with an awl]!" In fact, I was even sent out a few times to cut the birch handle, fashion and sharpen the extra-large nail, and bring her a new awl myself, just in case.

During summers, under the steady light of the *Sa Ra-ahyile* (Midnight Sun), there was no need to assign an older boy like me to start the fire. One thing I always tried to do, and never did, was wake up before Granny. She would always be sitting right there in the morning, with her cup of tea, surrounded by the warm, heavenly smell of the spruce-bough floor, patiently sewing and waiting on her precious grandchildren to wake on up.

With that warm Duhogah morning breeze there to gently greet you, it certainly was an idyll.

Today, I would say we got a front-row seat into the world of the elders. It has always come in handy to know of a very different way of being.

CHAPTER 2

Radelie Koe

Every time I went there, I wanted to see the picture of me and Archie in our rabbit fur parkas.

A typical First Nations community is, by nature, an extended one, so our little town of Radelie Koe was very tight-knit in those days. My generation of Dene was born on the land, and we thought of ourselves as being country folk. When in town, people lived in their own log homes.

Visitors from Kabami Tue set their up their tents here and there, often after the sixty-two-kilometre walk overland, coming out to the Duhogah River at Old Baldy, a prominent hill just north of the town. A hundred and sixty kilometres south to Norman Wells was yet another world.

One relative, Addy Tobac, who visited our humble little home, was probably the first to ever give me an art lesson, or pointers, anyway. As I drew a can of Carnation milk, she pointed out the way the object curved and how to show that visually.

Our next-door neighbours were Uncle Charlie and Auntie Louise Masuzumi. She always had cookies in a tall clay jar for eager little fingers to reach for.

In terms of the possible scope of family, we had an early start indeed. Uncle Charlie's father, Hiroko Masuzumi, originally came from faraway Hokkaido, Japan, a place we could not possibly fathom in terms of distance.

From Vancouver, this Japanese man, a Samurai warrior who

fell out of favour with family, worked on one of those old steam-wheeler boats servicing the goldfields of the Yukon. Hiroko came over to the western Northwest Territories with grandfather Peter Mountain Sr., and Hiroko's son Charlie married my Aunt Louise and raised a family. So I had cousins who were Dene and Japanese.

My cousins, sons of Charlie and Louise, were called Alfred, Walter, and Barney. They were a pretty rough and tumble bunch who always tried to outdo one another. Of the three, I spent most of my time with the youngest, Barney. I would pester him so with questions about the world "outside," as we called everything that was not Radelie Koe. The oldest, Alfred, was the inventor, the mad scientist, always up to some new gizmo or new way of doing things.

Farther down the dirt road toward the Point at the southern end of town lived my godparents, Antoine and Henrietta Kelly. I was named after the former. Godmother Henrietta was the one who patiently taught me to make a fire.

Whenever I went to visit them, one of the first things they always did was find and show me the picture of me and their grandson Archie wearing rabbit skin outfits. We were seven or so, and these covered our entire bodies with only our scowling and crying faces showing! Could be that one day was too hot to be covered in warm rabbit fur for pictures!

In a communal extended family, all of our elders regarded us children as their own and often used special Dene words and phrases to make their point, like gohsheneh, meaning to do things carefully, be neat and tidy, and to watch exactly what you are doing to make sure you get it right the first and every time. I found out later that this is the same for our southern Dineh, the Navajo.

Two Pieces of Candy
One for me and one for Judy!

Although most of my time was spent in our two-storey log home, I usually stopped at the home of my grandparents, Peter and Marie-Adele Mountain, to get water to bring home. They lived up Ohndah Dek'ieh Leline, Jackfish Creek, where the water was cleaner. Often Peter and my other grandfather, Michel, would be there, talking like older men did.

I would ask them for "two pieces of candy." When asked why two, I would say, "One for me and one for Judy!" Michel called me over, and Grandpa Peter said that they could already tell that I would be a very kind person, having already started thinking of someone else.

The book learning at school in Radelie Koe was one thing, but the way the old-timers thought was very different—someone who was "smart" also thought with their heart, and knew the Dene way of doing things properly.

Peter Sr. surely already knew of my interest in art, for he was an artist himself, able to make just about anything with a simple carving knife. I think he also overheard me asking his other grandson Barney so many questions about the big ol' world. At one time, he told me, "To make anything of yourself you have to go a long, long ways from home, Grandson." That always stayed with me, along with another saying in which he talked about the "tracks one makes in one's lifetime."

"In your life, Grandson, you will make many trails, more than you will ever be able to recall. But one day you will come upon a set of footprints you will not recognize. Those are the ones you are making right now, as a child. And the same ones which will take you the rest of the way home." He always said whatever he had to say in a way you would understand, even though in the Dene way it often took years to fully appreciate it.

At the time, there was little of the idyllic pastoral in our northern homeland's shoreline, a place rather taken with continuous waves that was sticky, soft, and muddy, up to a metre or more in some places. If we didn't have our moccasins on, then it was the black rubber boots, which, when caught by the grabbing muck would have to be left unceremoniously behind, to be carefully gotten back, probing stick in hand.

What one should also know is that our stories, and even legends, are often intentionally just like this, they seemingly leave the listener hanging. Yet it could very well be that the purpose is to leave the rest of it up to you and to learn to appreciate the way in which life itself is best left, a mystery. Or better yet, a gift best opened slowly ... day by day.

And even though it has been years since their telling, those words I heard as a child are yet as light as the notes of a bird perched on a branch of the Tree of the Ancestors. Forever and yet merrily hopping over my own faltering footsteps.

Making her own greeting to the rising light of a new dawn.

Diamonds in the Dark

Most of what we did in winter in Radelie Koe was to simply keep warm. This meant a lot of the work and chores we youngsters did had to do with collecting wood, sawing, chopping, and stacking it all indoors for later use.

But life was certainly not all work-related. We had the wondrous *rayuka* (northern lights) to keep us company, and what better way to amuse ourselves than to go "sliding down," as we affectionately called sledding.

Fort Good Hope not being such a large place at the time, was more of a place where people did things together. When the evenings were fair and the lights played across overhead, everyone turned out to either slide, or just to watch and laugh.

The main road running through town was not steep enough to sled, so we all gathered at the one closer to Ohndah Dek'ieh

Leline. There were log homes on either side of this narrower road, which you had to make sure to avoid hitting, especially the one way down at the bottom: Albert and Dora Lafferty's.

People had all kinds of sleds, usually the shorter flat-bottomed ones sold at the Hudson's Bay Company store. The larger regular *becheneh*, dogsled, could hold a lot more people. When it tipped over, sending all within sprawling in deep snow, it was something of a disaster!

All of us boys wanted our own homemade *chaleh*, a kind of racing sled with the taller runners and handles to steer it by. In summer, we would be on the lookout for the wide metal straps used to secure the larger crates that came on the barges. These made the best runners to tack on to the sled for greater speed.

With your face only inches from the frozen ground, you could really hear the metallic cutting sound these fast sleds made on the icy road surface. You would try to jump off at the bottom of a dead-end run, still holding the sled, and kinda flash that at the young girls! Of course, you would sometimes fall flat on your back, with iced-up and slippery mukluks on, and a chorus of braying laughter following a shameful walk back up.

The packed snow made a crunchy sound all the way back up the hill, with the stars glistening off the snow's diamond surface. It was a kind of a cooler paradise with your breath visible, and the air so clear it was like drinking fresh water.

Other things we did in winter in town also involved sliding, but with a big ol' mound of snow, up to two metres high, halfway down the run. We would go racing toward it and simply jump as high as we could with our sled soaring up, up, and come crashing down, hopefully to keep going.

The old Department of Transportation (DOT) hill, where the community complex building was, was one good spot for these daring plays. I totally wiped out doing this once, and my cousin Walter told me that when they got to me and asked me if I was okay, all I came out with was a feeble "Yeah!" not wanting to sound weak.

The older guys were always trying out new ideas. One of these was to tunnel right under the frozen ice at the Point, at the very south end of town where the barges tied up upon arrival in summer.

My family was very strict about our curfew, so whatever we got ourselves into, we had to be back by nine or be locked out. I don't actually recall any locks being on doors, but you had to do as you were told anyway.

Mystery Caroler a-Jolly!

A strange song hung in the quiet pre-dawn air, tinsels hanging in echo.

Midnight Mass at Christmas was one of the biggest events of the year in Radelie Koe. Moms, aunts, and sisters busied themselves with sewing and embroidery through the long winter months, after having gone out in late fall for the trapping season.

By the time Christmas rolled around, everyone was dressed in their beaded and silky best, the men on the left side of the aisle at Mass, ladies on the right. After midnight, people would gather, shaking long-awaited hands, then head home for some early celebration.

Such was the scene in the Jim and Thérèse Pierrot household, as everyone was treated with *lebo lat'eh kolee,* a potent concoction of yeast, potatoes, and canned fruit.

As the hostess, Thérèse, tells it:

> We only gave enough time for people to see each other again, after all this time out there on the land, and to have a quick drink, then we sent them all home because the next day, Christmas Day, would be the real one for people to really come around and party. Now it was time to go to sleep and rest up.

Me and Jim both went to bed, and I was just drifting off to have myself a good dream, and here I heard some kind of Christmas song. When I listened close it was somebody singing "Silent Night"!

I got scared, and right away I shook up my husband, Jim, woke him right up and told him to quit singing.

"You know I was sleeping. What you wake me up for now, crazy woman?" he scolded me.

I told him, "There's somebody singing 'Silent Night' and I thought it was you."

"You know I only sing our Dene songs, and I don't even know any Christmas songs. Just go back to sleep."

Same thing happened again, and I woke up Jim again.

This time we were both getting mad, and I told him to just light up a candle and have a look around the house. He did, looking every place in our cold house in the middle of the night. It took him a while, but he finally found out what it was. There was old Ehse Theodore Tobac, lying flat on his back under our bed, way over the wall, just under us. *He's* the one that was singing "Silent Night"!

Such were the entertainments in our merry little town.

Alehlekeh

My circle of friends was a rather large one, always hanging around our place, waiting for me to come out and play. Summers were usually spent out in fish camps with only a limited number of children, but either there or in town, there were a lot of things to do and lots of fun to be had.

Year-round most of our time was spent outdoors, and we would not really be allowed in until bedtime. We lived in a place where it was cold, period, from the first week in September to the end of June, so we never thought of the seasons as such. Winter for us was like spring and summer anywhere else, really.

My closest friends nearby were my cousins, Barney Masuzumi, David, and Fred Kelly. Fred would later make his mark in the sports world, as the famous Kelly Express, for his full-bore ski-racing style.

I will forever feel bad for playing a rather cruel trick on David, although the thought of things going wrong wasn't a part of childhood reckoning. We were watching an *alla sho*, barge, going by when I got him to jump off the steep Duhogah bank, saying I would catch him. He did jump, but I stepped away, and he broke his leg!

Our group of little boys was quite a bunch of rascals indeed. Early summers were spent at either Fiddlesticks, a popular swimming hole along Jackfish Creek, or at the Point, at the south end of the community on the big river, for the same watery mayhem. The littlest ones did the dog paddle, cupping their hands for fins and kicking behind as they went.

Sometimes our games could get rough. The gang got a hold of me once when we were fooling around near a trash heap. They swung me and threw me into it. I fell on something sharp and ended up with an ugly gash on my lower arm. It was simply wrapped and left me with a huge scar.

Growing up on the land, we all knew, for the most part, how to handle a knife, gun, and axe. We made all kinds of things out of wood—from carved boats, with little propellers shaped from Copenhagen snuff cans, to bows and arrows. Bows were made of an older willow called *k'ats'ah*, carefully carved over several weeks, immersed in water, and fire-hardened. With so much prep work, to see it splinter and break when you first went to bend it was heartbreak indeed!

We had real out-and-out wars against the older boys with these bows and arrows over the girls, who were our captives in forts. You had to be quite daring to get right in there and capture them, too, with all kinds of danger awaiting you. Good slingshot sticks were sought after. They had to be paired with the right kind of rubber tire. It had to be the "fast" kind rather than the "slow" one, which would just stop when pulled.

Besides my cousins, I associated for the most part with Walter Edgi. He was a super runner and always had some good snacks, a radio, and even records at his home, which was some ways across town, high over Ohndah Dek'ieh.

At that time, everybody was listening to country music. Some people had records, and Walter had classical records. A couple of early albums I recall were the Righteous Brothers and, of all things, the American Van Cliburn's historic win in the inaugural International Tchaikovsky Competition in Moscow, Russia, 1958! He played Concerto No. 1 in B-flat minor.

Of course, none of us budding pre-teen standout Dene athletes could tell you what a B-flat was, much less the minor key, or a Tchaikovsky, but something in the soaring aural waves in the upstairs log building bound us to this classical music from the start. Where Walter's father, Cassien, got these discs is anybody's guess. He was also an amateur photographer and a bit of a local legend.

Radios at the time had huge batteries, the covers for which were slick and made for great sleds! We thought there were little people in the radios who did all the talking! As for the music, how an entire orchestra might fit in even the largest radio was anyone's guess.

My friend Donald Modeste's parents were from farther down the river in Tsiigehtchic, as were others who settled in our town. Another friend, John Turo, would later figure in my first trip to art school in Toronto.

From Bear Rock Mountain

Other friends were John T'Seleie, Stephen Kakfwi, and Richard (Dicky) McNeely. Richard's father, old Bill McNeely, had a store on the way to school, where we would stop for a Superman candy bar. Dicky's mum, Darian, made the best pies in the world and was a very kind-hearted person. Stephen went on to a life in politics. John would later figure in my first times at the residential school, Grollier Hall in Inuvik, some 161 kilometres farther north.

When I think of what awaited our small group of innocent children, I often wonder what it would have been like to just stay as we were, a younger version of a traditional community.

Then again nothing ever works out that way. Everything changes.

Even then we were of diverse origins, from the grandson of the original Chief T'Seleie, who signed Treaty 8 on behalf of our people, to the son of a northern Métis trader.

History, like it or not, was about change. And we were in for more than our fair share of upheaval.

Of all these *alehlekeh* (friends), John T'Seleie was the one who lasted from start to finish. Through the trials and tribulations of life, he kept friendship the simplest by adhering to the vision of what our cultural hero Yamoria meant by being Dene: not picking a friend like you would a nice jellybean out of a jar but knowing that once decided there is no personal choice.

As it turned out his father called me *Seh Leh Beyah* (My Friend's Son) after his feelings for my dad.

We had our very basic differences, mind you, but never enough to start looking for a way out, as some others chose to do.

Ol' Time Fun in Town

We made our own joy! Living all the way up the river on the seventy-metre cliffs of the Ramparts, you clearly heard the first sounds of the drums. When the drummers got going on their caribou-hide drums to celebrate some occasion, there was no stopping the dancing during the midnight sun.

In fact, that far north, a day could easily last a full month and a half, with the sun just barely touching the horizon on a late evening and going back up yet again. After a long winter of only five hours of daylight, we looked forward to a time of relaxation. When you were used to cutting a lot of wood and chopping ice for water in the world's coldest place, lazy summer days were exhilarating.

When drum dances were held in winter, it got pretty hot in the ol' log dance hall we had. It wasn't anything fancy, just a bigger log building with a full-size oil barrel woodstove for people to come together to enjoy themselves.

The drums went on for as long as people felt like dancing. During breaks we would go outside and say "sek'e niyuh [breathe on me]," to cool off.

Quite often there would be a fiddle dance to round off a night of fun. Some of the drummers were Gabe Cotchilly, George and Antoine Abelon, John and Edward Gardebois, and some of the elders, like Gregory Shae and Louie Boucan.

In terms of our extended family, Antoine Abelon was a relative of sorts. He called me Sheuyieh (Shares My Name), a form of affection between people whose names just happened to be the same.

Everything in Dene culture reinforced this concept of the group.

The idea of celebrating one person's birthday was foreign to us, as in most other First Nations tribes, although when it was recognized at a drum dance, for instance, the child would be placed in the centre of the room, with the rest of the community in a circle, celebrating.

Of a time, too, they would set up for hand games, a kind of team guessing game with the drums going. An equal number of players would square off on each side, and the captains of each team would try to find out with nods of their head, which side of their hands held little tokens. The winner got to be on the side holding all the counting sticks.

The drummers would set up a fast-paced chant, and the team members hid their tokens from a guesser on the other team. This play went back and forth until only one side held all the sticks, and that was one game. In older times, these hand games would go on for days, with breaks only for naps and to eat a little.

Fiddle music started in the far-off Orkney Islands of Scotland and was brought to the North by the Métis who intermarried with Dene women. To our town of Radelie Koe came Albert Lafferty, for instance, who worked on the boats bringing supplies and modern goods. He showed some of our locals how to play the fiddle, and it carried on from there.

After a night of hard rain, the floor of the old dance hall would still be covered with water. It didn't make a bit of difference to people intent on jigging, so you'd have these great splashes of water wherever the high-stepping happened!

Of particular mayhem were the square dances, with the caller trying to be heard above the din.

After the ol' dance hall was torn down, we never did have action quite as heated and exciting.

Sports Day in Town

He would be waiting for the rest of them, cigarette in hand.

Although we spent almost all of our time in fish camps of a summer, we did go into town for some events. July 1, then called Dominion Day, was one such event, with sports being a big feature.

One of the things that always impressed me was the adults' foot race, and especially one runner from our Radelie Koe, Edward Gardebois, who would take on and handily beat all comers, even with big ol' gumboots on! He would even stop and wait for them, idly chatting with a few spectators.

Another thing I found out early was that, even though I was of a slighter build, I was actually very athletic and won most of the events I took part in.

Before Japan, the Dene/Dineh

It was one of those days that blossomed like it would just go on forever in the Land of the Rising Sun ... and in a way, it did.

As the world changed, life in Radelie Koe went on. Yet, we were touched by faraway events. At eight-fifteen on the morning of August 6, 1945, an almost cloudless day, the first of two atomic bombs, the uranium gun-type Little Boy, was dropped over Hiroshima, detonating at 580 metres. It was the equivalent of sixteen kilotons of TNT. Three days later, on August 9, another, the plutonium implosion-type Fat Man bomb, was dropped over Nagasaki. An estimated 120,000 Japanese were killed, nearly all instantly, from the first-ever, horrific nuclear blasts.

In terms of the overall effect, no one knew even as the blast happened, just how long the fission would continue in its wake, like a stone tossed into a calm pool of water. But serious debate over the use of this massively destructive weapon goes on, even today.

Oddly enough, years later, I would find myself in Italy, reading about Nobel Prize–winning physicist Enrico Fermi, who was first credited with discovering nuclear fission—that is, splitting the nucleus of a uranium atom to unleash the tremendous power it contained.

A gigantic step away from simple solar power.

The first test bomb set off by the Manhattan Project, at 5:30 AM on July 16, 1945, at the Los Alamos, New Mexico, site, completely vaporized the metal stand on which the bomb sat, melting all the surrounding sand at Ground Zero into glass.

We Dene/Dineh were not, of course, caught in the blinding doom when these gates to Hell burst open, but just as surely, our people in Canada and the United States were the first human casualties of these bombings.

In 1942, the Eldorado radium mine near Déline was appropriated by the Canadian government and, over the next three years, produced hundreds of tonnes of uranium ore for the top-secret Manhattan Project, which developed the bombs that ended the war in the Pacific Theatre.

Although the Canadian government knew about the dangers of this raw uranium ore, it was carried out to barges on the backs of Dene workers, who later died of cancer. Farther to the south, starting in 1944, our Navajo Dineh relatives also came under direct contact with uranium ore mined in Navajo Nation for the same purpose.

In both the northern and southern Dene/Dineh Nations there were many deaths from cancer from exposure to this uranium. No one can doubt that we paid the price of "freedom."

For our northern Dene, the damage was foretold in the prophesies of Etseo Ayha in the tiny fishing village of *Déline* (Where the Waters Flow), on the shores of the Sahtú/Great Bear Lake, one of the five biggest freshwater lakes in Canada.

This man of God spoke of the atomic bombing of Japan, and he was even consulted by high military and federal government officials about the dangers of Nazi power to the Western World.

CHAPTER 3

Icy Fingers of Change

There is a cold blast of air that first hits you when you step outside in winter, getting right into your lungs and taking your breath for a moment.

The difference between our small town of Radelie Koe and Inuvik, where we went to residential school, was just as drastic. The Mackenzie Delta was certainly physically colder, and there was a new kind of coldness awaiting us young and innocent children at the residential school there. I was nine, and my sister Judy just seven when we went on September 19, 1959.

Back at home, everyone was a relative, and most were close. In our Dene way, it was up to all the people to raise every child. In contrast, at our appointed confinement, we were in the charge of priests and nuns preaching the fire and brimstone of the early church. They were definitely there to let all know that hellfire awaited anyone who dared disobey, with the Canadian colonial state on side. My poor sister had never been away from home.

The building itself was imposing, and, right from the start, boys were separated from girls. In my case, Judy, who was a constant companion at home, now might as well have been living on the moon.

Our parents were strict with us, yes, but once a chore got done, we could pretty well relax again, in the easy affection of comforting country surroundings.

We would soon enough learn for ourselves that places like Grollier Hall were designed to literally "kill the Indian in the child."

Ahso, Grandma, Getting Smaller

She just stood there on that shrinking shore, getting smaller.

Something about the way she didn't move at all, not even waving as we were taken away to go back to residential school for another year, bespoke a profound sense of our future without meaning. This was often the last time during the break that we saw our beloved grandmother, Ahso Begho Honleh, by the water's edge, at Warih Dahgun, a fish camp up the Duhogah a bit from town.

The fish camp air became sharper around the middle of August and the water much colder when you went to check the daily nets.

> ... and a different and somehow more real kind of chill
> descended as sure as the passing
> of the season of midnight sun.

When the camp started to bale up all the fish from the summer catch for the coming winter, we knew that our longed-for summer break from residential school would soon be over. As children, though, we also looked forward to seeing more of the world than our little riverside camp.

> Yet when time and the RCMP police boat came for us
> we could not help an entirely empty feeling
> as if the place blown into a blue balloon set aloft
> watching dear ol' Grandma grow tinier
> there in a suddenly lonely camp
> she with her universe
> back down to ONE
> for yet another winter
> in her dwindling
> few
> left.

Some Wild Bush Plane Rides!

Those earlier northern times were about the famed Beavers and brown paper bags! The de Havilland Beaver was a plane specially designed for its durability and its ability to get in and out of, with relative ease, the countless small lakes that dot the northern landscape.

For we students bound for Inuvik, almost 317 kilometres over the Arctic Circle, all six passenger seats were taken out and about twenty of us were crammed in, many for their first airplane ride ever.

Nothing had prepared us for that wild ride!

Except, of course, for my cousin, the Mad Scientist, Alfred Masuzumi! His favourite game was to have each of us smaller friends and relatives line up for paratrooper duty, that is be grabbed by his brother Walter, tied up to an old blanket, and summarily tossed off the seventy-metre-high cliffs at the Ramparts, right next to our Farahezen fish camp on the Duhogah.

Alfred had put together these homemade parachutes with rigging, a blanket, and some kind of harness to hold the chutists, in this case, us.

I was the first to go, being the lightest. Smooth sailing all the way down, to alight on the ground far below. Check one success story.

We all made it down, buoyed by wayward Duhogah breezes. Everyone, that is, except Barney, who had a stockier boxer build. His "chute" wouldn't open, and he dropped straight down and broke his leg! Alfred and Wally's plan was to just leave him there, and they would have but for their father, Uncle Charlie's, questioning when they had to reveal their evil doings and caught heck for it!

For the insane rides over to Inuvik, there were none of the ease and comfort that modern airplanes provide, just you, your bag, and the sight of barren, frozen ground far below. The idea was to get as many of us youngsters, some at five or six years old, from one place to another. The plane went as much up and down as forward, with frequent freefalls that would leave your stomach, and much of its contents, in your throat!

There was never a good enough supply of the brown paper "puke sacks," which filled up pretty quick.

That bush plane ride pretty well set the tone for what we were to expect from the residential school itself—basically being thrown unceremoniously into the deep end of the pool.

September 19, 1959

Ahso reminded me that she had put a dollar bill in a white shirt in my plain, beaten up ol' suitcase, but it got lost in the confusion. Strangely enough, besides all the mountains of abuse, that lost one-dollar bill was one of my most traumatic memories of residential schools, probably because it was the one thing I had from dear ol' Grandma.

September 19, 1959, a Saturday, will always stand out as the time me and my sister Judy were taken from our home in Radelie Koe to go north to school at Grollier Hall. I had been north, like many of our people, to the tuberculosis infirmary in Aklavik a couple of years before.

We flew north to Fort McPherson and went to an Anglican Church service with the students there. Then we went to the old hostel in Aklavik to continue to Inuvik by Bombardier.

When we arrived at the Grollier Hall hostel building, we were separated, and I didn't get to see Judy but on special days. This was the hardest for us, I believe, because we had been so close back home. Judy had always insisted on coming along with me, even when I went out playing with the rest of the boys.

That separation at the doors of Grollier Hall, our official welcome to the land of the Mola, was what began the long process of tearing our family apart.

Thinking about it now, some sixty years later, that was when the "disconnect" from siblings, family, and culture really began, the physical and emotional pull away from everything you knew and loved.

Sadly, survivors of these traumatic places have a marked tendency to want to avoid any kind of human contact and certainly any intimacy, anything that might result in some sort of connection.

For want of a better word, this is the real legacy, if you will, of these residential schools. To become part of Canada, you had to lose everything you cared for.

> Up to then no amount of minus thirty or forty weather
> could have possibly hurt as much.
> The stinging cold
> no comparison to the long years ahead
> away from HOME.

Each in our own way, we began to learn that even with hundreds of others around in exactly the same sad state, the loneliest feeling ever in this big ol' world was being in a foreign bunk-bed, the cold arctic night creeping in.

> No familiar, steady heat
> of woodstove
> soft Dene tones
> nor friendly hiss of gas lamp
> dogs howling at the moon.
> Just a blank wall
>   to turn to . . .

One way or another, the Roman Catholic Church found its way into the North with the traders and now began its payback, on behalf of the Canadian government.

We, the innocent children of the First Nations, were the victims in this vicious circle. There was no doubt that we were a part of a truly colonialist regime and that this was cultural genocide, beginning with taking the children from their parents and home.

All First Nations were very much right in the middle of a major transition.

After some thirty thousand years or so of life on the land, we found ourselves in town life. This created a lot of major problems, not the least being too few resources to go around. On the land, there were never more than a given and limited number of people in any one campground for a very good reason. With their intimate knowledge of the land, our elders always thought ahead before moving anywhere for an extended period of time. The idea was to not fish nor hunt out any one tract of land, and to leave places with a chance to restock.

Now all of these people in town had to compete for the available jobs and resources. The only choices were with the outside businesses: the Bay, or Hudson's Bay Company Trading Post, the Department of Transportation (DOT), and maybe a couple of jobs with the RCMP.

Were that not bad enough, our relatives were now told they could not keep their own children.

The way the new town of Inuvik was created was a perfect example of the new forces at play in the North. The reason given for the new town was flooding at the former government centre in Aklavik. This explanation is questionable, since Aklavik is still very much alive today, some seventy years later. Except for the need for utilidors, above-ground conduits for water and sewage, the basic structure of the town could have been any Canadian suburban scene.

Meanwhile, when I arrived at the junior boys' wing of the Grollier Hall residence, the rest of the boys were out at the nearby Sir Alexander Mackenzie Federal Day School, where our classes were held with French Catholic and Anglican students from the community. I marvelled at the size of it. Up until this time, the biggest place I had been in at home was the church building. Even just the junior boys' wing of the residential school seemed huge to me!

When the boys got back, they crowded around me, knowing that I only spoke our language and wanting to hear of news from home, hundreds of miles to the south. After the novelty wore off, the one guy who stayed with me was my lifelong friend John T'Seleie. He warned me that I was not to speak our Dene language again.

Of course, ignoring his advice got me into trouble time and time again.

Along with my lifelong hell-bent lack of respect for any kind of authority outside of our Dene elders, somewhere out there in the ether of human existence floats my little beaten-up brown suitcase, along with thousands like it taken from Jews on their way to *Shoah*, the Nazi death camps.

Kill the Indian
The idea, so dangerously biblical . . .

The thought behind the saying "Save the child, kill the Indian" goes all the way back to before Europeans even landed on the shores of America. There was even a papal bull from 1491, predating manifest destiny, setting down how Indigenous Peoples were too primitive and ignorant of "civilization" to be involved in "progress."

So the stage was set for any itinerant explorer to wander around, often completely lost, claiming lands for foreign governments by simply planting a flag on traditional country, which our Peoples had lived on for at least thirty thousand years.

To impress the ignorant savages, there was a great show of fancy clothes, gifts, and paper, official papers, showing who would be the new boss.

Our Peoples saw these treaties as friendship treaties, but the

Mola saw them as a transfer of land. Through this series of outright thefts, much of the damage we see to Mother Earth today was officially okayed—at least on the side of the oppressors.

In 1876, not ten years after Confederation, the *Indian Act* instituted residential schools as an Act of Parliament. Just one of them "co-incidences": set up Canada and then "kill the Indian."

Since then, some 150,000 of our First Nations children have become fodder for cultural genocide, the next best thing to just killing us right off. Of course, all of this didn't make much sense to a group of several hundreds of us at Grollier Hall in the late 1950s, when it first opened.

We would, though, as all survivors of war and other related trauma do, suffer for a coming lifetime.

With Each Whack

The evil thought behind each vicious strike with brush or strap began long, long before the actual beating. Medieval zealots had formed the mindset of the Roman Catholic missionaries long before there was any such thing as a residential school in Canada. But we were now trapped in this new life.

Heathens and pagans, like Indians, would go straight to Hell!

But the two ideas came from the same source, whether found in the Bible or the Constitution.

As with each and every step of oppression anywhere in the world, we of the First Nations had what Europeans wanted: land and what they like to call "natural resources." In short, we had all of Mother Nature.

Of course, none of this made much sense to me as a little boy of nine. Sitting forlorn on some steps waiting for whatever else was going to happen, I was joined by someone I knew from back home: John T'Seleie.

He asked me if I knew what was going on, and when I answered him in Dene, he told me right off that we were never to use our own language or else we would "get the strap."

Having just been in an institution in Aklavik to be treated for tuberculosis the year before, I was only too familiar with the pain such a punishment left in your hand and, more, in the deep hurting shame we never felt at home, no matter what we did wrong.

Stubborn as I was, I knew if I spoke Dene, I would be told on to the head nun, Sister Hebert, by her favoured "pets," snitches who would turn you in on even a suspicion of any supposed wrong.

And, of course, I was right.

Besides the strap itself, one favourite penalty for a "black mark," or several, was to be handed a shovel and sent to spend movie night up on the roof of the huge dining room, cleaning off the thick accumulated snow. You could hear the sound of the film, with all of your friends laughing merrily along below. One punishment reserved for the really stubborn kids was being forced to stand in a closet while the others slept.

> Another I got used to and expected on any given night
> while the rest slept the long night away
> was a simple closet.
> Standing in a corner inside the whole time.
>
> Even this closet held that familiar
> odour of pent-up
> need
> for anything remotely human. A mix of various unspent
> funks of life.
>
> In a complete and utter dark, except for the small doorway
> crack of light behind
> separating me from
> all the Good Little Indians.
>
> Never did want to be one anyway.

A Perverse Need for Order

The only time I saw the same measure of confusion as I felt at Grollier Hall was in an episode of *The Twilight Zone*. A man somehow gets trapped on an abandoned street, only to find out there are murderous Nazis all around him and no place to hide!

I came from a family that prized neatness above all. Grandpa Peter Mountain Sr. said that the way it is around you is the same as it is in your mind, either it's messed up or well kept. Especially out on the land, you simply needed to keep order around you.

Mom especially insisted that, "*Baghareh goded'zah* [anything extra only creates a mess]."

But the manic insistence at Grollier Hall on an overregulated day didn't make much sense—and being told what to do in a foreign language only added to our confusion.

Just for a moment, imagine sleepily shuffling your way to the washroom, and on the way back to bed, encountering the cold arctic dawn that followed close on a night of muffled cries, as a hundred or so children as young as five try to sleep once again, away from the arms of a loving mother and the comforts of home.

Wake-up call was mayhem as we tried to get our beds just so, with the corners tucked in at the right angle.

A miserable line-up of the poor boys so keyed up, so psychologically traumatized, that they could not help but wet their beds.

The fact that these were always the same little ones only showed that it had to be something eating at them inside in the deep of night when they needed their rest the most. They were made to stand in line holding their stinking sheets front and centre for all to see.

Even in the dining room, we had to maintain some kind of order in the rush to eat on time, in the arctic north, where winter is basically one long night.

Breakfast was invariably a pasty blob of lumpy porridge with maybe a splash of watery KLIM-brand powdered milk on top, sour or not.

Both lunch and supper were usually some kind of overcooked fish, all bones and dried-up flakes, with maybe the odd plate of overcooked reindeer brought from Europe.

There was no attempt at all to bridge the vast cultural gap between the old French background of these priests and nuns and our traditional First Nations roots.

They prattled away among themselves in French, our church services were in Latin, with no regard to what we may have wanted to know of them.

> Natural childish curiosity
> soon gave way to sullen gravity
> like a stone carelessly tossed and
>   sunk
> into a muddy bottom.

We were all marked for failure, except, of course, for the pets, "sister's pets"—the cuter ones who did who knows what for the nuns in private. For the pets to keep their favoured spots, though, they had to snitch on everyone else.

There was little doubt that we were only *les sauvages*, savages, dirty Indians in need of some serious straightening out!

In an unspoken loveless language, though, we did learn from the start that it was rule by fear.

Even acts of kindness had an element suggesting we were nothing but a pack of stray dogs. On special occasions, the nuns would throw handfuls of hard candy or peanuts over our heads and we had to fight the people around us to get anything at all.

Our mail was invariably read and parcels opened before they got to us. The Inuit children's parents must have thought more of them, for they usually got the best stuff.

The rest of us just sort of sidled up to them, going, "I'm your friend, huh . . . huh, friend?"

Each child had a little pile of personal, pitiful trinkets under their pillow. Every once in a while, you would ask someone, "Lemme see your junks." Looking back, I do believe this is where a lot of us were early on grafted with a sense for the neurotic, not to mention anally retentive, for a lifetime.

> Where really, this Holy Spirit
> raised on High in daily mass?
>
> And, to whom, pray, held aloft
> above a needy world
> but to their missionary selves
> saving us from ourselves.

The real part of this living nightmare was, and is for too many thousands of us survivors, the PTSD slowly seeping into our life-blood—with all official eyes intentionally turned away—like the poison in the cloak given Hercules by his wife.

> Only an echo of this can be heard
> from Bear Rock Mountain.

In time, the only parallel I ever saw or found was with the Nazi death camps—Auschwitz, for instance—where this same kind of brutally enforced pace of blind obedience eventually turned a once-proud people into neurotic adults.

These missionaries gave up unresolved lives back in France when they got the "calling" from God. But reality caught up with them, and they took it out on little children. Put a priest or a nun in the farthest, coldest outreach of a foreign country, away from their familiar France, deprived of any human sexual outlet or emotional warmth—another kind of poverty—and you have the recipe for some psychotic "norms." All of *that*, without the benefit of any kind of court for us, the presumed guilty.

One could only wonder why these Christian missionaries, even full of their own brand of blind, unforgivable faith, would so soon have forgotten the jackboots recently endured back in occupied France!

Unless, of course, we Indian children were as dangerous as the Jews, hell-bent on taking over their stifling world.

Truth be told, none of us had ever been in a place with more than several hundred people, much less known there was anything beyond East 3, one branch of the Duhogah.

In more ways than one, we had been brought to the very edge of the universe and dropped off in

F
  R
    E
    E
      F
      A
      L
      L

Child in a Cage

There are differences we cannot ignore and damages that
trail lives littered with negativity.

Decades after I had gone through residential school, I presented the Truth and Reconciliation Commission with an image to be used as a poster in our northern schools:

It was deemed too "harsh" for present-day Disney-influenced

schoolchildren and was outright rejected, very likely because I had dared to suggest that we needed real survivors to sit on such commissions. This only goes to show how insidious this kind of official "Kill the Indian in the child" abuse really is, coming as it does from a supposed higher order that is going to set the world right.

My talent as an artist was recognized soon after I got to Grollier Hall, and the nun, Monster Hébert, the most bullish of two-legged inhuman terrors, had me paint copies of pictures—dog teams and such—on the wall as decoration while balanced precariously high on a stepladder.

> No one dared stand up to this menace
> from the lowest bowels of Hades itself
> a monster
> if ever there was one!

By then I was a genuine veteran, having survived my share of her tortures for speaking Dene, with the blistered and aching hands to prove it. But unlike anyone else, I never had any qualms about speaking up for myself, and much though I appreciated being indoors on a winter day, I told her I just couldn't copy the pictures, period. I wanted to at least use my own colours, a major no-no in the strict residential school way of doing things, anything, really.

No personal form of individual expression, ever, or else!

This is exactly how it was when I was at the dreaded Grollier Hall, from the late 1950s to 1965.

> A lonely and miserable child sits
> eyes and face downcast, behind bars
> in a sorry prison he had no choice in.
> A Christian cross frames his miserable form in back.

But in all tales of survival, there are signs of hope.

In the case of we, the First Nations of the Americas, it has to do with our sense of survival, having already been here with our Mother Earth for over thirty thousand years. This kind of resiliency is also shown in the fields of fireweed—a symbol of hope—for this is the flower that first blooms after a forest fire rages through the land. It is also in turquoise, a sacred colour God knows you by.

> In a semicircle below
>   and reaching for this child in a cage
> is the sacred fireplace
> of the Native American Church
> which eventually saved me from demon alcohol.

> Here and there to punctuate
> and eventually rust and break
> the bars of steel
> blossoms of our Mother Peyote.

CHAPTER 4

The Wider Picture

We were doomed long before the RCMP came in boats to
take us away.

Although our grandparents were spared the indignity of the
residential schools, they were no less a part of the Canadian
scheme of cultural genocide to rid this world of more bothersome
brown people.

The assimilation into European culture began with a de facto
Act of Parliament at the time of Confederation, no less, way back
in 1867. But to get a truer idea of just what was in store for our
First Nations Peoples, you have to go all the way back to the days
of the fur trade.

The best furs in the world came from my home Sahtú, the Great
Bear Lake Region, and the fur companies did everything they possibly could to ensure the best profits. Dene trappers trading for a
weapon would have to stack up their beaver furs to the very top
of a long musket and were very likely charged extra for the lead
ball and powder too. There was even a wooden press to make an
almost solid block of fur for easier handling. The lead balls used as
ammunition were so new to the North that a hunter would often
have to look for many hours to find the projectile for reuse.

The Roman Catholic Church jumped right on board, too,
having been brought up to remote villages on company boats.

Right up to our grandfather's generation, Indigenous Peoples
had been subjected to these religious zealots and their hellfire

and damnation sermons. Whatever remained of our Dene cultural beliefs had to be stamped out by any means possible. Even in my earliest times, we said all of our prayers in Latin.

It is no secret that the German madman Adolf Hitler took careful note of how our First Nations People were treated for his devious plans for the Jews and other "undesirables" in Europe.

One particular case in point here in the North was an Oblate priest, Father Henri Posset, who committed suicide right in the mission building in Tulita rather than publicly admit his guilt for sexual crimes there. It took this drastic act to convince our Dene elders that, yes, a supposed man of God could do and did that sort of thing.

Some Saving Grace

There were those *whew* moments—one of them came right on my first day after being out in the hallway trying to figure out my next move. Standing there with my cousin David Kelly and a few others, I was trying to think of what to do next, which class to slip into. I had been to a day school back at home before, but nothing as daunting as this strict residential school.

My friends were all heading for their respective classes at the Roman Catholic elementary wing of the Sir Alexander Mackenzie Federal Day School, a few hundred yards from where we lived at Grollier Hall. Not knowing what else to do, I just picked a higher grade to duck into: Sister Leduc's Grade 3 class. In all the confusion, she didn't say anything. She was busy with what looked like a stack of bits of paper in front of her. It turned out to be paper money, which she was using to reward those who got the right answers.

When I arrived in late September, I was way in the very back of the room, trying to make myself as small as possible so I wouldn't get kicked back to a lower grade. By the time Christmas rolled around, I was sitting right in front, with my own stack of bills up to about twenty-five dollars or so. Whoever knew a stack of bills would save me! And I not even knowing what *somba* (money), was.

For a final quiz and five big smackers, Sister Leduc asked for the spelling of "wasps," which, when completed, added to my total. I had earned the first pick of toys high up on a shelf running all around the entire room. When she said for me to go ahead and pick one, I instead asked her what would happen to the students who didn't have any money.

She calmly replied, "That is their problem for not paying attention."

Just as poised, I volunteered my pick to whoever this might be. All eyes turned to little Roy Goose, who as usual was busying himself drawing airplanes, very advanced for a child under ten. He was one happy little child as he proudly stepped up on a chair and then the desk and reached for a big ol' bright red fire truck that was almost as big as his desk!

I now had a friendship that far outlived a simple toy.

Sister Leduc, though stern as a proverbial ramrod on ice, had an artistic side and took to producing the entire school's yearbook, the first with a canvas cover. Knowing that I, like Roy, was often sketching behind a shielding arm or hand, she got me to do the artwork, beginning a long line of such work, all the way to high school.

No Coloured Bubbles

Early on, I found some ways to at least mentally put the hated present of Grollier Hall on the back burner and go on the best I could. One was the first feel of a basketball in my hands, bouncing it on the gym floor just below our junior boys' wing. I naturally took to basketball, along with any sport, for that matter. I was also good at writing, though it wasn't accepted because it was counter to the indoctrination we were experiencing.

One particular reminder that I was now living among a bunch of children in church chains came when we were asked to write an essay about some way that we wanted to be. I wrote that I wished to be Inuit; even that small grasp for a bit of freedom was greeted with derision.

> "No, Antoine, you are in prison here
> and no hope
> of even expression!"

Another time I was given the book *The Wind in the Willows* as a prize for being good with words. Although somewhat pleased to have some sort of recognition, I simply could not relate to this Mola reference to some English pastoral bliss, so far removed from this ultimate arctic cold.

Besides, I could already feel that ol' "Good Indian" noose tightening around my little neck, the kind that made my peers try to be favoured as sisters' boys—that invisible brand of Roman Catholicism that led the sheep to slaughter.

> It came with the morning dollop of slop porridge
> watered down with prayer recited
> and brought home
> to confused Dene parents
>
> Without quite knowing it
> I was also well on my way
> to simply shutting off
> emotionally
>
> Although the will
> was there
> already real enough

At twelve
when all the magic bubbles
were supposed to pop up .
in living colour!

It would take about a half century to put a name to that drifted feeling and realize that cultural genocide was already an institution of First Nations life by the 1950s, buried as it was under a mountain of hypocritical good Christian intentions and downright denial.

One thing that did take root, though, was my love and respect, right off, for the written word. It was more than the idea of books per se—the way a string of words put together in different ways had the power to create worlds of their own.

I found that reading was more, far more, than simply an escape, which could be done easily enough. Very likely it was just this idea of words being worked over so they would fit together to make sense and then enclosed in a secret-enough place—on a page, in a specific chapter, even within a sentence—like we little children in residential school ...

Waiting for a time
and place
like this one
to be read
thus freed

at least
in the mind of someone else.

Uncle Joe's Dogs

Just being together again in the warm sled with Uncle Joe steering in back was a renewed ray of joy!

In a world of dulling monotony, we longed for any memory of home. The constant and unchanging menu of porridge and dried-up fish marked our days at the residential school in a long, grey wintry stretch of hell.

Once in a while, there would be a mail call, with letters and parcels from home, but the clutching hands of the Church reached into even this vital link with our distant relatives. What little we did get from parents who could neither read nor write was often opened and tampered with—the idea being we were not to have any drastic comfort, I suppose.

Judy and I were some of the very luckiest ones though, with relatives in town. Every few weeks, we were allowed to go out on a Sunday with Uncle Joe and Aunt Edith Gully. Their little camp on the edge of town seemed like a palace to us, compared to the confining hallways of Grollier Hall.

They always had Dene *berreh* (real country food), lovingly cooked bannock, caribou, and fresh fish, which we ate with relish. It never failed that Uncle Joe would hitch up his dog team just for us and take us flying through the Delta channels past East 3, the original name for Inuvik, for an hour or two.

Although it was cold out there on the frozen ice, we were warmed for a brief time by real loving concern, not the kind with threats of damnation attached.

Needless to say, these times are our best memories of Inuvik.

Beatles and Dylan, a Glimmer of Hope

One feature of residential school life was the utter boredom of the routine. What we boys found so hard to deal with was the constant prayer—before and after every single event—all day long. A dull and absolutely tasteless menu was something else we could very well do without.

But once in a while, we could relate to something new that came along. We heard on the radio over the intercom at school about a new heavyweight boxer named Cassius Clay who would later become the youngest world champion. Never before had we heard a non-White person have the nerve to call himself the greatest!

And there were other distractions from the boredom. Whenever I hear an instrumental version of "The Last Date," it brings back the sound of Floyd Cramer's piano drifting across the row of beds in the senior boys' dorm at Grollier Hall. It signalled the end of the Saturday night late show from the local CBC affiliate, CHAK Radio, which had an Inuit announcer, Elijah Menarik, at the controls—a brief respite for us.

True, there was always good ol' Elvis Presley to sing you a lover's lullaby, but the thoroughly new and exciting sounds of the Beatles and Bob Dylan made you wonder what there could be beyond that Arctic horizon after all.

Another activity that numbed the pain for us a little was the chance to play all the sports we ever wanted. My favourites soon became basketball and cross-country ski racing with a bit of hockey, as a goalie with my fast reflexes.

Nights of 'Oney and Benz

We had our humble beginnings, to be sure.

When Coach Father Mochet put a call out for students at Grollier Hall to try out for cross-country skiing, we did not know what to make of it. But always being up for a challenge, and just to get out of the hated halls of that dreaded place, my best friend John T'Seleie and I decided to go and see what all the fuss was about.

We had no idea what skis were and just strapped on those heavy, wide army surplus ones, with broken hockey sticks for poles! Out on the training track, with skimpy light bulbs strung out every ten yards or so, we went back and forth, to and fro, all through those cold high arctic nights.

Indoor training found us doing the same thing, in wooly stocking feet, over and across the gym floor, creating loud static electric sparks when anyone came near.

One of our other coaches, Guy Vézina, whose English was spotty at best, kept telling us in his thick French accent that what we needed was plenty of "'oney and benz," meaning honey and beans.

After I got the hang of the quick-kick technique our coaches, Father Mouchet and Bjorger Petersen, demonstrated for us, I eventually got to be the best skier on our team. We travelled to races in the south, mainly in La Belle Province, Quebec. I was simply amazed to count at least ten hockey rinks on each side of the airplane as we landed!

Besides the traditional French assortment of breads, my favourite part of every meal on those trips south was not just one but two banana splits!

Others from our hometown were Fred "the Kelly Express," Harold Cook, and John Turo, who had an indomitable will. We each had our own fans who said that we went faster uphill than they did racing downhill!

My Green Bear

When I was yet in grade school, I thought I would try my hand at painting.

The bear just sort of stood there in the otherwise bright classroom, immobile, with a dull sheen all of its own. I got a few colours together in class and just started drawing the bear. The simple effort of putting something down from my own mind was such that I felt great all during our lunch break.

But when I got back to it, all that greeted me was a dullish green bear with only three legs. But by then it didn't matter to me.

I had begun my painting career and that was that.

To this day, I wish I still had that green bear . . . yet I have to wonder what such a bear would say.

> "For this we wish above all
> to simply be allowed
> something to say
>   and when given the chance
> we want more, and what's more, we want the best."

Little Hearts Tearing Apart

The family break-up began, I believe, as soon as we—brother and sister—were physically separated at the residential school doors upon arrival.

I only saw my sister on special days, when we ate together, or a time or two at the skating rink. Even in the main chaotic dining room, we could only maybe catch an occasional glimpse of a family member on the girls' side. The seating at church was the same way. There was simply no way to make out a single face in such a large crowd.

Over the years we stayed at Grollier Hall, we were left no choice but to grow apart in our own ways, depending on just how much we were affected by the alienating influence.

At the best of times, we the Dene are not an emotionally demonstrative people. Even after a year, a light touch of hands will most often pass for a greeting, along with a simple statement of what you are doing at present. We are wary of the Mola's ways of verbally gushing right from the word go; we find certain traits, like asking direct and personal questions, very rude. Too, most First Nations Peoples will simply not look a person right in the eyes, out of respect. It is regarded as an intrusion of privacy and considered not polite at all.

These comparatively restrained ways may have well been the result of a martial past, when our people were at war with the Chipewyan to the south, for instance. And even more recently, the heavy losses of relatives during the 1928 influenza epidemic left a lasting mark.

Of course, living in the coldest place in the world doesn't exactly make for the most relaxed ways of relating. Yet again, those are tribal traits and not subject to change from outside forces. So the imposition of a new order of cultural genocide was clearly felt, even though the intent itself was not so evident to us until much later.

We are by nature a forgiving people, to a fault.

Being the more sensitive artistic type, I found myself intentionally shutting off emotionally. Over the first four years of my stay in Inuvik, my circle of emotional trust went down to almost zero.

Our parents and elders must have felt this right from the start, too, for we had now lost our more carefree ways as a community. In town, alcohol abuse was something that was not there before, and so there was no demonstrated way to deal with it. Many of our own parents, including my father, had gone through the residential school experience themselves and had lost any parenting skills as a result.

Having had to deal with an essentially more zealous, earlier order of the Roman Catholic missionaries, our parents had it drilled into them that they were the spawn of the devil, no less, and faced certain hellfire and damnation as a result. The Canadian government, for its part, certainly did not help matters by giving over the responsibility for our education to the churches. Some of our parents had to endure an average of five years far away from home. They lost their Dene language out there and had to also relearn all their lost skills of living on the land.

One can clearly see, then, that going all the way back to their inception in the late 1800s, the residential schools were an out and out attempt to destroy our way of life: cultural genocide.

But for the time being, our parents had the advantage of now being full community members. As students now, we became transients in our own homes.

Being so far away in an alien land for ten months of each year had a lasting impact on our ways of relating to each other. Although my generation was born on the land, we found ourselves gradually being drawn away from our own Dene and Métis culture.

Although we as a family still spent our summers at the usual fish camps, people became short-tempered with each other, and there was now this new sense of confusion and lack of direction in life.

The residential school's effects had an insidious way of creeping into our once-happy lives.

Best Clean-Up Boy

We had always been encouraged to keep our living space neat. My mum must have picked up this habit for tidiness from my grandfather Peter Mountain Sr., for I recall him telling me, "Your place around you is the same as in your mind."

So, when I was in junior boys at residential school, I was already in the habit of making sure everything was in order. This must have caught the attention of someone, for at that one school year's end, I was awarded a nice trophy of a young boy standing with his arms stretched up to some heavenly places.

Granny Elizabeth had her own moments of near divinity, too.

These usually happened when she wanted my sister Judy and I to just dance for her. She herself was no country-singin' Dolly Parton and could not carry much of a tune, but she did know what she wanted us to do. We would both stand patiently in front of her, and she would begin her Dene chant to get us moving:

"Heyeah-heneh ... Neyeah-heney ... Heyeah-heneh ..."

All we had to do was stand there and kinda move around a little, to her great delight!

Granny always had a lot of visitors, people seeking her advice on many things they needed to straighten out in their lives. So, when they would get together, she would make it a habit of taking my Best Clean-Up Boy trophy from its proud perch on top of our old dish cupboard and set it in the middle of her and her friends as they solemnly prayed, thinking this was a religious icon of some sort!

My sisters, meanwhile, would be just killing themselves giggling.

First Jobs

Got started picking weeds.

Because we were so poor and I wanted to keep busy during summers home from Grollier Hall, I started my very first job with my sister Judy when I was twelve or so. With the twenty-four hours of summer daylight, any kind of vegetables would grow in a northern garden—and so would the weeds.

One of the RCMP officers hired us to pick weeds. The lemonade they gave sure tasted tart and good in the hot sun. And it was the very first I ever heard of a tip, a whole dollar bill each, for doing such a good job!

The old Hudson's Bay store used to be right on the riverbank, so the barges that brought in the supplies could be unloaded right there on the shore of the Duhogah. The manager, John Cormack, was a busy Scotsman who had a very kind-hearted wife named

Kay. They were both much beloved, especially Kay. We Dene call her kind of people *Dene bezieh golih* (people with a kind heart).

When I was about fourteen, I asked Mr. Cormack if I could work at the store, and he told me to come in a week, which I did. That was my first official job.

For the first time, I had my own money to help out around the house with expenses. I also made sure to buy the occasional ice cream cone for Judy. I more or less wolfed mine down on our walks to the Point, while I was amazed that she could patiently lick hers to the very end.

I had a watch and would tell her the time every few minutes. I must also confess that I stayed up late just to see the date change to the next day.

Grandpa's Mehkoih

Going on the land with Peter Mountain Sr. was a trip home! Our old-timers sure did love the land!

Former priest René Fumoleau told a lot of stories from his memories of our People. He once came upon my grandfather Peter Mountain Sr., as he was about to leave for some winter hunting. He had six dogs hitched up in tandem, with a sled that looked almost empty for a run out in forty-below days and even colder nights.

When the man of God asked him if that was all he was taking, Grandpa said it was.

"Well," says the priest, "where is your tent and stove? Aren't you going to get cold out there?"

"What for?" answered the Dene man in his parka, mitts, and mukluks. "This is all I am going to need."

"What about the cold? You are going to freeze to death for sure!"

"I have matches and an axe. I can make a *mehkoih* [brush shelter] from three poles and a few big spruce branches for the back and sides and to sleep on. With a fire in front, all I need is a warm canvas tarp."

It sure makes me smile when I think of the heavy loads we used to take even for an overnight run to Kabami Tue by Ski-Doo!

CHAPTER 5

The Door Swings Open, WIDE!

Up until the summer of 1965, my world was still relatively closed in, including as it did only a totally colonialist Northwest Territories with an occasional trip south with the Territorial Experimental Ski Training (TEST) Ski Racing Team or as a gifted writer/artist.

Things had begun to change at home. Judy and I were now too old to jump around in our silly dance for Grandma. We just kinda stood there sheepishly until she got the idea. And around that time, I first heard the rumour that I had been left to die at birth by my parents. I overheard it being talked about in casual conversation at my aunt and uncle's, I believe. After that, I intentionally disobeyed my mother, a first ever.

One day in the summer of 1965 when I was back home in good ol' Radelie Koe, I received an envelope with the return address of a place called Grandin College in faraway Fort Smith. The invitation to go to a different residential school included a photo of a couple of modern buildings in a pristine setting.

There were a few of the older boys, including cousins Barney and Walter, who had already been there and who spoke of its wonders compared to Grollier Hall. As for myself, anything away from that dreaded hostel had to be a better choice.

I decided to go to Grandin College, and after a long airplane ride and a ride into town complete with a genuine singalong, we found ourselves in our rooms, with only one roommate! Were that not enough, the junior and high school, Joseph Burr Tyrrell, included many more Mola students than we were used to in the Far North.

We were formally welcomed by Grandin's director, Father Pochat, who told us that, yes, there were rules for us to follow, and if we did not follow along, we would be free to leave. Then again, who in their right mind would ever want to go away from such a place?

The regimen, which now included morning exercises, was tough, but we were already used to these kinds of marching orders and took to the place with a renewed vigour.

The Sixties!

The sixties were a time to wake up . . . and live!

The thought among the youth was, "Whatever it is, we are against it!" Even from our confines in the residential schools and northern British colonialist outposts, we could still see that a new world-wide awakening was taking place.

As an extension of the ideas put forth by Aldous Huxley (*Brave New World*, 1932) and George Orwell (*1984*, 1949), the Canadian philosopher Marshall McLuhan coined the term "global village," in good part explaining how a single event anywhere in the world could spark an entire series of other happenings. For instance, students in the US, France, Germany, Britain, and even Mexico rose in revolution to change what we needed to know and how we learned it. All social norms in clothing, music, drugs, sexuality, and racism were up for question.

As in the fifties, we in our isolated North still would not take our fight into the streets but we were definitely part of these essential changes toward the end of the famous sixties. This was the era of the controversial Vietnam War and Civil Rights. With every segment of society affected by these social uprisings, we also saw the birth of the American Indian Movement (AIM).

Meanwhile, life remained pretty well the same back home in Radelie Koe, where we didn't even have television until the seventies.

Barney's Famous Mile Run

My cousin Barney told me that there would now be a sports day at Grandin College and that we could pick whichever sport we thought we might be good at. I was interested in the javelin, and I just wanted to throw the spear.

"Naw, you wouldn't be any good at that, compared to all the rest of these football types around here," Barney said. "Here, I'll tell you what. You just lay on back and watch what I do, just this time around. In future, I want you to do whatever you see me do today. I'll show you what sport is all about!"

So he lined up with about twenty other guys at the start of the 440-yard track and they all took off like a bunch of demons, with girls watching for the hero of the day. Barney rounded the first bend way ahead of the pack, and by the time he reached the middle of the next stretch he was one complete round ahead of the panting, seething mass.

Slowly but surely, they caught up with that poor cousin of mine, and when they did it was not a pretty picture, nor even something you wanted to write home about. In fact, they were so disgusted with this guy for making them look bad in front of their girls that they ALL ran right over him! As the race was over, all Barney saw was a cloud of dust where he should have been prancing to female adulation.

So forlorn did he look, all covered in dust, scrapes, scratches, and shame, that I thought for sure he needed some help. When I went to give him a hand to rise, I asked him if he was okay.

"Thanks, Cousin," he said, "and you know what I told you about doing everything I do?"

"Yes," I stammered.

"Well, don't you do *any* of that, Antoine. You run your own race."

With such humble and contrite beginnings, did my fine track career begin.

More Ski Travel

We two huddled in the basement of the St Pat's Rectory,
just listening to records.

To keep on with the Territorial Experimental Ski Training (TEST) program, my roommate John T'seleie, Coach Ed Beaulac, and I had to overnight in *Somba K'e* (Yellowknife) on our way north to Inuvik. Given free rein of the rectory building, John and I wandered on downstairs, where we found a record player and some old records. We sorted through the selection and spent some time listening to Danny Kaye's comedic skits.

One record, *Peter and the Wolf*, followed the antics of the old hunter and animal scenario. Another favourite, a traditional Bantu African story, had to do with people trying to guess the name of a tree, uwungelema, to win the king's daughter's hand in marriage.

At the qualifying race to stay on the team for southern races, I did the "impossible," according to my teammate John. Though it was a short run, I came in, as I simply had to, a full minute ahead of the rest. To my mind, at times like this you have to physically think and transform yourself into an animal, in this case, a rabbit, to do the required moves.

At the southern races in the Laurentian Mountains of La Belle Province, Quebec, we, having gotten used to training at −34°C or −40°C, simply found it too hot. To the spectators' amazement, we raced in our T-shirts!

In our spare time, we got a hold of a bunch of miniature hockey sticks from somewhere and spent hours playing pick-up games in the halls. One memorable evening we were invited to attend a hockey game at the old Forum between our absolute heroes, the Montreal Canadiens, and the New York Rangers. Meeting the likes of the legendary Jean Béliveau and Henri "Pocket Rocket" Richard (he was shorter than his brother Maurice "Rocket" Richard) was definitely *the* highlight of these times, and we got a kick out of Montreal's goalie, "Gump" Worsley, a portly fellow out of uniform, but dapper in a checkered worsted wool suit!

Grandin's Regimen

Our dearly beloved director at Grandin, Father Pochat, actually came from a military past, and it showed in our new everyday lives. He believed in a sound mind and healthy body, so each and every morning started with the whole lot of us doing jumping jacks and push-ups before breakfast. We were expected to keep our rooms neat and tidy, with Saturday mornings given over to cleaning the entire residence, top to bottom, as clean as a barracks. Study was compulsory, three hours a day and five on the weekends.

We had our own student government, and, although I was a guy and a girl typically held the role, I was allowed to be the secretary/treasurer, using my skills as a writer to invent hilarious episodes involving a hapless man named Lover Lawrence for our weekly reports.

One thing you could absolutely not fault Father Pochat for as a director of this experiment in northern leadership was that he always, always kept his door open, for whomever wanted to just come in and talk about things. His was a strict order, yes, indeed, but done with love for the students first and foremost. This made all the difference in the world in the way we learned to perform out of respect, rather than the fear we had known up to then.

Yet there is little doubt that we were picked and trained as an elite group of students; our lack of choice was the underlying flaw in our present situation.

Burn, Baby, Burn!

While we at the elitist church-run Grandin College were happily numbed by colonialist forces, the outside world was going through some catastrophic changes, mainly through the efforts of youth. In most places, the only voices daring to be heard were those of youth, who, in many ways, had nothing to lose but the certainty of the status quo.

Far from the inner-city ghettoes of America, where it found its most explosive expression, the Black Power Movement began as a political offshoot of the Lowndes County Freedom Organization (LCFO), also known as the Black Panther Party, in the southern state of Alabama.

While we in the North were still being lulled to sleep by agents of Canadian colonialism, southern Blacks were making their first moves away from racism, toward a real voice in American democracy. The first steps involved simple voter registration. Like South Africa years later, the counties in the rural south were overwhelmingly black, but all of the power was with white votes.

Incendiary civil rights leaders like Stokely Carmichael voiced it best, wanting to move away from the non-violence preached by Dr. Martin Luther King Jr., saying that after his twenty-seventh arrest and six years of protest without any tangible results, he for one was ready for Black Power, Black Power, Black Power! Thus, the LCFO was born.

There had been a spark from the likes of Malcolm X, with his fiery call to revolution, away from the White man devil, "by any means necessary."

One direct influence of Malcolm X was the Black Panther Party for Self-Defense, formally organized by two college-educated ghetto youths, Huey Newton and Bobby Seale, in Oakland, California, to combat police brutality. With the idea of "by any means necessary," members took to carrying weapons in clear view. They would also quote Chinese communist leader Mao Tse-tung's motto for revolutionaries: "Power flows from the barrel of a gun."

Under intense scrutiny by FBI director J. Edgar Hoover, Newton served several prison convictions, one for manslaughter, but continued with his education, earning a Ph.D. in social sciences.

The chairman of the Black Panthers, Bobby Seale, was also subjected to intense surveillance by the FBI's COINTELPRO (counter intelligence program). This branch of the FBI specialized in surveilling and disrupting domestic political organizations, targeting, among others, civil rights leaders.

Malcolm X was brutally assassinated in mid-speech at the Audubon Ballroom, flung back from the podium by two sawed-off shotgun blasts and a number of direct handgun hits as he lay bleeding. He was killed because of the threat he posed to Elijah Muhammad for the leadership of the powerful Nation of Islam. This most exemplary of Black leaders lives on as a martyr to the cause, of our continuing attempts for human dignity.

In the summer of 1965, the Watts riots swept through south central Los Angeles. During the riots, thirty-four people died, over a thousand were injured, and there was $40 million in property damage.

White power and government backlash was ready and immediate. As a result, part of President Lyndon Baines Johnson's antipoverty bills pointedly excluded any services or social assistance to those involved in these cases of civil unrest.

Throughout all of this, Dr. Martin Luther King Jr. increasingly found himself shut out from his civil rights following, many of who wanted more violent expression, and official Washington support for much-needed social programs.

A possible ally, Robert F. Kennedy, then head of the Justice Department, even reluctantly signed the okay to have the FBI wiretap King, looking for incriminating Communist ties.

Yet these flames of civil unrest could not possibly quell the new spirit of the Black voice. Eldridge Cleaver, himself originally from the Watts ghetto, penned the incendiary *Soul on Ice*, from Folsom State Prison. There was no doubt that, right or wrong, the only way, for the Black man at least, was an all-out and continuous rebellion against White domination.

The one stipulation regarding social assistance from the Johnson administration brings to mind a very similar situation to residential schools in Canada: any parents attempting to withhold their children were threatened with having their social assistance, family allowance, cut off.[3]

In Germany, Spain, France, Mexico, the United States, and elsewhere, students rose as never before to rid society of an archaic way of setting the standards for life.

> He who learns must suffer—
> and even in our sleep
> pain that cannot forget
> falls drop by drop upon the heart
> until in our own despair
>   against our will
> comes wisdom
> through the awful grace of God.

These words, by Greek poet Aeschylus (525–456 BCE), and publicly spoken by another soon-to-be martyr in the name of freedom, Robert F. Kennedy, could also well serve as an epithet to all the social calls to arms of this seminal year. Kennedy spoke those words the night of the brutal slaying of civil rights leader Dr. Martin Luther King Jr., one of a handful of sane voices in these turbulent times.

One particular group that rose to prominence in this drive for change was the SDS, Students for a Democratic Society. The group took over Columbia University in New York City as a show of increasing dissatisfaction with the influence of the military on campus and in Vietnam. One feature of this action was that the school was planning to build a segregated recreation facility in the Harlem community. Although there was a dispute over tactics, the plan resulted in a de facto coalition with the Black students and the occupation of separate buildings. The weeklong event ended when the New York Police Department violently removed students, but not before they had gained worldwide attention.

The Weatherman Underground, a radical wing of student demonstrators, was put on the FBI's Most Wanted List after a number of government-owned buildings were bombed and targeted for more violent action. They eventually had to shut down public bombings after a number of their members accidently blew themselves up making explosives.

The Black Panthers, an outgrowth of the civil rights movement, was not non-violent in practice, as the movement had been up to then. The average age of members was just seventeen, speaking to the kind of commitment young people had at the time to a social cause.

> The sparks
> knowing not of the fire
>   this nor the next time
> were soon turned into a tumult
> highly visible scream of indignation over our
> blinded psyche.
> No longer would voices like theirs fall silent ...
>
> but not before many fell silent
> in our midst.
> Valiantly
> echoed in a meaningless Tomb of an Unknown America,
> once
> so blessed.

Tom Longboat Award, 1968

Without knowing a thing about it, the medal itself looked mighty good, nestled as it was in a Birks jewelry box, in some kind of shiny, silky bed.

We in Grandin Hall remained unaware of the turmoil of the outside world.

One day I was stopped in the hall unexpectedly and given a medal. There wasn't any kind of the ceremony that a White student would have gotten. I was just handed the medal and that was it. It came as something of a surprise that I received the national Tom Longboat Award, not even knowing it existed! I am quite certain to this day that were I a White student, I wouldn't just be called out of the classroom by a teacher and simply handed this coveted medal in the hallway like a bus pass.

Little did I know that Tom Longboat, an Onondaga man from the Six Nations Reserve near Brantford, Ontario, was at the very top of the running world in his day, competing in the 1907 Boston Marathon and in the 1908 Olympic marathon.

I had learned early on, even way back to my days at home as a young lad, that I was a gifted athlete. By the time I got into Grandin College in 1965, I also continued to be something of a brain, maintaining straight A's.

I was still involved with cross-country ski racing, but without the team I was part of in Inuvik, it wasn't quite the same. Yet again, I travelled with the NWT TEST team to Quebec City for the first-ever Canada Winter Games and managed the best times for the team, fourteenth out of thirty-five racers. At the Canadian National Junior Championships, I placed seventh out of thirty-six, less than two minutes behind first place!

To do anything that requires a superhuman effort, you have to train your mind beforehand to think of ways to cut every corner until you get to the point where there are no reasons to fail.

John T'Seleie, my roommate at the time, was a great help, as we made an extra effort to go on our own daily morning run before group exercises. We made fun of ourselves, spoofing the CBC, and calling this the "Northerners Run." I preferred to run the mile barefoot for added speed, and am quite certain I did it in just over four minutes, without a lick of training.

We even had our own mini-Olympics in our room! We just made your basic obstacle course of pillow and books and raced around, play-acting our dreams.

Basketball, too, was a favourite sport, as I made the Court Kings, on the way to the varsity team, the famous Canucks.

Although this was almost the height of my athletic career—the territorial championship of basketball was still to come—I was already pulling away from it all, with the drop in grades to prove it.

One has to understand that sports at these residential schools followed along the same lines as everything else, do well and keep the powers that be pleased with you.

> Which was fine, as far as winning went.
> Only I never saw myself as
> the Good Indian it took
> to be like that.
> Never was, and never would be.

So treatment like this, having to live with swallowing one's pride as a First Nations person, was par for the course in our colonialist North and still went without question, no doubt because the Indian in us had steadily been drummed out, certainly almost completely by high school.

I saw it most in some of the other members of our TEST program, like my cousin Fred "the Kelly Express." His shyness and willingness to please meant he never stood a chance!

As for the Tom Longboat Award, just knowing of the sheer existence of such fine recognition, with the medal in its silk-lined Birks jewelry case, was honour enough for me . . . then. At least it was something, at a time when you were just another face in the crowd, more or less

> Aside from it all, though
>   in a time somehow suspended.
> In the long, long race
> you are all alone.
> Totally on your own.
>
> Your eyes and mind refocus
> on their own
> when anything
> EVERYTHING
> is possible
> as never before.
>
> You are held in there
>   mystified.
> in the realm of Eagle, Wolf, and Bear
> too terrified
> to even leave.
>
> Mesmerized
> emblazoned
> to GLORY.

Athletes considered for the national Tom Longboat award were judged on their top three sports events; mine were cross-country ski racing, playing basketball, and running the mile.

We on the NWT Cross-Country Ski Racing Team had our own heroes, Nordic skiers from Norway, Finland, and Sweden, but in the North, we had yet to have access to TV, so I couldn't see my basketball heroes.

Besides other athletes, the one person I could identify with was Jim Ryun, the first high-school student to beat the four-minute mile, in Kansas. At the 1968 Olympics, Ryun won a silver medal in the 1,500 metre, in Mexico City's high altitude.

I eventually learned that only four First Nations athletes ever won the Tom Longboat Award, making it, as a fellow TEST ski team racer said, "Like a gold medal for a First Nations athlete to win!"

High praise, indeed, for such a competitor.

In *Kabami Tue* (Colville Lake)

After dear old grandmother Elizabeth had a stroke and become disabled, there wasn't much to hold me to my hometown of Radelie Koe.

We had close relatives in the neighbouring and much smaller town of Kabami Tue, and we had a house there.

Once I moved to Kabami Tue and was reunited with my parents and cousins, I really did enjoy the summers in a place where time seemed to just go on, with no divisions like days and even weeks. The days just rolled into one another.

In this place of almost total isolation, the presence of a smallish, bearded anthropologist, Joel Savishinsky, all the way from New York City, made for a curious sight. He eventually wrote a book of his studies in Kabami Tue called *The Trail of the Hare*, the "hare" being a commonly held misnomer for our People. According to our own history, we are the *K'isho T'ineh* (Big Willow People); our traditional enemies to the south are the Chipewyan *K'it'seleh T'ineh* (Small Willow People).

Not being familiar with our complicated Dene language, anthropologists and other "experts" have the tendency to confuse the words *k'ieh* (willow) and *gah* (rabbit).

To his credit, though, this twenty-five-year-old author was tuned in to the sixties mentality. He saw it wise to mention the turmoil in the USA at the time, the shooting deaths of both Martin Luther King Jr. and presidential hopeful Robert F. Kennedy.

It would have been more topical and relevant for Savishinsky to do research on any place larger in the North to study the effects of stress to get a bigger sample size. At the time, we were going through our most trying times, away from the land, freshly into community life.

A record like my book in your hands, though, gives us a picture of the colonial times we survived. And, too, of an age before outboard motors and Ski-Doos, when dogs and paddling canoes were the only way to get around.

Ol' Joel did make as much of a commitment as any visiting outsider would, staying in Kabami Tue year-round and choosing to live within the community itself and not under the wing of either the trader or Mola priest.

One of the chapters in Savishinsky's book about Kabami Tue talks about the rivalry between the only two white men there: the trader and the Roman Catholic priest, Bern Will Brown (1920–2014).

A perennial presence since the village of about a hundred Dene found its present home on the shores of the lake, Brown was a multi-talented builder, pilot, artist, and photographer. Over his sixty years in the North, he became something of a legend, this former American from upstate New York, and he was certainly a mainstay of our colonial life.

For the longest time, this "authority" on the natives of the North let it be known that we the northern Dene simply did not have, nor know anything of, our own history.

He even went so far as to claim that we prefer the name Slavey, a thoroughly derogatory stamp given to us by an early 1780s explorer for the North West Company, Alexander Mackenzie. Of course, we don't get to know the part about this famous but lost adventurer believing he was on his way to the West Coast, on our Duhogah, which flows only to the Arctic!

Our language is just too hard for any foreigner to learn. In fact, our language is so difficult to learn that a sister version of it to the south, Dineh, was used in the Pacific Theatre during the Second World War by the Navajo Code Talkers to do its fair share to save democracy and freedom for the West. That Navajo Dineh military code itself was never deciphered by the Japanese and, in a very real way, saved Western democracy.

These kinds of early cultural damages live on too, even in the media, with this equivalent of the "N" word—*Slavey*, an intentionally derogatory word that wrongfully implies our people were slaves—being bandied about with no regard to its real meaning. Of course, a deeper racist need to brand others to one's liking is not all that far from its real intent and purpose.

Even after having established himself and the church and living in our midst, Brown still insisted that he wanted a book written by a Dene, to refer to and quote, for our history. Like being an auto buff and wanting to study cars, but only the red ones that go fast!

For the most part, we remain an oral culture for good reasons: one, to keep our language and essential culture alive and two, simply because we do not trust the written word to fully capture anything of our ways and beliefs. In the very same way, storytelling is a living and vital First Nations tradition to help keep our memories alive. When your People have lived with nature for the best part of thirty thousand years, the last thing on your mind is to write it all down at the cost of all the trees!

As distasteful as the man was to one who has grown up knowing his own culture and language, I must say that Bern Will Brown is valuable, but only as a classic study in the way colonialism itself works. Disguised as concern, this is the very kind of arrogance, built on ignorance, that cements the stones of the wall separating us.

Whilst preaching about a mysterious God who just happens to share a good part of our traditional Dene values—sharing and love for your fellow man—he also had a way of ingratiating himself to people, to such an extent that he got a lot of free and/or dirt cheap labour to build his church and tourist lodge there, which just happened to be what he chose to do after leaving the priesthood and joining our civilian ranks.

What also leaves a sadder and lasting impression, though, is that Brown had this lazy habit of picking and choosing the parts of any erroneous research that agreed with his outdated ideas and passing them along as the real deal. For instance, he claimed to have visited a part of the Navajo Reservation in Nevada, a state hundreds of miles away from Kabami Tue, to check with students there about similarities in our language.

There are similarities, of course, and we are related, but it takes much more work to come up with real answers about how. His kind of dubious legacy would have to have been one of a person stubbornly clinging to colonialist ideals amidst the crashing waves of change on a continent in transition. Having built on shifting sand, you just have to find ways to convince yourself and others that you are yet afloat.

In reference to Bern Will Brown's last book, *End-of-Earth People*, I have yet to hear of anyone calling themselves the Dene version of end-of-Earth anything. Indeed, a good deal of this man's "legacy" is full of these kinds of hokey, touristy tidbits of "authentic" information, sure to be passed along for future generations as historical truth.

Thus the wheels of outright misrepresentation keep turning, and an all-too-familiar pattern of our First Nations People being helpful, as is our tradition, only to be taken advantage of yet again.

For the most part, then, this has to do with sifting through the "legend" to get to the real story. The saddest part, though, is that too often people are just too lazy to figure out the real story.

Ts'iduwe Ta Beragodehwe
(Unto the Ancestors)

A kind of ending came for me in January 1969 when our beloved grandmother Elizabeth finally succumbed to her debilitating paralysis. For a number of years, she had not been able to move as she once could; to their credit, my sister Judy, Uncle Thomas, and Aunt Denise did what they could to make her life as manageable as possible those last few years.

It took quite a number of years to be able to get around to giving our family matriarch a small measure of the honour she deserved. It was in the form of a headstone I sent from Peterborough, Ontario, where I just completed my first year of Ph.D. studies.

When I went to see another elder, Lucy Jackson, with a question about a phrase used when an elder passes—she thought for a minute and simply stated: Ts'iduwe Ta Beragodehwe. Our Dene language, like Navajo Dineh, is very complicated, much more so than English, which sounds lifeless in comparison. This saying, which I had inscribed on our grandmother's headstone, basically states that while her body has been interred, her spirit, too, is going through a time of being honourably accepted back by the *Ts'iduwe* (ancestors).

We also believe in reincarnation, and one of our sisters, Betty, is actually named after our venerable granny. She has spent most of her adult life as a teacher, with students looking forward each year to being in Miss Betty's class!

As for our grandmother, I often think of the rest of the family, many of the girls, still carrying forth our Dene language, to the point of being experts.

> Unto the ancestors
> She returns

One other and rewarding feature with all of this is that, without even knowing about it, I had somehow already begun ingesting these ancient traditions of my People, the Dene, along with the inherent ethical lessons they entail.

CHAPTER 6

Electric Storm

Even as a very young child, I always had a song in
my heart.

When I was young, as our boat went along the Duhogah to or from town, I would sing along with the designs on the water.

The songs I would sing were nowhere near the dull country and western music everyone else was so fond of, although I did know those lonesome numbers too.

When I got to senior boys in Grandin, I made it a point to go on up to Felix Lockhart's room to ask him if I could join his rock group, Electric Storm.

"Well, let's have a look at your mouth," he said.

We went to his mirror, and I opened wide while he looked intently in, searching for what I had no clue.

"There!" he suddenly exclaimed. "Your tonsils, they're hanging just right!"

Such was my entry into the world of music.

It took some hours of practice with Felix at his guitar playing rhythm for the song "Hey Joe," but I finally got the idea. I must say that in the following year or two, we lit up many a stage at Grandin College, Joseph Burr Tyrrell High School (where we went to day school), and even on to other towns and halls far and wide, including a summer of music in my hometown years later.

Other members of the group were the supremely gifted Herb Lafferty on bass and Angus Lennie on drums.

Our Famed Canucks

When we were clicking there was no way we could lose!

Grandin College produced some of the best basketball players I have ever seen. When I got there in 1965, these guys were already legends: Jerry Ruben, Ernie Bernhart, Peter "Slush" Silastiak, Nelson Green, Fred Zoe, Tony Mercredi, and others.

For my part, I was most impressed the first time I saw Johnny "Grease" Catholique play, and I thought for sure that he and I, on our own, could take on any team, anywhere!

Then again, everyone from the junior boys' Court Kings on just wanted in on the varsity team: the Canucks! This team had either won the Northwest Territorial Championship or given any of the top teams from Yellowknife or Inuvik a good run for the top spot for years.

So of course, I was thrilled to wear a forward's #31 for the team and to take on other local contenders like the teams from Breynat Hall and the Town of Fort Smith itself.

Our coach, Father Ed Beaulac, had a Jesuit background, so we were getting the best of any basketball finessing. He was a good player himself, which he proved playing against us for the town team.

For practice, though, I always wanted to be up against one of the fastest players, just to work on my speed. This, along with a patented rainbow jump shot I especially developed to prevent any interference, assured me twenty-eight points in one game alone, with fourteen assists and a few blocks too.

In Rebel Mode

I had always read, of course, but the choices I had in the North were limited alms from the colonialist world we of the First Nations found ourselves in.

Although it was billed as a "leadership school," Grandin College was more an exercise in formulating an elitist group to more or less head up the future of the North, as is, and certainly not in recognition of our own native cultures.

The new rock 'n' roll music of the rising hippie culture was what really caught my attention now. School and sports were always important to me, but I found myself more and more just getting lost in something to read and in thinking of the music we were doing with the Electric Storm. And, increasingly, art: a lot of drawing and some painting.

As it turned out art was not even a subject in school. To the college's credit, though, an art club was formed. We went out on frequent sketching tours with our instructor/supervisor, Ed Beaulac, and Violet Shawanda, originally from the Six Nations in Ontario. There was even a separate band room above the gym for the Electric Storm. Where before I wasn't happy unless I was the pitcher for a ball game or a starting centre for basketball, I now just preferred being in left field, reading *The Catcher in the Rye* by J. D. Salinger, about another unhappy, misplaced student.

The result of this widened circle of interest, was, of course, my failing grades. I didn't feel myself losing any of my mental abilities. Those were never in doubt. I was just now beginning to want to think for myself . . . in rebel mode.

What was happening, of course, was that I somehow knew these old restrictive ways of thinking were not for me. I was "dropping out," before the phrase caught on a few years later.

Morning after Shades

It was common enough, yet disheartening . . . We as a
People had not quite known how to voice our new lives.

The shift in place and lifestyles—from living entirely out on the land to moving to new communities—came at a price. One of the first changes was the new government log homes built in town, which were heated by wood stove. Also, larger freighter canoes with outboard motors replaced the simple ratting canoes people were used to, so fuel had to be brought to the communities.

Given the larger number of people in one place, especially in winter, you now needed a Ski-Doo to range farther and quicker for wood, fish, and meat. All around, these new stressful changes to our traditional life on the land created problems now taken out in drink.

The women were the first to feel the full brunt of this new way of life; you would often see your own mother or aunt being beaten at home. It became common to see them with them big dark sunglasses on after a weekend, a big purple/blackened spot around the edges still clearly visible for all to see.

The neglected youth had only a few recourses. You either looked the other way, moved out, or started drinking yourself to drown the pain. In a First Nations culture, where we did absolutely everything together, this marked a real spiral downward for our People.

About the outright violence, though, it took quite a while for enough people to start turning things around. Then again, wife beating was definitely one of the things we agreed with the Mola law about, and it had to stop. The fact that many former wife beaters still laugh their behaviour off, even decades later, proves that we were right all along.

We Dene were just too, probably not cowardly, but traditionally obliging, to ever want to make any of the real cultural adjustments we needed in a changing society. Our ways of being decreed that we were not to make too much of our own accomplishments, but I knew this would never work for me. I knew for a fact that a big part of the hunting experience, for instance, was the returning man recounting his prowess in great detail to an adoring audience.

When I looked further into it, this "kill talk" was an integral part of our First Nations world, to bolster self and community, pride and honour. When I dug deeper into our own culture, I also found that a person who hit a woman could "no longer call themselves a man," for he would be even worse than a common animal.

Truth be told, after having set a pecking order, even a wild animal would never do such a thing to one of its own kind. Violence against women is clearly a human sickness.

This was the kind of traditional knowledge fast disappearing with our older generation. My grandfather Peter Mountain Sr. told me as much, saying that those we called our elders didn't know what our real Dene culture, from his time, was all about.

Art Shines Through

At Grandin College, the only releases from the intense academics were either sports or art. Fortunately, I was good at both and played in the rock band the Electric Storm. The only other musician at the college outside our group was Phoebe Tatti, who dubbed herself both our number one critic and fan.

I always kept myself busy with one thing or another, an ever-present book in my back pocket, jeans more often than not splattered with oil paint. What with the artwork for Grandin College, the residential school, and the yearbook for our day school, Joseph Burr Tyrrell High, I was always in demand for posters for various events.

One person who surprised me with his ability with a brush and colours on canvas was Stephen Kakfwi. Other than the one painting I saw of his, the other artistic expression had was singing, eventually even composing and producing some CDs.

With so many changes crammed into these few short years at Grandin, there was no way to tell who you would ever spend any time with in future, but one who I did was Jim Antoine, from Fort Simpson. I always made sure to line up against him for basketball practice, simply because he was so fast, and, as centre for the team,

I wanted to at least be able to keep up with the speedy forwards. He also ended up being a lifelong supporter of my arts, buying up what I had right from about then to this day. His daughter, Melaw, became quite an artist in her own right and an excellent moose-hide tanner.

And I cannot fail to mention that I sold my very first canvas, then, to an early supporter, Dennis Bevington's sister Sue.

Drum Cover Cracked

Soon after getting over the novelty of being in a residential school not so severe as Grollier Hall, I could feel my brain systematically being whitewashed, my Dene self slipping away right out through Grandin's antiseptic walls. So, it wasn't long before my usual A-grade average became spotted with B's, C's, and worse.

Before I knew it, there we were in the director's office, talking about two very different matters. I had entered Grandin College four years before as the pride of the First Nations, an exemplary straight-A student. And yet the divide between that gem of the Roman Catholic North and the simple folk I came from in my hometown of Radelie Koe was too wide for me to fathom just yet. I was, however, deliberately going through these rebellious acts set in motion by my Dene heart of hearts, even before it became the thing to do. How could I ever explain to my own relatives that we were quickly becoming too far apart to ever hope to bridge the gap?

Yet I always did have a notion in the back of my mind of making a fine priest someday, but with no idea of what the mysterious "call" to religious orders was all about, and, failing this epiphany, the idea just faded off into the shadows.

I must also admit that, perhaps because of being summarily yanked away from home at a very young age, I was simply always going to be bucking the system and anything that reeked of authority.

For its part, though, Grandin did all that it could to support us as students through very difficult and changing times. There were others who were let go from this leadership school though, like my cousin Barney and basketball great Johnny "JC" Catholique, who we would line up against at Akaitcho Hall in Yellowknife. Luckily, these were the sixties, and there was a new and rising awareness of being yourself.

I had never been allowed to be what I really was: a Dene artist yet unrealized. I could either smile wanly and go along with the program or go Dene. Besides all that, I intentionally added on much more of a load, getting involved in my own and school and residential school art projects, our politics at the time, which started to expand and be influenced by the 1960s mentality, and as lead singer in Electric Storm.

Needless to say, I was eventually summoned into Director Father Pochat's office, with members of the high school administration and supervisory staff present. I was simply asked why my grades were so poor and what my plans for the future were. I reminded the director of Grandin College that he had originally clearly said that any student who was not pleased with the residential school could go home, which I was prepared to do. I only then learned that my parents would have to pay for the return fare. I knew that there was no way my relatives had that kind of money. After a lot of back and forth, we eventually compromised—if I agreed to write the final exams, I would at least get a passing grade.

Such were the terms and conditions of what success was to be expected then, in my case anyway.

What we were actually talking about were two very different things. They, of course, had a valid reason, being concerned for my education, knowing that I was a naturally bright student. Without being able to say the words, I wanted to know why I was now a brainwashed victim of the colonial agenda. Without really knowing it, I was beginning the long road away from the evil construct of the residential schools.

Similarly, anyone who knows about caribou hide drums will recognize the signs of it being in a foreign place. The only place this kind of drum cover will ever crack is in an office, far away from its intended place of use. The hide, for no other reason than not feeling its home close by, will often give out and split right down the middle, giving up the rest of its songs.

Especially
in artificial,
lifeless
air.

The Dene people who were taken from the land were like a caribou hide in a foreign place. Our culture, like the drum, split and cracked.

Grandin College did its part to produce some leadership for the North. Those people, in turn, went forth with institutional blessings but basically served as just one more a cog in the wheel of colonialism. What started out, for the most part, as a genuine devotion to faith was eventually watered down by the actual experience itself.

Even in comparison to other religions, which allowed their clergy to live a normal married life, these poor souls sent to the farthest corners of the North could never even hope to satisfy their real human needs.

Deprived of even the most basic natural expression, everything for them slowly became a sinful abomination, not in their own responsible eyes, mind you, but in the all-seeing cyclops of some overzealous lord present to snoop and dig into everyone else's lives.

To this day I will always associate
that dried-up stench

of simple want
in the confessional
with that.

Some secret,
sickly sweet.

Cloying
abomination
never meant for
any kind of light.

What I was really going through, without quite being able to articulate it, were the symptoms of Post-Traumatic Stress Disorder (PTSD), exactly the same kind of battle fatigue and outright cultural shellshock every soldier on the battlefield experiences.

After twelve years of these residential schools, I just wanted out—to be Dene again.

Far off
    in the Barren Lands
    of my country
wolves howled.

Back from Season 249

When I first arrived at Grollier Hall, I was given the number 249, which, for all intents and purposes, served to stamp me the same way the innocent children at the Nazi death camps were. Issuing someone a number is dehumanizing: make every attempt to take away humanness in favour of a lower and more beastly savage grade.

There were no attempts to recognize our Dene culture or language, just a blanket refusal to own up to a common humanity.

My own snap-out of this church-and-state imposed slumber began with the book about a Jewish prisoner at one of the places for Hitler's Final Solution. The recognition, in fact, of what author Eugene Burdick had to say was immediate. I would eventually gravitate toward veterans of various wars. I felt we shared an experience, both assigned number and rank, and both fighting in our own ways for freedom.

> Both produced a searing
> unspoken memory.
> In this particular marathon
> I had hit
> that proverbial wall
> only to have it morph
> and become carried within
> for everyone else
>   try as they might
> to reach into.

It would take me some fifty years and many depths into various versions of Dante's *Inferno* to touch on other recognizable episodes, one in fact self-penned for Bonnie Devine's course at OCAD University; it was titled *The Residential Schools: Our Canadian Auschwitz*. A bit later I came across Eric Larson's *In the Garden of Beasts*, which chillingly mirrored then-Prime Minister Stephen Harper's administration's stranglehold on Canadian rights.

One of the articles I wrote for my column, A. Mountain View, in Yellowknife's *News/North*, called "The Past as Prelude," referred to the book *Auschwitz* by Laurence Rees, parts of which tell an all-too-familiar tale of the Jewish children taken by train to their doom, more than one quarter of a million from just over one million dead in Auschwitz: a sad debacle and departure from human decency.

A Deeper Cultural Divide

We children were caught right in the middle.

Besides being forcibly separated from our parents for ten months out of every year, the timing of the separation was all wrong. The months of the year we were taken to the residential schools, from September, just when our People would return to the land for winter, was traditionally a time for young boys to learn the art of hunting and for girls to learn how to sew with caribou and moose hides.

We returned home in June to go out to the fish camps, yes, but we boys were not expected, nor even allowed, to handle the fish as the girls did. They, in turn, didn't have access to the hides needed to make moccasins, gloves, and other clothing for most of the year.

We all grew up not knowing what it meant to be a part of a society that respected those who could provide for the community. Of course, our parents were happy to have us back, but they had been pushed to the side, in a very real way, as far as our cultural education was involved. They had no way of bridging the emotional and psychological gaps to our way of being, which was largely one based on survival.

Even our grandparents were helpless to step in to help. The churches saw to it that anyone who still had anything in the way of traditional medicine ways was shunned, with their savage and evil ways.

In time, all we could do was go through the motions of life as we knew it before—even to the point of being glad to be going away again.

The kind of deep-seated lack of identity that we developed is something we yet have to resolve, and perhaps never will.

We were definitely guinea pigs caught in a foreign culture that only valued the way we could think, our intellect. All First Nations cultures place just as much importance on how much a person cares for others, the ability to do a great number of physical activities on the land, and a spiritual connection to the Dene way of life.

What makes the residential schools a genuine cultural genocide is that our own People were eventually made to feel that they did not have a right to their own children and, by extension, to the future of our First Nations, be it Inuit, Métis, or Dene.

In Sand-Blown Epitaph

There is always this feeling of something missing . . . like a drum that never gets tuned, you live condemned to a life on hold.

For us survivors of residential schools, that something missing was our real selves, snatched away overnight way back when, just when we most needed to just be loved and appreciated for being Inuit, Métis, or Dene.

> For some
> the cracks started to show early on.
> One of my very best friends
> just shut off
>   and stayed off
> as I did
> at twelve.

Only his was for a life lived on with nothing to give, especially to those who most wanted to hold him. Others went through the motions of making it out of places like Grollier Hall alive. Being old enough to drink was an open faucet you never had to shut off.

Some even had the best jobs, but one too many nights in a

lonely hotel room, standing in for the People, took a life to limbo . . . from there God only knows. Others cried out as best they could. Too late for the coming of that human light.

The worst, though, just had to be the little guy, JoJo Pascal, who really could make you smile when you were down, even without a word.

> . . . but with no one there
> to do the same
> for him,
> he ended it in an agony
> of Drano,
> pain, and
> a forgiving end in
> blissful silence.
>
> Yet the echo of these
> who chose their own end
> lives on
>   feebly
> in faded words
> etched
> on cold stone markers.
>
> In their time
> toppled back
> to sand
> The Near Room.
>
> Meanwhile
> in a parallel
> mirrored King/Kubrick *Shining*
> fated eyes
> slowly losing off.

Softer focus
brings to mental means
a place for each

Some cruelly cast aside.
    Supposed rancid fruit
    from original sin

Others
    closer
mine somehow
rescued, yet black-wreathed still
to these indecipherable
psychic depths.

From this Mother's womb
Our gaze up, up . . .

Envision

Waving far beyond
a silent grave

Lapping starlit home
in shores sublime

Steps to this
Near Room
afforded only
of spirit light.

Beleh Dezen (Black Wolf)

Counted out by institution and family.

Now that my days of residential school were coming to an end after twelve long years, some more serious problems reared their ugly heads.

Ever since hearing the rumour that I had been abandoned to die as a child out in the freezing cold, I had been trying to face that sad truth. I had begun working away from home a number of years before, but each time I returned, there was always a sense that I did not belong at home and never would.

For their own reasons, both my parents always blamed me for being born when they were in their teens, and that feeling was not about to change.

> I was on my own
> having been born to another time.
>
> To this changing place
> I became a Rubik's cube
> with many parts missing
> only the elders knew about.
>
> It was years before
> I realized that.

My other grandmother, Marie-Adele Mountain, angrily asked me why I wasn't spending more time at home. When I just laughed about it, she slapped me, hard, right across the face!

> . . . a long moment passed
>   in shock
> until she grabbed and hugged me close.

Without even knowing it
I was still right in her
ancient Dene world
with no fear
of wolves or men
while my life was in
freefall.

Too far removed from this immediate reality, the Roman Catholic Church, for its own selfish reasons, completely failed to offer any kind of an explanation, other than to outright deny its collusion with the Canadian state and its responsibility to us, the survivors.

Being left out in the cold, we had the added internal terror of PTSD. In his book *Strong Hearts, Wounded Souls* Tom Holm talks about the Native Americans of the Vietnam War, writing, "While the war itself had been a shared experience, like a war party of old, the actual homecoming was not."[4] The same can be said for those of us who went through the Canadian government's exercises in cultural genocide.

In fact, we were blamed by all and sundry for not being able to be as Dene as we once were, adding to our sense of alienation, set apart from the People. This kind of an emotional upheaval, especially in a generation just then at its height, came back as rage against any and all authority, thus upsetting, in its way, the kind of respect there once was for tradition.

In terms of each survivor, a deep-rooted self-loathing could not but help set in, and worse yet, without any kind of community support to explain and deal with it. Meanwhile, the church could simply sit back and still play the part of communal confessor, with no fingers pointed at it, ever.

The only time we really recognized one another as Dene was when we made it a point to follow along with our own Indigenous spirituality in ceremonies like the sweat lodge. Too many never found these ways back to the Good Red Road and to this day remain brainwashed, to one extent or another, no matter their education or position in life.

In Dene terms, a permanent kind of bitterness set in at some point, lodged, innermost in the survivor's psyche, never to return the person to serve the community as an elder.

> That was
> perhaps
> the deepest
> of intentional cuts.

The Japanese have a practice to deal with these kinds of damages called *Kintsugi*, where a crack is filled with gold and then held in treasure.

> At my most wounded I sat
> head in hands
> with only etched ghosts
> of those who went before
> as muted guides
>
> as a silvery cloud passed
> high over the walls.

For any veteran or survivor with PTSD, the kind of bitterness grown of betrayal of your basic humanity never does go away. What remains, though, is what you choose to do, or not, with it.

The most effective way to use these severely traumatic memories is as a fine-honed tool to help you both adjust to your new life and succeed when others fail. And effective tools you need to address the convoluted concepts of being the oldest in a family from another lost generation.

The only way to turn all of this around is to personally do something, anything, to help today's youth.

Family does have a way, as life does, of setting some of it back to rights, though. As when one of my sisters honoured me with the name *Dene Bezieh Raseh* (Strong Heart Man) and another, the Adventurous One, as a warrior must be to go out on the warpath.

Broken Pillow

You come back to it
alone
    a kind of sad fact
tucked carefully away
in a deck of cards
used by many hands.

Just that familiar smell
of simple want
and endless need.

All around
a younger forever
ending in tears
on a broken pillow.

PART II

Social Awakenings

1969–77

CHAPTER 7

Summer of '69

To Grandin's credit, I was allowed to stay on and work on the buildings with the maintenance man, Brother Pelletier, even though I barely got my high school diploma.

Although the times we lived in were definitely stacked against our First Nations' culture, there were people in authority who were good people, and this member of the clergy was one of those.

Frère Pelletier always took the time to joke with the boys, and we spent our spare time in his room, cadging cigarettes and teasing him. What I found out that summer was that there were people out of our bubble of school life who really did have to work for a living—and to make life easier for us besides.

Frère could do it all, from inspecting the boilers, to reinstalling failed electrical systems, to his favourite, I was sure, carpentry. He could easily swing that extra-heavy hammer with either hand and handle any piece of lumber at the top of the long ladder.

Although I was there to work, I also found out that Frère Pelletier was a dedicated worker and would be sorely missed when he passed away a few years after we left Grandin College, which finally closed its doors a few years after that.

Although rock music and some of that freer thinking had reached the North, we youth didn't quite outright celebrate this hippie spirit for a couple of more years.

This was still at a time, let's not forget, when it took a week for us to see a replay of a hockey game.

Media Back Door

After graduating high school and spending the summer of 1969 working on maintenance of the Grandin College buildings in *Thebacha* (Fort Smith), I went to the territorial capital of Yellowknife to figure out what to do about my immediate future.

After a more or less 180-degree turnaround in high school from being a straight-A student who didn't even check in with the school's guidance counsellor to an almost dropout, I had limited possibilities. One thing going for me was that I could usually think my way out of various situations and this, though a major issue, could be solved.

The mining town of Yellowknife—or Somba K'e, which translates to *where the money is*—had been designated as the capital of the North two years earlier, so the government of the Northwest Territories was new. It was still more personal than bureaucratic, so I marched right on into the Department of Education, then in the Lahm Ridge Tower, and asked what my options were.

Some rather unexciting prospects were presented, but all it took was the mention of something to do with the media, in this case radio and television in Fort William, Ontario, to make me want to take a chance.

Not that I had much to do with even attempting to broadcast a hockey game over the residential school's PA system, as some did, but I just knew that this was going to be as close to what I really wanted to do, studying the arts, as I was likely to get in this stifling colonialist world.

Four Dead in Ohio

We in the North existed in a kind of bubble. Even Canada, for the most part, was still apart from world events. The federal government's White Paper, which advocated doing away with the *Indian Act* and having us Indians be like every other Canadian citizen, was still a year away. But events everywhere else were a different story. Students, particularly overseas in France, Germany, Spain, and Britain, were actively protesting, and closer to home, Mexican and US students were too.

A good deal of the turmoil in America had to do with former US President Lyndon Baines Johnson lying about the Vietnam War back in '64. The Gulf of Tonkin resolution gave him some rather wide latitude to conduct the war there. Also, the end of college deferment for the dreaded draft now made all students fair game.

The most vocal of these public outcries took place on the campus of Kent State University in early May 1970. Now with the Nixon administration's bombing in Cambodia, an escalation of American military imperialism meant more combat deaths, with just too many young soldiers being sent back home in gruesome body bags. Demonstrations had been going on at Kent all that weekend, with the Ohio National Guard called in and now on campus. On that fateful Monday, May 4, protests quickly got out of hand, and live bullets were fired in the confusion. Clearing smoke and tear gas revealed four students dead in its wake, two of whom had nothing to do with the protest.

As never before, it also became clear that this time the buildup was not simply student protest but increasingly the voices of ordinary American citizens who were just plain tired of being lied to by the government.

Bury My Heart, Too!

There are just some books that take a hold of you and won't let go. Such was *Bury My Heart at Wounded Knee* by Dee Brown, a true-to-life account of how the American West was lost. I read this book some years after I left Fort William, Ontario, just about the time I was first at the Crow Indian Agency in Montana, and I wanted to continue my personal studies into the Indian Wars. I got to about halfway through this well-researched account of the way European thinking, such as manifest destiny, made it "imperative" that other nations standing in the way of invasive expansion were outright murdered for their lands. Like a generation of like-minded youth, I made a commitment to get involved. In the North, that meant with the Indian Brotherhood of the NWT.

There were just too many questions: with the world yet mourning six million Jews killed in the Second World War, how could my own missing eighty million Indigenous relatives go unnoticed?

In comparison, why would the Mola claim to have discovered America when my people had already been here thirty thousand years and quite certainly longer? It all got to be too much for me to bear, so I simply had to put the book down, to reconsider for later, if at all.

About six months later, I picked it up again, thinking, "Well, like it or not, Antoine, this is your history, which you need to know, to go on in this life."

In a way this printed tale carried right on with my own life, being taken at the age of seven to a residential school, as a continuing and concerted genocidal plan. Just like my People in the book, I made what I could of a very tough situation. And I turned mere survival into a way to the future.

Like everyone else of the First Nations, I well identified with Lakota warrior-patriots like Crazy Horse. Even more like him, I never did have much truck with the way others of my people wanted for social gatherings. I would much rather spend most of my time away from people, yet learning as much as I could about our own culture.

Tashunka Witko (Crazy Horse) was instrumental in leading the final charge on the foolish General Custer's command at the Battle of the Little Bighorn, known to the Lakota as the Greasy Grass. He was led to his death at Fort Robison only a year after wiping out the *Wasichu* (people of European descent).

There was a brief time in that last year when it was viable that things would carry on as normally as was possible. The great warrior himself was even made an Indian policeman and made a strong suggestion, wrongly interpreted, that he could help wipe out the entirety of Chief Joseph's band to the north.

But intertribal jealousies held sway, and his good army friend, Lieutenant William Philo "Whitehat" Clark, was persuaded to lead the great Oglala warrior-patriot back into the fold, and maybe go along on a peace mission to see the Great White Father, President Rutherford B. Hayes, in Washington, and finally be allowed his own agency.

But in the end, a prophetic warning from his original vision became grim reality, with his once-best friend, Little Big Man, holding his arms while a soldier ran him through with a bayonet.

Now mortally wounded, Crazy Horse lay dying in the arms of another good kola, the seven-foot giant Touches the Clouds, who reached for the dead warrior's chest, saying, "It is good. He has been looking for death for a long time, and it has found him."

The other notable holdout, Sitting Bull, came back from exile in the grandmother's country, Canada, but was himself slain at his very doorstep on the banks of the Grand River.

A last-ditch hope to bring the millions of buffalo and their former way of life back brought the fleeing Minneconjou Chief Bigfoot's band to Wounded Knee Creek, the site of the worst massacre of First Nations—over 150 unarmed men, women, and children. They fled, in the dead of winter, from massive firepower, including four six-pound Hotchkiss guns each spitting a .45 caliber shell every second.

After I was done with this Indian history of the American West, these words of Lakota Holy Man Black Elk, himself a witness to the original Wounded Knee Massacre, echoed and resonated with me:

I did not know then how much was ended. When I look back now from this high hill of old age, I can still see the butchered women and children lying heaped and scattered all along the crooked gulch as plain as when I saw them with eyes still young. And I can see that something else died there in the bloody mud and was buried in the blizzard.

A people's dream died there.

It was a beautiful dream. [5]

Particularly galling were the twenty Medal of Honor citations handed to the troops of the 7th Cavalry responsible for this senseless tragedy and the fact that the slain were Christian converts on their way to find a safe place from trouble all around.

So, when the site of the original Wounded Knee Massacre of 1890 was taken over by the American Indian Movement in 1973 in response to a brutal federal government–supported regime on the Pine Ridge Indian Reservation in South Dakota, it also awakened all of our First Nations from a long sleep.

Once again, it was proven that we each and all had hope in this modern world, rekindled by our ancestors. In one other unexpected way, this unblinking way of looking into the past helped us in the present.

I began to think of my own curiosity as an education in itself. I wanted to at least objectively know about other cultures. Also, their beliefs steeled me to our own everyday realities.

I better understood how our story was the same as the Holocaust. How, for instance, the Roman Catholic Church's papal bull, Doctrine of Discovery, written a good half-century before the hapless Columbus voyage, set into official order the "right" to every "discovery" on non-Christian lands for whomever set sail on behalf of foreign powers.

True, it is
that history is written
in the blood
of the conquered.

Native American Church

From a simple plant, our salvation! This ancient helping
peyote religion began with our People, the Dene.

In one story, an Apache Dene maiden became hopelessly separated from her fleeing people, with the blue-coated enemy closing in. In her despair, she found a place to hide herself and her young one for the night, falling into tear-filled sleep. In fitful dreams, she saw a teepee set up, and a wonderful shimmering light therein.

She cautiously scratched at the doorway and was bidden entry. Within were all of these ancient ancestors, elders who were busy with an all-night ceremony. They made room for her, and she stayed until a dim light started to catch at her uncomprehending eyes. She was told that, when she awoke, there would be a plant beside her that she should eat and continue with her journey.

As she turned to leave the teepee, she noted that each of these elders, lost in prayer, was now some kind of a cactus plant, with a white, glowing top.

In the newly arrived dawn, the woman was surprised that she and her baby were yet alive, and that, yes, there was a strange small cactus plant right by her head, as if awaiting her rising.

She remembered her instructions to eat of this holy medicine and filled her bag with some of the plant and continued, stumbling on her way. It did take a while, but she managed to find her people again, as instructed.

As with traditional custom, she brought the supply of the special plants to her uncle, who prayed over it, ate some, and declared that it was not only safe but could be used in a new way of prayer.

Over time, as members of the Native American Church, we use our Mother Peyote for three reasons: it can educate, protect, and even heal the user. At the end of the Indian Wars, an utter sense of despair walked like death throughout the lands, stalking our First Nations. With little hope for our future, many just took it that the Indians would simply die. The herds of millions of buffalo had been systematically killed off, leaving our People at the mercy of government handouts, often rancid and rotting when finally delivered.

Just when everything was at its absolute bleakest, a prophet from Nevada, named Wovoka, let it be known that, yes, the old free ways would indeed come back. The Paiute holy man had meant for this to be a way to ensure the survival for the future, but when the warlike Lakota began to take the message as a way to return to the old ways, government agents sent in soldiers.

The end result was the Massacre at Wounded Knee, where hundreds of innocent people, including women and children, were mercilessly shot down in the cold snows of December 29, 1896.

§§§

Meanwhile, far down to the south, along the Rio Grande, Texas/Mexico border, the Lipan Apache had been using a sacred plant, peyote, for ceremonial prayer. Some anthropologists began to gather information on the use of this sacred plant as a religious practice.

Eventually, a group of Comanche and southern Cheyenne adherents to this new faith went to Washington to see to formalizing its use with the protection of federal government law.

Thus the use of peyote was formally incorporated into the American constitution in 1928 under the American Indian

Religious Freedoms Act, making it legal for our members to use and transport it in a sacred manner. In the late 1960s, the Peyote Religion was also formally incorporated into the Canadian Constitution.

Telemedia and Movies

My second year studying radio and television arts in Fort William, Ontario, 1970–71, was not as chaotic as when I first arrived there from the North, but just as disconcerting in its way. My little clique of artsy hippie "freaks" was now closer-knit, and we ended up renting an apartment downtown, where friends invariably got together for music, drugs, and fun. We also got into moviemaking in a more serious way, or at least shot a lot of film, in the company of a dentist who fancied himself a filmmaker. A lot of it, of course, was a chance to party, which this person didn't at all mind.

Having gone through the audio portion of our studies in year one, we now ran our own virtual TV station, complete with commercials and ad campaigns.

On a more personal front, I learned a great deal about my life-long interest in music from my best pal, Ted Huff. He taught me to really listen, especially to the lyrics, to how songwriters like Paul Simon and Neil Young could put words together to make a simple and effective yet lyrical statement.

Now being apart from my high school bandmates in Electric Storm, I had no choice but to try my hand at the guitar, which I pounded away on for nine months just to get a decent song together.

But my residential school past had a deadly way of rearing its ugly head, and under the influence of strong drink, I must confess, I even attempted suicide. One Mola student told me that the day after one of our school parties he found me unconscious out in the snow and brought me back in, just short of freezing to death.

It seemed strangely forgiving, somehow, that history, which had anonymously picked me to offer to the Gods of change also sent a total stranger to the rescue.

I would not say that I was in any shape to have graduated at the top of my class in Media Studies, but I did get the required certificate and that would have to do for now.

I was also eager to help out my People at home through these changing and social times.

Yamoria and the Dineh Twins

Legends based on twin brothers are common to both our Northern and Southern Dene/Dineh.

Our Dene version of these ancient stories comes from a time when the world was new. People still spoke with our animal relations and mammoths and mastadons walked this land.

There were two brothers, one a peacemaker named *Yamoria*, or One Who Walks the Universe, and the other a warrior, Yamoga. The former chased harmful giant beavers all the way from Artillery Lake in Chipewyan Country and finally caught up with two of them at *Fieh Tehni-ah* (Bear Rock Mountain). He killed three of these great beasts there and tacked their hides to the mountain, where they are still visible today.

He also made a Forever Fire, which appears to those who will be granted a long life.

He finally shot two arrows into the waters where the Bear River meets the Duhogah. Even with the annual break-up and swelling of these rivers they are yet visible today.

When the Indian Brotherhood of the NWT was originally set up in the late sixties, the elders said that, as long as we remembered these legends, our nations would thrive into the future.

The Indian Brotherhood

Finally, a voice for the Dene!

Eventually, the student protests of the sixties in the rest of the world began to penetrate the North. These were the first heady days of social consciousness in the early seventies, some years before the Dene Nation was formed. We were a ragtag team of youth determined to come home to set the record straight on our rights.

There was talk about a possible pipeline to take our natural resources south. Eventually, the famous Berger Inquiry was commissioned to find out more about how our people felt about the pipeline idea. Our work as staff of the brotherhood, as it was often called, was to help prepare our Dene people for the upcoming Berger Hearings. It was the first time we as a group had any say in our own lives, so these times were like a fresh springtime breeze blowing our way, for a change.

During the hearing, the air was so charged with energy you could cut it with a sharpened tomahawk. As these words accusing President Bob Blair of Foothills Pipeline echoed off the walls of the gymnasium of the Chief T'Seleie School in Radelie Koe, they also reverberated across Indian Country and history.

Chief T'seleie told Blair,

> You are the 20th-century General Custer. You are coming with your troops to slaughter us and steal land that is rightfully ours. You are coming to destroy a people that have a history of 30,000 years. Why? For 20 years of gas? Are you really that insane?[6]

To drive his point home, Chief T'seleie vowed to lay down his life for his beliefs. The hearing's presiding judge, Thomas Berger, was federally commissioned by the Pierre Elliott Trudeau government with the daunting task of collecting evidence from the People of the Norwest Territories, which he did in a series of community visits.

The Dene and Inuit people in the North would be directly affected by any major industry, in this case a pipeline to take natural gas from the Beaufort Delta south to northern Alberta.

Yet it was this seminal moment in Fort Good Hope that reflected the united and concerted opposition to the pipeline, resulting a few years later in a final decision to at least postpone the question of any major development until the treaty and land settlements were completed.

Custer's ghost, to be sure, stayed clear of the North.

The proposed pipeline was a focus in which we, the Dene, made our stand against unwanted economic intrusions on our traditional lands. Although logistically demanding, the Berger Hearings themselves went pretty much as expected, with widespread opposition to the pipeline. The eventual decision against this Canadian megaproject came as a welcome one, though.

We had an office set up on the second floor of Harold Glick's Tog Shop right in downtown Yellowknife. From all I had learned being in the South over the last couple of years, I was eager to do this kind of work, although not sure where I would fit in. I simply walked in, sat down, and started typing up something. Two weeks later, I was hired.

Because of my experience in the media, I was put in charge of our fledgling radio department and given two students to train. I had known Phoebe Tatti from back in Grandin College. Peter Hope was the other student. I drilled the idea of discipline on-air into them, as it had been drilled into me, making it a point to fine them what turned out to be their lunch money for mistakes. To this day, Peter is the best I have heard of First Nations broadcasting on air.

We also travelled to the communities in the North. This colonialist time began about the turn of twentieth century, when even the word "Dene" was a novelty. We had been taught to keep our mouths shut and just go along with the colonialist program.

The long road ahead, waking up our own people and fighting for our rights, made for a truly wonderful time in the North and in Canada.

When I arrived in Yellowknife in the summer of 1971, the Indian Brotherhood of the NWT had been going for a few years already, having started as a response to the White Paper that laid out a way to abolish the Indian Act and, in effect, end the treaty-bound legal relationship between our Peoples and the federal government in the name of "equality." The White Paper drew widespread First Nations opposition all across Canada and resulted in a common purpose that unified us.

Ottawa handed the responsibility of education and health to the new government of the NWT in 1967, the centennial year of Confederation.

The brotherhood's central and overall goal, though, was to see to the recognition of our rights written into Treaties 8 and 11, both of which were signed in the North, in 1899 and 1921, respectively.

We certainly had our work cut out for us.

The North then was nothing like the advanced New Democratic Party supporter it became later.

Truth be told, it was very much like the old Wild West, with an "anything goes" mentality as far as Dene lands and rights went. One has to remember that the Klondike Gold Rush had happened only at the turn of the century, a few short generations before, so much of those freewheeling ways still remained.

We were, however, determined to set our world back to its rightful place. All in all, though, and in practice, we were more idealists than revolutionaries of the Fidel Castro, Che Guevara, or Nelson Mandela ilk.

There is no doubt that this was serious business, though, at the time of Vietnam, all-around civil unrest, and "Tricky Dick" Nixon.

In a mini, northern version of Watergate, our Indian Brotherhood office was broken into and files taken. Some of us were under investigation by the International Criminal Police Organization (INTERPOL) and denied travel overseas.

I was still under investigation some twenty years later.

To this day, I identify with the old Italian man in the 1970 satirical movie *Catch-22*, based on the Joseph Heller anti-war book, who told the young American soldier, "I've been an anarchist all my life, and I will never know what it means."

Given all of this, our rebel, anti-government cover and act was all there—jean jackets, headbands, and braids—but on the inside, all we really wanted to do was act the part: wild Indians on the loose!

More pragmatic than martyrs, all we wanted was to basically stop the pipeline and live our own lives.

Little Castle on Latham

Jimi Hendrix's "Star Spangled Banner" echoed on down
Morrison Drive at 4 AM on the weekend.

One weekend, I welcomed the former bass player of our high school band, Electric Storm, musical wunderkind Herb Lafferty of Fort Simpson, as my guest. Electric Storm had now been separated for a number of years, but, as a consummate musician, Lafferty always had at least a guitar in tow for moments like this one, early on a Saturday morning.

I got warnings that our noisy weekend parties were disturbing the Dene people living in little colourful houses in the far valley, but this was at a time when this kind of news just took a hasty exit out the other ear.

My neighbour, Father René Fumoleau, was a good one, and we did some writing together besides. One end result was the book *As Long as This Land Shall Last: A History of Treaty 8 and 11, 1870–1939.*

Another book, commissioned by the brotherhood, was called *Denendeh: A Dene Celebration*. It included this, one of the poems I began to write:

Our Drum

The sun is the drum
That the Dene play
Music in the ripples
across singing rivers

The wind is our hair
That blows
Through tall trees

Where is our song
But in the promise
of tomorrow
Where is our heart
But in Denendeh

Our dance
Is life itself

Reclaiming our Dene rights, then, included taking back our identity from the grip of the hated church. Not everyone was as committed to our Dene cause just then. Some didn't catch on to it until they settled on it as a career move, a mindful alternative in the expensive North.

My involvement with the Indian Brotherhood to wake up the social world and turn it upside down had begun a few years before, so there was work to do to decolonize the North and ourselves, but this was also the famed seventies, after all, when the serious git-down partying begun in the mid-sixties was just hitting full stride. No one quite knew who was with whom, but that was the least of our worries.

After taking my one and only (ever) bank loan to buy and move a trailer from Fort Rae (now Behchoko), I was living with a young lady from Pine Falls, Manitoba, in our li'l castle on Latham Island (now Ndilo). We had a dog named Boss who insisted on following me, even to work, which now included TV productions at the Tree of Peace Friendship Centre, across the Ndilo causeway.

So ol' Herb and his spot-on rendition of the immortal Hendrix was part of a regular weekly schedule of fun at home, which usually began when the dance was over at the Elks or Legion. Partiers would come on by, and there was always a straggler or two to wake up to yet another warm, sunny Latham Island morning.

Stephen Kakfwi, my pal from back home, turned out to be one of these regulars. He was actually teaching in Fort Simpson at the time, but he would drop by for a weekend. Far from his eventual leanings to Bob Dylan in years later, he was then more your hard-core country and western George Jones type, given to bouts with the whisky bottle. In fact, none of us would turn away a shot at that, either.

One of my fonder memories was of he and a rather heavyset blond California surfer, an out-n-out hippie, who could always be counted on "to get his head into" this or that. Them two would get to arguing over whose turn it was to use the one foam mattress to sleep on for the night, still grumbling over the same piece of furniture in the morning, with our dog Boss wondering what was wrong with just curling up on a piece of ground.

They probably each also wanted a bit more of what the other guy was all about, Mr. West Coast to be a little more stand-up and ol' Steve to be Mr. Natural, whatever *that* was all about.

Northern Dene Treaties

René Fumoleau was commissioned to do some research for a book about Treaties 8 and 11, which were signed in the North.

Since we were also next-door neighbours in Ndilo, Yellowknife, René Fumoleau asked me if I was interested in working on a book about Treaties 8 and 11 with him. He said that he asked a person before me, a young First Nations woman, if she "knew anything about the Fort Good Hope band." She answered that she didn't know "Fort Good Hope had a rock and roll band!"

Having an interest in history and already being familiar with writing, I agreed. Right from the first day of work, I was impressed with this man's work ethic and his unflagging ability to go through the thousands of pages of notes, with bits and pieces taped on, just to produce a page at a time, over a number of years.

The project, which would eventually become the definitive word on these two legal documents signed in 1899 and 1921, respectively, took us all over the place, first to the Hudson's Bay Company archives in Winnipeg, Manitoba, and on to the National Archives in Ottawa, Ontario, to dig up records of exactly what had taken place way back.

One thing I always noticed, liked, and admired about René was that, no matter how busy and harried we got with the piles of paper all over the place at the mission, he never did pass anyone up on the road for a ride, going into or coming back from town.

Yet even for a humble priest, he was as much caught up in the ego of a fledgling writer, or what he may have thought of as a celebrity of sorts, for I couldn't help but notice that when the book came out there was not a single mention of all the typing and editing I helped out with. Neither was he averse to changing the titles of my poetry for another publication.

We actually ended up going even further afield, all the way down to Iowa State University in the American Midlands, where doctors June Helm and Beryl Gillespie had been going through their own records from when their school sent researchers to the North way back to the late 1890s.

What we eventually uncovered told a very grim tale that included government and church collusion and outright forgery to make it appear that our Dene ancestors had signed away all of their rights to our northern homelands. Also that government inaction and neglect made for a one-sided relationship built on misunderstanding.

Up until we at the Indian Brotherhood began to seriously question these treaties, the official interpretation was that we had signed away all of our land and the rights to it.

Whichever way you look at it, *As Long as This Land Shall Last* remains, today, a scathing indictment of official corruption, duplicity, and outright neglect.

This Poetic Land

A mirrored
language of colour
echoes in the wind
through chattering birch and poplar
on the way
to breathless heights

Far off
tinkling heavenly bells
float
amongst grassy flotilla

Sparkling plays
along misted surface
over a canvas

Silvered waters of life
even on to the fading
light holds its especial noble
magic twilight

Multicoloured threads set aloft
by Ehsieh Gosieh
Grandfather spider's web
fair catches and weaves

Even you
into your rainbowed nest

On the Air

The airwaves were dead for our People.

The president of the Indian Brotherhood, James Wah-shee, called me into his office one day, and we talked about how the radio department was doing. At our Naedzo Studio, named after famed Sahtú Holy Man Joe Naedzo of Déline, I was keeping busy training Phoebe Tatti and Peter Hope to be broadcasters. Peter, in particular, did us proud by working at CBC Radio for many years after.

Mr. Wah-shee and I met with the manager of the local affiliate, CFYK, and got right down to it, letting the man know that as far as our Dene were concerned, CBC Radio, often the only outlet to the outside world, might as well have been broadcasting in Lithuanian, for all we were getting out of it.

Eventually, he agreed with us, and I ended up hosting a weekly Friday evening show, the first of its kind in the North.

Now the three of us at the Indian Brotherhood Radio Department worked on a genuine production of our own.

One person who came in handy for these regular programs was Chief Baptiste Cazon, who loved to talk and could fill in whatever time we had left at the end of a half-hour show.

From our humble beginnings with the Indian Brotherhood, our dreams became more local. Georges Erasmus asked me if I wanted to join him and some others on the board of directors for the Tree of Peace, a northern offshoot of the National Native Friendship Centres.

Addy Tobac, a close relative from my hometown of Radelie Koe, Doug Leonard, and a few others banded together, and we soon had our own working space in a building in Old Town, across from the Back Bay float base.

The idea for the name came from an ancient legend from the Six Nations that tells of how the Great Peacemaker, Dekanawidah, eventually put an end to warring tribes by having the People throw their weapons into a hole at the base of the original Tree of Peace. This great tree would shelter and protect future generations of formerly warring nations.

I now worked with Pauline Douglas and was training my old high-school pal Johnny Catholique of Lutsel K'e (Snowdrift) to produce television programs for the Tree of Peace. JC, as we called him, showed a natural affinity for the camera right from the start. The Tree, as we called it, also put out a newsletter called *Tsigoindeh* (the *Talking Tree*).

Along with all the television programs we put together, we were going through the motions of rebellion and moving away from an older colonialist order.

Of course, it would still take a number of years for us residential school survivors to be proven right, but so goes the struggle.

CHAPTER 8

Straddling That "Then" Gap

The church was trying for an impossible balancing act.

For us at the Tree of Peace, absolutely everything was up for question. As a part of the worldwide youth movements born of the sixties, and now just coming of age, we had no problem shutting down any and all of the old order.

This all-encompassing assault on social attitudes and norms also meant a turn away from some of our own Dene traditions and lifestyles, leaving us somewhat isolated from our own homes. Wearing braids, for instance, as a return to an older time of no scissors, was a step too far for my own father, Chief of Radelie Koe.

In the long run, though, we were on the same side.

In particular, we didn't want to have anything to do with the colonialist territorial government, now dubbed the "terrified government," and tried in every way to simply shut it down.

For its part, the archaic Roman Catholic Church was simply too entrenched to be easily, if ever, budged, although there were also efforts from within. Namely, "outlaw" priests like René Fumoleau and Emile Piché, nephew of Bishop Piché himself, went through the motions of rebelling but couldn't quite find the confidence to completely join our ranks.

They went so far as agreeing to meet with us at the Tree of Peace to talk about possible ways to work together, but as soon as I heard that they would only do so in instances when the church noticed a "sin," of all things, being committed, I simply got up and left them to stew in their own hypocrisy.

Given their closed minds, they were clearly not able to effectively work away from the church's utter abomination of everything good and natural we wanted to save of our Dene, Métis, and Inuit worlds.

Singing Sage along the Bow

You could just stand there on the riverbank and breathe in the musky scent of sage all day long, coming back to Indian life!

One of the features of a lot of the social unrest going on in the sixties was its aim to offer solutions to existing social conditions and problems.

In April 1971, James Wah-Shee from Behchoko was the president of the Indian Brotherhood, which was later renamed the Dene Nation. One of the prominent leaders in our small group of determined youth was Georges Erasmus, who later took the lead for the brotherhood. It actually did not take long for strong leaders like Alexis Arrowmaker, Lazarus Sittichinli, and Joe Bird to emerge from the communities. They were already there, just not formally recognized.

Of course, with all of the rapid changes going on, each of us was involved in a number of different projects and overlapping areas. I used my artistic skills to design the first logo for the Indian Brotherhood of the Northwest Territories and to paint signs for the first of our national assemblies, starting with nearby Behchoko.

The second and remainder of the decade-long series of Indian Ecumenical Conferences, taking up most of the seventies, was held in Morley, Alberta, on the Stoney Indian Reservation, a truly magnificent country, bordered by the majestic Rocky Mountains. This was the first time our group from Yellowknife was ever exposed to any real native spirituality. We had been basically kidnapped from our mothers' arms at a very young age and subjected to an out and out attempt at cultural genocide.

Even in the North, where our people still lived close to the land, the hold of foreign Mola churches was yet too tight for any Dene roots to show.

All around, for the ten days
in Morley
that smell of sage
your mother's loving care
from teepee
to arbour
and powwow!

Only our elders, like the Anishinaabe Ernie Benedict and Cree Albert Lightning, could clearly see the damage we were just beginning to do to ourselves with drugs and alcohol. Their gentle call back to the circle was the first we had ever heard, sadly.

Speakers would take turns at the sacred fire, under a willow arbour, holding forth on our spiritual selves and needs. Most of it was talk, true, but people like Cree elder Ernest Tootoosis for one made us at least want to try our own ways, such as the sweat lodge. In fact, we made our own and would jump right into the ice cold, glacial Bow River to cool off between the four "rounds" of the ceremony.

Ernest always made it a point to call on us "braves" for whatever needed doing, like help with a teepee, wood, or water. This kind of a cultural reminder went a long way to encouraging us to continue on the path we had chosen.

This was also the very beginnings of rebel groups like the American Indian Movement (AIM), it did not take much to get our hot blood boiling!

We took to braiding our hair, Indian style, and to wearing jean jackets, and red headbands. Real badasses with one foot in the hippie world!

Every night there would be an old-time git down Oklahoma Choctaw stomp dance and forty-niner led by the jovial Dick Hill. Man, those were fun! Eventually even a powwow was added to the merriment that was Morley.

Some nights, I could just make out the insistent and rapid water drum, and I did meet a few of my distant Navajo Dineh relatives, but the Native American Church was still too far removed from my party life to make much of an impact.

I will always recall the smell of the sage that grew all along the top of the banks of the Bow River, where everyone camped out for the ten days in July with the drums going almost all of each night.

What was really happening was that, for a while, at least, we were away from the Mola need to compete with our fellow man. Instead, for the first time, we were taught to be grateful for what we had, and to find ways to be in our everyday walk of life. At the same time, we realized that we were strangers to each other's Dene selves, though being as close, otherwise, as the movement required.

Johnny Catholique explained it best, saying that the White world produces specialists; each person is expected to only do one thing well, so losing a job to them means a traumatic event, an ending.

We Indians, on the other hand, out of necessity, had to learn to be a good at a wide range of things and could fall back on something else, if necessary.

Regardless, it would still take years of life to appreciate these new lessons.

Sitting Bull's Vision

After dancing in the hot midsummer sun for three days,
Sitting Bull offered up a "scarlet blanket," one hundred
pieces of his own flesh, to Wakan Tanka, the Great Spirit,
and saw a great number of soldiers falling from the sky,
upside down, with their ears cut off.

Because the *Wasichu*, "Europeans," would not listen to the Lakota
and uphold and respect the Fort Laramie Treaty of 1868, and with
gold-seekers swarming all over their sacred *Pahá Sápa* (Black
Hills), the Lakota would die, and soon, at the Little Big Horn,
known to the Indians as the Greasy Grass.

At the head of the bluecoats rode George Armstrong Custer.
The headstrong and ambitious "Long Hair" Custer came upon
a huge gathering of the Lakota and their Cheyenne allies at the
historic Battle of the Little Big Horn, with mounted warriors num-
bering in the thousands.

Sitting Bull, who had called this assembly of eagles, had been a
war chief before, but now, getting on in years, he was more a holy
man, able to foretell the future.

The ones who did serve on horseback, including Crazy Horse,
were prominent in turning the tide of this fight, and, along with
Gall and Crow King, rallied the surprised camp to drive Custer's
overwhelmed force back up the Medicine Tail Coulee to defeat.

General George Custer's command was completely wiped out
on that day, June 25, 1876.

One warning Sitting Bull gave from his vision, not heeded, was
to leave the dead Wasichu where they lay and not seek to plunder
the spoils of war.

From that day on, the same Indian Wars have continued, in one
form or another, forever seeking to have us First Nations assimi-
late with the rest of society.

Two Simple Teachings

Do not be jealous of anyone, nor feel sorry for yourself.

Our elders were charged with the enormous task of getting the youth back into the circle of life . . . and right from the start, they kept it simple, so we could understand, as a baby taking its first steps.

In the sacred arbour at the annual Indian Ecumenical Conference held on the Morley Indian Reservation, just outside of Calgary, Alberta, those who could still recall our ancient Indian ways taught them to us.

As we all sat on the ground, with the central sacred fire burning day and night, the first lesson we heard was to not be jealous of anyone, period.

There will always be someone who is better at doing that one thing than you are. That is just the way it is. But there is no one in all of the history of mankind, right from the start, who can be as good as you in being you—no one. So be proud of who you are. Especially that you are Indian.

The other main teaching we heard from more than one older person under the rustling leaves protecting us from the hot July sun, with the smell of sweetgrass and sage wafting from the fields:

> Never feel sorry for yourself.
> You will have to learn about life the hard way
> and the only way to do that is to live it
>   to do it for yourself.
> There is no book for this.
> No one can be an Indian for you.
> You are the only one.
>
> Again, be proud of yourself
> where you come from
> those relatives and ancestors

of yours
and everything will be all right.

Dum Diversas, the Stacked Christian Deck
Our fate was sealed from June 18, 1452!

Years before Christopher Columbus's hapless landing in the Americas, the Roman Catholic Church was already dealing sharp, stacking the deck in favour of stealing our lands. The original papal bull, the Doctrine of Discovery decreed by Pope Nicholas V, was expanded almost a half century before in Romanus Pontifex, during the so-called Age of Discovery.

An intellectual and humanist in the Renaissance Era in every sense, Pope Nicholas V came from the powerful Strozzi and Albizzi families in Florence, Italy, where I would eventually take my third year of art school.

According to these decrees, explorers like Columbus now had the God-given right to claim lands "discovered" for their Christian monarchs. Among other features, these papal bulls sanctified the seizure of non-Christian lands and actively encouraged the enslavement of non-Christians in the New World.

With these spiritual edicts in hand, converted pagans could be spared. If not, it was either be a slave or die.

Given that the people onshore when Columbus's crew alighted from *La Niña*, *Pinta*, and *Santa Maria* had already been in the country for at least thirty thousand years, the only history that was made that day was which of the three—Christianity, slavery, or death—they would be allowed to discover. With these choices, the names *Christianus*, *Servitus*, and *Mortis* would suit far better as names for the three ships.

So much for thou shalt not steal and thou shalt not kill!

How symbolic, then, that the monastic order started by Saint

Francis, whose central teaching of utter humility through poverty, stressed by his monks not even owning a Bible, was to become a papal order, no less, for the transfer of Indigenous lands into the hands of the mighty church!

Throughout all of this, and to this day, nothing was nor is ever mentioned of the one hundred million of our First Nations Peoples already here, waiting, one would suppose, to be "discovered."

In terms of the impacts on the thousands of First Nations tribes already calling America home, these religious manoeuvrings were eventually translated into manifest destiny, a convenient way for American imperialism to push our People aside and simply occupy the country.

Historian Frederick Merk described this territorial expansion as a way for an almost-established America to "Redeem the Old World by high example ... generated by the potentialities of a new earth for building a new heaven."[7]

In of the case of papal order or manifest destiny, humanism definitely did not include the original and rightful owners of this land, nor were the acts to usurp our rights to it even seen as any conduct unbecoming of "founding fathers."

Captain General Colombo

Tuesday, October 16, 1492: "The people have no religion, and I think would be very quickly Christianized, for they have a very ready understanding."

This from the ship's log of Cristoforo Colombo, a.k.a. Christopher Columbus, an Italian long held to have "discovered" America. The idea was to just sail west and eventually come upon Cathay (China), to find gold for his sponsors, King Ferdinand and Queen Isabella, reigning Catholic majesties of Spain.

Born in Genoa, in Italy's northern Liguria region, Cristoforo Colombo made a total of four seagoing voyages to what was then termed the New World, although history, as we know, favours those who write it.

After learning to read and write and from a lifetime of sailing, Columbus learned enough to put into mind what was possible, with the limited knowledge of worldly navigation available at the time. Thus sailing was as much an act of faith as any skill at hand one might happen to have, the fear being that at any moment your ship would simply drop off into space.

Fellow Genovesi and world traveller Marco Polo had to dictate his memories of continental Asia while jailed back at the turn of the twelfth century. Ol' Cristof must surely have been going, "Well, Marco there made off to walk his dream and ended up in yon grim castle keep, I believe, therefore, I shall cast mine dice at high sea!"

Even the most educated guesses had Cipangu (Japan) where Cuba now is and China round about southern California, so it was definitely, "Go west, sailor boy!"

A good majority of the crew leaving Genoa that fateful August of 1492 with the seagoing Captain General Colombo were actually Jews being officially expelled, so in truth, if America was discovered at all, it would've been by Jews, adding a decided dash of naval chutzpah to the mix!

One can imagine the Star of David secreted somewhere on board for whatever sands presented themselves for the claiming, in case pirates made off with the flag of Spain.

The fact that one of Columbus's first impressions had to do with the *Indios*, the Indians he met having been made in the image of God, could well serve to explain the name Indian. After all, far from his wanting to find a trade route to India, he was actually on his way to China and Japan. Yet the hope was still to find gold, for which he took some captives to "help" in this quest for riches.

The name America itself came from Amerigo Vespucci, a banker and sailor who backed Columbus's second and third journeys to this rich new frontier. Martin Waldseemuller, a German painter, proposed Vespucci's name for the new land. Could've been worse: a country called Waldseemuller inhabited by a bunch of Mullers just doesn't have the same kind of impact.

With his sending five hundred natives back from his second voyage, one could well argue that Columbus, said to be more devout in practice than most priests, was also a genuine slave trader of the first order. Clearly his religious observations did not extend to the natives he much admired.

> Christian bells now tolled in
> civilization to America
>
> The gospel mixed with
> a liberal dose of exploitation.
> The new national anthem.

A crewman, Bartolomé De Las Casas, so disgusted by personally witnessing the beheading, dismemberment by dogs, and raping of three thousand natives in a single day, turned to the priesthood in sheer disgust: " . . . Now I tremble as I write."

The entire local Spanish rule was judged a disaster, and the hapless Columbus, along with his two brothers, were sent back to Spain in chains. He was pardoned and returned to the Americas a fourth time. This is the same monster America named Columbus Day after, a national holiday for a serial killer still pompously celebrated to this day!

Far from any pretense of ecclesiasticism, the Roman Catholic Church itself had long turned a blind eye to a lack of celibacy in the papacy, clearly for political reasons. Stories from the time tell of the Borgian Pope Alexander VI being entertained by his son, Cesare Borgia, running down convicted men in the square of Saint Peter's Basilica, shooting six condemned men as he rode by on horseback, bow in hand, right on the same grounds devoted present-day Catholics await the white smoke signalling a new pope!

Indeed, the church's head himself rode out as a general, fronting the Papal Army, to show to all and sundry the might of God's word on Earth. None of this ever reached our innocent ears as altar boys in residential school. Instead, chalice held high, the priest had us believe God was boss!

Another Genovesi, Giovanni Caboto, a.k.a. John Cabot, made a successful landing in Labrador, in June of 1497, laying claim to Canada for England. The flag he planted, however, was Venetian. In the convoluted reckonings of the time, if Cuba was Japan and California was China, then Cabot must have thought for sure he had "discovered" Mongolia!

For our part, the Denendeh in the seventies, we were trying to relearn our own history, a newer, decolonized reality, a bid to cast off our past supposed "education," a kind of intellectual baptismal fire, if you will, not always with the exact facts ready at hand—and often through a bliss of marijuana and hashish purple haze.

Unlike ol' Columbus, though, we knew we were on the right track! This particular theme, the lost explorer, would come up again to the light of day, years later, at an art show featuring Anishinaabe artist Bonnie Devine at the Peterborough Art Gallery.

The show, *La Rábida, Soul of Conquest: An Anishinaabe Encounter*, told of Devine's own artistic voyage in search of Columbus, all the way to La Rábida, the very place where a Franciscan abbey sanctioned his first probes into the mysteries of the unknown world.

Perhaps thanks to the spirit of Saint Francis, or darker portends, Bonnie Devine started having all kinds of problems with her computer and items falling off the shelves when she tried to take some of the soil from La Rábida back with her. She wisely chose to put it back.

While we're on the subject of the man who "discovered America," an Osage from Oklahoma named Wiley Steve Thornton tells the following story:

When I was a boy, I went with my mom and dad to one of the dinners that we had on Sundays after peyote meetings. Dinner was ready by noon, but everyone was still in the meeting at twelve forty-five. So, the cooks sent one of the men helping with the cook fires to see when the people were coming. He went to the meetinghouse, then came back and said, "Put everything back on the fire, they just now started talking about Columbus!"[8]

The Paulette Caveat

We were out to prove the treaties to be a fraud.
This involved several weeks of hearings of the NWT
Supreme Court.

At the core of the all-encompassing Paulette Caveat was whether or not our people understood the true intent and meaning of Treaties 8 and 11 that our leaders had supposedly signed in 1899 and 1921.

Chief François Paulette of *Thebacha* (Fort Smith) headed up the 1973 legal move to recognize Indigenous rights and title, in Judge Morrow's courtroom, to over a million square kilometres of land. On all other fronts, Paulette, the youngest chief in the North, best vocalized the meaning of our Indian Brotherhood movement, which very likely resulted in his intensive investigation by COINTELPRO, including his visa being revoked for international travel.

It was also found that our Indian Brotherhood offices were later broken into and files were missing. Staff members were approached to collaborate with authorities.

At stake: over a million square kilometres (400,000 square miles) of traditional lands our people had hunted, trapped, and fished on for well over thirty thousand years. We were up against the Mola who, comparatively, were like a five-year-old child in terms of residency.

Our primary concern was to see to it that our original Treaties 8 and 11 would be upheld in the way we understood them, as friendship rather than signing away our lands and rights. With this in mind we organized for the Paulette Caveat to recognize our right to our lands in the North, which we managed to win in the NWT Territorial Courts in 1973.

As for these legal documents, it also soon came to light that there was a huge and definitive gap in the way the treaties were understood. According to the government, we had signed over all of our land for five dollars each per year, plus the right to "free" education and healthcare. But individuals like Julian Yendo in Fort Wrigley recalled that there was no mention of the land at the signing back in 1921. These legal agreements were understood to be friendship agreements, for northern White visitors to have free access to the goldfields of the Yukon.

After a month of testimony, Judge Morrow ruled in our favour, legally recognizing our Aboriginal rights in the process. Eventually, however, the Supreme Court of Canada overturned this decision but did not question the judge's findings on Aboriginal rights. Looking back, this particular episode of Indigenous Resistance marked one sure chapter in our quest for Northern rights.

Another Wounded Knee

The world held its breath for those seventy-one tense days!

The memory of hundreds of Indigenous men, women, and children brutally massacred at the first Wounded Knee on December 29, 1890, was reawakened in no uncertain terms on February 27, 1973, as hundreds of Oglala Lakota and American Indian Movement warriors seized and occupied the town of Wounded Knee on the Pine Ridge Reservation for seventy-one tense days.

This drastic move followed close on the heels of frustration at the failure to impeach the corrupt tribal President Richard Wilson, also accused of abuses to opponents of his political regime. Also, there remained some very basic and outstanding treaty obligations with the United Stated federal government.

Throughout these events, the combined forces of the United States Marshals Service, FBI, and other law enforcement services cordoned off the area of Wounded Knee, leaving two Indians killed.

After negotiations and a peaceable end to the conflict, charges against AIM leaders Dennis Banks and Russell Means were dropped.

Richard Wilson was re-elected and his GOONS (Guardians of the Oglala Nation) went on to be suspects in over sixty violent deaths of their opponents.

Although there was a definitive statement made on behalf of Indigenous rights, more and pointed questions came out of this attempt at resurgence, such as the case of a Canadian activist Anna Mae Aquash and, ultimately, the role AIM leadership played in her sudden disappearance from the scene.

First Glimpse from A. Mountain View

A cheque for $750 bought Giant Mines a Dene child.

It took several years from when I started with our humble radio department at the Indian Brotherhood, but with a dedicated group of very talented people, we created our very own Native Communications Society of the NWT with the bi-weekly *Native Press*. A favourite feature was "Dene in the News," basically a snapshot of whomever was in town and what they were doing.

One of the biggest stories, of course, was the very real threat of the pipeline we were all definitely against.

Another and more local story surfaced: the death of a Dene child from Ndilo, on the far side of Latham Island, from eating some contaminated snow.

The parents were given a cheque for $750.

The nearby Giant Mines could be the only culprit, spewing forth billows of arsenic. When it closed in 2004, one of Giant Mine's legacies for our future northern generations, after a half century of steady pollution, is some 237,000 tonnes of deadly arsenic trioxide buried in abandoned mineshafts, to be kept frozen, somehow, forever, at a cost of two million dollars annually.

It is one of the most contaminated sites in Canada.

One of the editors I worked with, Lee Selleck, eventually wrote a book, *Dying for Gold*, about the issue.

Selleck and his co-worker Bruce Valpy also had the foresight to initiate the first series of my A. Mountain View columns. They wanted siss-boom bah-humbug and that is, for the most part, exactly what they got, even if it took a furtive Selleck on the phone line, trying to catch every nuance of an angry Dene trapper 965 kilometres to the north in Radelie Koe, calling collect, of course.

Ah-Li, Ah-Li, Ah-Li!

Ali pulled us All up!

Every time Muhammad Ali stepped into the ring, we were right in there with him. After having proven that he could take on, outsmart, and easily outbox a brute like Sonny Liston in 1964, the Greatest, Ali, made it a point to enter the political scene in a way that no other public figure ever had, by simply refusing to join the US Army, claiming that "no Vietnamese ever called me Nigger!" What he meant, of course, was that our real enemy was right at home, refusing us our rights, in a supposedly "free" country.

He paid the professional price by having his title stripped from him for four years in the prime of his fighting career.

Even after he came back from an officially imposed exile, somewhat slower than the "float like a butterfly, sting like a bee" boxer who "shook up the world," he still had enough belief in himself to win the Heavyweight Champion of the World a total of three times, a record very likely never to be repeated.

His novel training involved submerging himself in a swimming pool with lead weights on his ankles to increase his already incredible reflexes for the Ali Shuffle, a kind of dazzling jig to totally confuse and discourage his already outclassed opponents.

Along the way, this courageous man took a physical pummelling from the likes of Joe Frazier, George Foreman, and Kenny Norton that, along with Parkinson's syndrome, left him with limited mobility for the rest of his seventy-four years.

The incomparable Muhammad Ali was the kind of company we kept as we chose to represent our People on the stage of righting wrongs—before this corporate world we know today takes hold of even people in elected office.

Ragged-Ass Road

The old-town lifestyle went on amidst a jumble of miners'
shacks left over from the gold mining days.

Even though, or because, we were out to change the world, the way we lived was about as down to earth as it could be. All along the Yellowknife and Back Bay, there was this history of ordinary people trying to get by in the North. Many people who wanted a more relaxed and laidback pace preferred the waterfront shacks and shanties that seemed to have just sprung up, seemingly on their own, right out of the rock. There also began to be an annual summertime pilgrimage of hippies coming up from the South; they just parked their painted buses and station wagons and camped out anywhere. Most of us got paired up, and at first, I shared my trailer on Latham Island with a lady from Manitoba.

Some years later, I ended up with a media co-worker, Pauline Douglas, on Bretzlaf Avenue, close to the infamous Ragged-Ass

Road, right across from the old Slant 6 house. Our work schedule became pretty routine, with the occasional trip out of town for community workshops and meetings.

People just kind of ended up wherever they could fit in. Our co-worker JC Catholique lived at the Old Hudson's Bay staff house with a couple of friends, Rick Fader and Randy Glynn. Ol' Earl Dean, who came under suspicion in these times of political high life for having some blasting caps in his possession, frequented a cave, of all things, on Joliffe Island, with neighbouring tribes of merrymakers.

And in town, Friday night was party night, without fail.

Everyone met up at any of a number of bars downtown, usually wherever the best new band was playing, whether it be the Gold Range Hotel, the Yellowknife Inn's Rec Hall, the Gallery, Explorer Hotel, the Hoist Room, or any number of other makeshift dives.

Some of the better bands were the Stained Glass Illusion featuring the Tees brothers, John and Gary Tees, the Komatiks with Tommy Hudson singing lead, and whoever Terry Mercer was playing with at the time.

Weekends there would be dances at the Elks Club or the Legion.

One of the highlights of those years was the annual Caribou Carnival with its dog races—held right out on the ice in Yellowknife Bay. In typical fashion, we would begin the party a month before and, for good measure, keep up the springtime mayhem for another month or so.

As with everything at the time, it just seemed that it would never end.

CHAPTER 9

A Great Loneliness

> "If the beasts were gone, man would die from a great
> loneliness of spirit, for whatever happens to the
> beasts also happens to the man. All things are con-
> nected. Whatever befalls the Earth befalls the sons
> of the Earth."

—CHIEF SEATTLE

Words to this effect were supposedly spoken by the Duwamish/
Seattle chief, with a liberal sprinkling of poetry by Dr. Smith, a
settler who recorded the speech.

As happened with the case of Lakota Holy Man Black Elk,
these European writers who, knowing the old shining days of
the Indian were now over them thar hills, made it their personal
mission to romanticize our ways and culture.

This softening, polishing, and reworking process went on with
the movies *Dances with Wolves, Windtalkers,* and others, usually
with white leads paving the way for a "deeper" appreciation of
Native culture, with, no doubt, an eye to their bank accounts.

We were threatened with becoming unwitting victims of our
own love of America, now a part of this great loneliness of spirit.
Except for the fact that we were not going anywhere soon, least
of all to fading images on anyone's screen! In fact, a good part of

our newfound awareness of our own Dene culture had to do with returning to our homes, once we served our parts in the awakening political front.

Although we knew ourselves to be in the right as Dene at the time, it would take another great while, a part of this aggrieved "great loneliness," to fully appreciate our part, away from any political or revolutionary rhetoric, in this very human of schemes. It could very well be, then, that our forefathers were looking even further into the picture than we would ever know.

Wind and Caribou

The sight of thousands of caribou all moving slowly along
in the early morning is a wonder to behold!

We will probably never see caribou like that again, but there was a time when you could go more than twenty kilometres (13 miles) and not see a break in the herd. There is an ol' Chipewyan Dene saying that "No one knows the ways of the wind or the caribou."

Well, these are the least of your thoughts when you are done with skinning the ones you've gotten for the day and you and your friends are all there by the fire, sitting or kneeling on a carpet of spruce boughs, eating some fresh ribs, and maybe even roasting a head for later.

Except for the occasional deep snow, fierce winds, or really cold temperatures, most hunters prefer the cooler days of winter, when travel is smoother and there are no clouds of infernal "skeeters," mosquitoes, to bat at every which way while trying to do the skinning and hauling.

And then there are the "chucklers," stories. Well, these are to be had by summer or winter campfire, but that jolly fresh air, when each breath is like a drink of cool water, just makes for one like this one from Stefan Folkers, a visitor to Lutsel K'e:

Well, y'know I'd been there for a number of years by then and got used to the way the People like to do. You just choose your own spot, your own pace, and you fit in the way you want to.

So here we are, a whole bunch of us on Ski-Doos, going after a new herd someone had seen not far from town, out toward Christy Bay, out that way. When we got where the first small herd was, the young guys got all excited and just kept chasing them every which way, and I followed them up this narrow creek in the hills.

About halfway up I came to a bend there, slowed down, and saw someone sitting by a fire, just relaxing, drinking tea. It was ol' Joe Michel, not a care in the world, taking his time, sharpening an axe or something.

When I asked him what he was doing, he said, "This is the way we hunt in the old days. Don't worry 'bout nothing. Mind your own business, like this."

Well, for some reason what he was doing sure seemed to make a lot more sense than chasing all over the place and running out of gas or blowing a piston or something, so I just joined him.

He told me a few stories of how they used to hunt with dog teams, saying as how only the dogs could really tell where the caribou had gotten to. He was just getting ready to start up another pot for more tea when some of those same caribou started coming back to the open, just a few hundred feet away from us. Still, he was in no hurry, putting his full pot of

snow crystals on for tea. Calmly, he picked up his
gun and asked me if I wanted some of these animals.

I got to learn to just take my time like this old-timer,
and by the time them boys got back without a single
caribou between them we were all loaded up and
ready to go back to town.

A Four-Month Picnic

My good friend John T'Seleie certainly knew how to put
things into perspective.

John T'Seleie was talking about the way the Mola see our Dene.
"They have no way of knowing how we live, what we do out on the
land. They just see us go out and come back. They probably think
that we are out there for some kind of a picnic!" Yes, and one that
just happens to go on for four months in the dead of winter, with
average temperatures of $-30°$C to $-40°$C.

Although people prefer life on the land in winter because there
are no infernal mosquitoes to deal with and the cool is easier than
working in heat, it certainly is no picnic. After travelling over long
stretches of rough country for hours at a time, you still have to
set up camp. If you are travelling by dogs, you have to unhitch
them, tie them up, and feed them. It helps if you are travelling with
others, but you need to clear off a section of deep snow right down
to the ground using snowshoes for shovels.

You need long poles for the tent and enough spruce branches
to make a carpet for a floor. On top of this, the woodstove has to
be set up, with the pipes in place. If you've arrived in the evening
you have to deal with the lack of daylight and must be careful with
handling a sharp axe to get enough firewood for at least the night.

Once your camp is set up, you need to set a net under the ice for
fish to eat until you can do a proper hunt for moose or caribou. And

you need to build a stage to store your meat, away from foraging predators. You have to put up a tall antenna for the bush radio to stay in touch with people around you and in town, in case of emergencies.

Once everything is set up, you can start to relax, or at least get used to doing everything for yourself on the land, as our ancestors have done for thousands of years.

Just from this quick look at what the Mola like to think of as "camping," you begin to realize that this is no walk in the park for our People.

Yet we think of this as a good way to live.

Starlight Cutter

*A shade of blue would follow me from the time I first saw it
on high yonder vales.*

Kabami Tue was one of the first places outside of my hometown of Radelie Koe I could call home.

The artist and photographer who took the original photo I used as a reference for my painting *Starlight Cutter* was Bern Will Brown, perhaps the first to introduce this village on the edge of the Barren Lands to the world.

My parents, both being of a wandering heart, also had a home in Kabami Tue as well as upriver from Fort Good Hope, across from the oil company town of Norman Wells.

This view of the man clad in winter parka, heavy woolen pants, mukluks, and mitts is fairly typical in winter, early in the morning, when a blast of chilled air greets your first step outdoors.

Some chores, like cutting wood, had to be done every day. You also had to go down to a hole chopped in the bay ice to get the water for tea and cooking. Indeed, those were the days before such modern things as chainsaws and even Ski-Doos.

Every now and again, you would catch sight of a lone dog team returning from somewhere out on the great expanse of the lake, with bells a-jinglin' and sharp commands of "Jee" and "Jawh," right and left.

This is also the place that measured time forgot, where a day could well be a week anywhere else.

People just like it that way.

Selaw Bedew'ih

That's one of the only times you really wanna break down and cry.

You get a lot of memories for yourself when you spend a lot of time on the land. It usually starts when someone other than your brother comes around the house looking to meet one of your sisters. Or, having already done married your sister, he ends up spending a lot of time with you, either going for wood or out hunting.

Every time you do, you have to make a fire at some time, just for tea or to cook up a real meal, maybe even from your kill: caribou in winter or moose in the fall. Either one always starts out the same way: with you looking for them dried twigs at the base of the bigger spruce, complete with the really furry stuff that'll catch right off with a match.

As the years go by, you have quite a right collection of these kinds of events you can choose from to recall your younger days. And as times change, maybe one of you even passes on, you still go to those places you did when there were the both of you. And it was so much *fun!*

When you see those same trees standing there waiting for you, with the fire-starting twigs, you mentally go, "Selaw Bedew'ih":

> My brother-in-law's kindling
> and you just can't stop the tears
> coming on.

Poison in the Mix

There were still unanswered questions . . .

> They ran like a dangerous underground stream
> coming up for air every now and then
> like bubbles
> little pockets of air
> seeking to breathe.

The early 1970s—when we young Dene leaders were back from postsecondary schools—were like swimming shark-infested waters on behalf of our People, and colonialist waters at that. One member of our immediate circle was found with some blasting caps and explosives, questioned and released. Another, Ed Bird, was holed up one day right out of the blue, at home, with a gun, threatening police and was shot dead.

The day we found out that someone had broken into the Indian Brotherhood office, we still thought of ourselves as self-styled rebels, and most had some of that potential, yes, but we could never be compared to the likes of a Fidel Castro. For the most part, we were pragmatists, not martyrs willing to face long jail terms for our cause.

When it came right down to it, we were not completely against economic development as such, but wanted to have a serious say in what went on our lands and the unresolved treaties issues dealt with.

Yet in a very real way, we also had our own unresolved personal problems from the residential schools, which had a habit of coming up at the oddest moments. It may well have been that I was taking on too much for an unappreciated artist, for I also had to deal with an ulcer at a young age, and I must admit that I did pick up a time or two with suicide attempts.

In Support of Leonard Peltier

Everyone wanted to be part of the American
Indian Movement!

The rise of the American Indian Movement (AIM) was the first of
its kind, a real and vital voice for the First Nations. Like the civil
rights movement, ordinary people began to feel a real need to
stand up for themselves against the military/industrial complex
threatening to swallow whole any opposition to events like the
Vietnam War.

And there was no doubt it was a time for change, any change
from a prehistoric way of thinking! For their part, the police, commonly known then as "pigs," and politicians wanted to shut down
any kind of effort we put into individual cases, like that of political
activist Leonard Peltier. A few of us even went to Vancouver
when he was arrested in Alberta and faced extradition back to the
United States for the supposed murder of two FBI agents.

The incident in question happened on June 26, 1975, at
the Jumping Bull compound on the Pine Ridge Lakota Sioux
Reservation following the seventy-one-day Siege of Wounded
Knee in 1973. The traditional Lakota called for AIM warriors
to come in when sixty-three murders by tribal chairman Dick
Wilson's GOON squad went uninvestigated.

Two others, Darrell "Dino" Butler and Bob Robideau, who
went on trial for the FBI deaths were found not guilty on grounds
of self-defence. Yet Leonard Peltier was found guilty, despite
overwhelming evidence of both his innocence and of FBI coercion
of witnesses.

Another activist leader, John Trudell, whose 17,000-page FBI
dossier is one of the bureau's largest, believed Leonard Peltier
would never again see the light of freedom.

Peltier has been in prison for over forty years. In January
2017, the former prosecutor of the case requested that outgoing
President Barack Obama grant clemency to the ageing activist

due to inconsistencies surrounding his trial and appeal.[9] On January 18, the Office of the Pardon Attorney said the president had declined to grant clemency despite the evidence and Peltier's chronic ill health. Amnesty International condemned the decision, while Peltier's lawyer called it "a death sentence."[10]

Mystical Appeal of Crazy Horse
This story will never die.

The real reasons for the killings of Sitting Bull and Crazy Horse in the late-1800s and the lifetime imprisonment of Leonard Peltier of the American Indian Movement are so much a part of our First Nations identity that they will continue to live on.

Some other names continue to be associated with them, like author Peter Matthiessen, who saw it wise to set the record straight with *In the Spirit of Crazy Horse*, a deeper look into Leonard Peltier's story and the FBI and its war on AIM.

The Crazy Horse book was completed in the early eighties but did not see the light of publication until a decade later, for some serious and protracted legal suits, one from former Republican governor Bill Janklow of South Dakota and the other an FBI agent present at the shootings that resulted in Peltier's incarceration.

Both lawsuits were dismissed and, although meddlesome, proved important in terms of "media law," freedom of speech, and how the public has a right to know the facts in key events.

What Peter Matthiessen brings out in *In the Spirit of Crazy Horse* focuses on the widespread fraud and government misconduct in Peltier's trial.

Hands of Anna Mae

Her decomposing body was found by rancher Roger
Amiotte in February 1976 in a far northeast corner of
the Pine Ridge Indian Reservation, about ten miles from
Wanblee, South Dakota.

At first it was thought that this young woman, whoever she was,
had died of exposure. When no clues were to be found, her hands
were cut off and sent to Washington, DC, for fingerprint identifi-
cation by the FBI and she was buried simply as "Jane Doe." Several
days later, the body of Canadian First Nations activist Anna Mae
Aquash, only thirty, was exhumed and reinterred on Indian land.

The Mi'kmaq activist from Nova Scotia became a member
of the American Indian Movement (AIM) and took part in the
takeover at Wounded Knee in 1973. Several years later, she was
accused of being a government informant by AIM leadership in the
case of Leonard Peltier.

After several decades of investigation and three grand juries,
Arlo Looking Cloud of South Dakota and John Graham, a Yukoner
from Canada, were convicted for her murder.

One story had her kidnapped and taken all the way from
Denver, Colorado, to face questioning by her peers with AIM and
summarily condemned to be killed, execution-style, for being a
suspected FBI informant in the Peltier case.

For most of us, this remains but a footnote from a time long
past, but for Anna Mae Aquash, this must have been a truly ter-
rifying time for her as a freedom fighter, thousands of miles from
home summarily accused of betraying her paranoid comrades in
arms with no one to speak on her behalf.

I did a painting titled *The Hands of Anna Mae*, which I gave to
Vernon Harper in Toronto in the late seventies, during the height
of those turbulent times.

With the involvement of family members, Anna Mae Aquash
was finally reburied at Shubenacadie, Indian Brooke Reservation,

in 2004. Her death happened almost four decades before Idle No More and the shameful national issue of Missing and Murdered Indigenous Women, claiming upward of twelve hundred lives and counting.

At a time when America took great care to find each and every soldier killed in action all the way in distant Vietnam and bringing them home in dreaded body bags, dear Anna Mae didn't even have a name.

Geronimo, a Dene Patriot

When enemy soldiers heard he was coming for them, often with just a knife, they would start feverishly praying to Saint Jerome, thus his name, Geronimo!

The man who would later become the terror of the southwestern desert mountains was actually born on Dineh, Navajo land in Arizona in 1929. Geronimo was no chief, but a war leader bent on a brutal lifetime avenging the killing of his mother, wife, and three children by Mexican soldiers.

He took to the Apache war trail for over a quarter of a century in the Sonoran Sierra Madre Mountains, often also using his skills as a medicine man to affect the time of day and weather in order to slow down enemy troops.

When his band of Bebonkohe Apache finally surrendered to General Miles at Skeleton Canyon and were taken to exile in Fort Marion, Florida, they were only thirty-nine fighting remnants of a once-proud nation ruling the Southwest. This made him the last of all the fighting Indians to give up his freedom.

Never to return to the land of his birth, Geronimo died at seventy-nine and was buried at Fort Sill, Oklahoma, in 1909.

Antoine's Island

People must have gotten used to having me around,
for away from Lutsel K'e they would ask me when I was
"coming home."

I was accorded my own Antoine's Island, past Bricker's Lodge going north. Meanwhile, Lutsel K'e, that precious diamond atop the *Tu Nedhe* (Great Slave Lake), still shimmered in the sun. By this time, I was with the love of my life, Anne Turner from Manitoulin Island in faraway Ontario. For some reason, we had bought a large roll of heavy-gauge canvas from Vancouver and brought it north, to do what with I wasn't quite sure.

I was already much more interested in our traditional First Nations way of life but without the daily practice. I had been away from my home of Radelie Koe for almost ten years and would need a guiding hand to find my way back.

This came in the form of my lifelong friend Johnny "JC" Catholique. It may have also been that he was grateful to me for training him in the media and wanted me to share his own love of the land. Whatever the case, we ended up living with his family there.

His father, the late Jonas Catholique, a real character himself, immediately took a liking to me, calling me *Babah Duweleh* (the Able One) in his Chipewyan language, for some reason.

Life in any Northern community is lived at a much slower and relaxed pace than the major towns and cities, and before long we settled right in. This was before many of our Northern towns took back their traditional Dene names, so Lutsel K'e was still Snowdrift to one and all.

The mystery of the 272 kilograms (600 pounds) of canvas revealed itself when people came forth asking for some to make their own tents, canoes, and boat covers.

Anne, in her turn, got busy and we soon had a teepee. This started me on a number of years of life in this traditional home. I always have the best sleep in a teepee.

One time I was camped across from Jerry Bricker's Frontier Fishing Lodge, and I turned over just before nodding off to sleep to take one last peek to make sure all was well. What greeted me was a brilliant flash of light, a flame rising up in a good-sized fire! You can bet I made a beeline for the shore with my water pail and got back so fast in my haste I jumped right on through the big flaming hole! I did manage to put the fire out, but not before having myself a good chuckle about life's foibles.

In an all-out attempt to make a nice house one winter, I got busy building one, not having a clue, really, what I was doing. We did move into it but had to drape the teepee along the centre beam, because the cabin was too big for just two of us.

After I was gone from "Antoine's Island," as the place was affectionately called, my good friend JC took it all apart and put it back together as a warehouse in town. The code of country living: "Use it or lose it."

Into Tomorrow

Every trip out
a lingering note
from love's door

Time away   pages disinterred

Floating on a calmed surface

No line between
leaving off
and an unfathomed here
    ever circled.

Rich tapestry
of the North

woven through
tall dark trees

Against floated blanket
bright yellows . . .
rich orange hues

Velvety blues fairly envelope you

Twilight slowly descends

Drifting thoughts   awakening through currents
of suspended time

Unspoken truths

into tomorrow.

How to Skin Caribou

A roomful of hunters all gassed up brings to mind the ol'
Wild West!

Throughout the seventies, a group of northern Dene and Métis
were in Ottawa to present their respective cases to some government types. On one visit, after one of two meetings was done,
they had an evening to relax, and they did so in one of the hotel's
sumptuous rooms over beers and liquor.

After an hour or so, the scene became no different from any
night at the seedy and raucous Gold Range Bar back home in
Yellowknife, minus the bouncers. The talk, as usual, came around
to life on the land and, in particular, the right way to skin caribou.
This went back and forth for a while, until one of the Métis men
volunteered to demonstrate the proper technique on his brother
who was already passed out on the floor.

"Okay, boys," he began, taking his best skinning knife out of its case. "You all know this part. Start around and just offa the hoofs and slice on down to the body. No one does this any different."

As he was explaining it, he was cutting into his poor brother's clothes—the only set he had with him all this way across the country.

He continued. "But see here, when you get to this here section, the stomach, you all know to make sure you don't get right into the stomach itself, or you get that big ol' 'poof,' with all the hair comin' and flyin' into yer face! No, we don't want that. What we do want is to cut all around here, like the Dogrib [people] do, and take all this right out so you won't have that problem at all, an just throw this part away."

The lesson went on for a bit, the main part of his skills now explained, and they went on with their little party.

The following morning, the man who had done his skinning demonstration offered to treat the group to breakfast at a place across from their hotel. Clearly, he had something in mind. In a conspiratorial tone he directed their attention to the front door of the hotel.

"Okay, gang, I know my brother don't have another set of clothes to wear, and our next meeting is coming up soon. Ahhh, just keep your eyes peeled on that there door. He'll be coming out any minute now. I know him. Whatever happens he don't like to be late."

No sooner had he spoken than his younger brother stuck his head out, looking this way and that. Spying a taxi on their side of the street he took off at a furtive dash, wearing only a white bed sheet, fluttering in the morning breeze.

He came up to the cab driver and got directions to the nearest clothing store, which happened to be right next door to the restaurant his friends were watching from. Once he got his bearings, he thanked the driver profusely and gave him a tip for this vital and timely piece of information.

His bed sheet, though, had somehow gotten caught in the door of the taxi, so when it took off, he was left without a single stitch of clothing on, right there on a major street in the nation's capital!

Oh, the price we pay for vital family lore to be passed along to a questioning passel of greenhorns.

Long Waters Home

He gave me a long, baleful, sinking look of despair . . .
"Hey, Selaw, brother-in-law, I thought you told me this was
a good boat!"

As we slowly paddled upstream to my camp at Bluefish Creek, Michel Lafferty kept taking the rising water out of the back of my freighter canoe, plans for our moose-hunting trip now in serious ruins. We didn't have much else to do, so I told him how this boat didn't always look so pitiful, the entire cover just kind of flopped off, with the skeletal wooden slat frames all out like that for the weather to claim.

I had started my journey off earlier that summer in pretty high spirits—sixteen hundred kilometres (1,000 miles) to the southeast at Lutsel K'e, across the Tu Nedhe (Great Slave Lake) from Somba K'e (Yellowknife). It was the late seventies, and I had this dream of making it all the way home, the way I heard some people do, by water.

Chipewyan elder Noel Drybones had a canvas-covered boat for sale and could throw in a serviceable motor that just needed a little work on the fuel pump. A group of us took a look at it, and Ray Griffith got the motor going. Before we knew it, we were on our way to Yellowknife.

I had an idea for a book then, but travelling over one of Canada's biggest lakes all but did in our crew. We took some time off in Yellowknife and decided to take a side trip over to Stagg River. We paddled a canoe down to Great Slave Lake and returned to the city. From there, we got back in the long boat, getting a little lost on the way south to the other side of Great Slave Lake while making our way to Fort Resolution.

When I close my eyes sometimes, I can still see my cousin Barney, ever the sailor, rigging up a genuine sail and just a-kickin' back, pipe a-smokin', a flagon o' rum at hand, expertly skirting the treacherous reefs through Devil's Island, lake sprays of misted water just grazing his tanned brow.

Not wanting to get seriously stranded in the maze of islands on the way to Hay River, we simply loaded the boat, passengers and all, on one of the larger fishing boats and made it to the hub of the North. Most of the crew decided to go south to the Morley Ecumenical Spiritual Conference near Calgary, and only Ernest Boucher and I continued our journey.

It took us a while, but we eventually made it back to my home in Radelie Koe, camping out at the San Sault Rapids and even shooting a moose to take in.

My grandfather Peter Mountain Sr. was right proud to have a whole winter's supply of firewood delivered to his door.

This story didn't cheer my poor brother-in-law Michel Lafferty, who was still pondering how we were going to get our moose now that the boat we had started out in was beached for good.

Such is the life of adventure on the high seas of Northern waters.

CHAPTER 10

Bluefish Creek and Mountain River

Except for the great number of bears, Bluefish Creek was
some great place to camp for the summer.

When I moved on back home from Lutsel K'e in the mid-seventies,
I had my goods put on a barge and shipped north. One of them was
a teepee that Anne Turner had made and left with me. All I really
needed was a net in the waters of Bluefish Creek as the lazy days
of the midnight sun just kind of blended into each other.

The odd paddlers came by and spent a bit of time chatting about
this and that. As would happen later, this was just one of those
places I could well imagine spending a lot of time in, although
there were the forbidding rapids of the Ramparts between it and
Radelie Koe.

Another and more traditional spot I ended up at was at the
mouth of Mountain River for spring hunting. I took up an invitation from my brother Robert and his then-wife, Joanne. There
was quite a group of people there, including George and Florence
Barnaby and their family, Baptiste Shae and his family, and
some others.

René Fumoleau even came by to take some photos for an
upcoming book, and a filmmaker from Yellowknife came too.

Sah Goneh (Bear Arms)

He could lift just about any weight, and then some.

My two younger brothers, Robert and Fred John, were better on land than I ever was. Especially Robert, whom I ended up staying with for a bit of time at Mountain River, one of the places our People used to stop on their way into the higher country.

For my part, I will always be grateful to Robert and his wife Joanne for inviting me there. But I had to fill in as woodcutter, with direct orders from Cousin George Barnaby on behalf of camp leadership, to make amends for not actually bringing along any supplies for the weeks I spent there.

As resident elder, Baptiste Shae surely lent a tone from our treasured Dene past to what went on there. Looking back, those were the good times, though I never realized it then.

As siblings do, Robert and I would either unwittingly challenge each other or just not care about certain things.

Once we were on our way somewhere in spring, with that ol' sun beating down hotter every day. His Ski-Doo tended to heat up with the weight of both of us—and whatever else we put on there. More often than not, there would be a long blue flame coming out of the engine and reaching almost all the way back to where I was playing flagman on the back carryall. Even that motor backfiring and about to explode didn't faze a couple of daredevils like us!

Mountain River country is one of the prettiest spots in all of our home area, with the picturesque place where our cultural hero Yamoria took an axe to a giant beaver lodge to get at the pesky beasts who preyed on humans in the oldest of our legends. The San Sault Rapids cut up the waterway over on the other, steeper side.

Maybe that's what brought author, photographer, and priest René Fumoleau to the place, with a genuine filmmaker and crew all the way from Yellowknife. All I recall is that camp life took a decided Hollywood turn, with different people vying for the eye of the camera, without too much fuss, of course.

My brother Robert, *Sah Goneh* (Bear Arms), being a true Dene in his natural element, though, would have none of it and stole off spring hunting every chance he got, especially when the film producer had the gall to ask us guys to build them a twelve-metre scaffold to film the goings-on. I must admit, though, that René did take a great photo of me sketching in my teepee.

When we were together, Robert was always full of questions, and we even ended up building a sweat lodge and having a few beers to relax from strenuous bush life. We were just learning this part of our lives, and I still regret having abruptly turned dear Joanne away from sitting in on the ceremony with us because of a sexist notion that sweat lodges should be segregated by gender. There was the time we were sitting, in the peace of the inner woods, waiting there, all night, for beaver—for a big ol' fat one to skin and eat later, and maybe keep the pelt, if it was any good.

It was all well and good, but looking back to where our camp was, we saw some serious grey smoke coming out of the bushes. When we went back to check, we found that an old stump right next to our campfire, along with some moss, had caught fire and burnt up both our packsacks and all the supplies we had in them.

I do believe all we ever wanted to do was spend a bit of time together, taking whatever adventures happened in stride. Back in town, there were a fair number of things going on, it was difficult to keep pace with town life.

Whatever else is happening, the land brings out the best in you. Away from other people, money, or possessions, there is nothing to hide behind. All you have when out on an open lake, for instance, especially without a gun, are your own wits and strength of character. If a pack of Barren Lands wolves, as happened to Cousin Alfred once, a bear, or a wolverine comes along, you are definitely the hunted: prey.

Any amount of yelling, screaming, or running
helps even less.

You have to find a way to
simply ... belong.
At the very least, convince yourself.

That's what I got from Sah Goneh, Bear Arms
and my other brother, Fred John.

In the Chief's Lodge

Although Dad knew how to cut a few corners, it was a
traditional home.

Pretty well all of my siblings grew up in the twenty-five years our
father was chief. From about the mid-fifties, town life was something new for most of our People in Radelie Koe, so his position
was very much in the service of the public, as originally intended.

Some of it, though, did not make for much of a family life. Our
home was more or less open to the community, and we were taught
to always expect people to drop in. This was usually an elder, so
we had to stop what we were doing and ask if there was anything
special we could help them with. Often they would just want
someone to talk with, so along the way, we got to know what they
had to say about the older days. If they were hungry, we would
cook for them and we would just spend some time with them.

But we had our problems like everyone else, not the least of
which was my dad beating on poor Mum when there was strong
drink around. It certainly was a confusing time for us youngsters,
having been taught the old ways of respect for our elders, yet
being helpless in our own home.

Not surprising, we all chose to leave as soon as we could.

Moose Hunting

Nothing like the sight of a big ol' bull standing there on the shore, just waiting on ya.

Hunting in summer is actually harder than in winter. This time of year, you are usually in a boat, which has more drag than sliding over packed snow on a sled. Then there's the heat and the swarms of mosquitoes to put up with.

The hunt starts with a few of you setting a date in fall when you think you might have some days of clear weather ahead. One of you has a boat, so you just have to put your money together to get enough gas to last a few days and maybe some extra. A few boxes of rifle shells, and some for ducks, your grub box of canned goods, a packsack, and a sleeping bag and you are off.

That first time on the water is often the best, before the hard work of skinning and packing actually starts. All you really have to do is keep a sharp eye out for anything big and black. This often turns out to be a bear, which most people don't bother with and for good reason. When skinned, this relative looks too much like a human being!

Anything you are not after, you just let go, including caribou or muskox if all you want is a moose, or several.

Being such a large and easy target to hit, the actual shooting of the moose is not the hard part—as long as you know where to aim so as not to damage the hide or the precious internal organs. One of you is usually a more experienced hunter who knows how to expertly cut up the big animal. The hide is tough, so your big skinning knife needs to be continually sharpened. After skinning, the real work begins, with a hind leg that takes a full-grown man to carry any distance.

But if you are in no hurry, with those fall leaves all pretty and a lot of ducks around, you can just make a big fire, hang all the meat up, get smoky, and let the meat tender up a bit. There's plenty of time for storytelling and enjoying the weather before you get enough for a good load of meat to bring back.

That ride just getting into sight of town with all of your waiting relatives is the best feeling of all! The word gets around pretty quick that a boatload of moose meat is coming in.

It is Dene tradition for the women to do the rest of the butchering at home, with people coming by for a share and maybe even a drum dance to follow.

Ol' YCI

I never got the impression I was with criminals.

There were a couple of times I served my time as a guest of taxpayers at the old Yellowknife Correctional Institute (YCI). One of the times was for simply refusing to enter a plea in court and letting the Justice know that I did not recognize this court of law on Dene land.

Neither was an extended stay, mind you, but I didn't have the feeling that I was somehow caught up among career criminals. Rather I agree with one good friend there in the capital city that these people behind bars were the "misunderstood."

Being a survivor of residential schools, I've always had this feeling that among all the bad feelings still very much present from those haunted days, there is one that is very much alive: that we want to get caught, we want to be punished for being bad.

Almost all of my fellow inmates never really had a chance to know what it means to be Dene, not that the people on the outside do either.

There is a very real need for law and order, but there is a full docket of cases to be heard every time the circuit court comes a-callin' in our Northern community, hauling away more of our youth.

Louie's Baseball Game

Storytelling in the North is a great and honoured tradition.
One kind is the tall tale, and our humble town of Radelie
Koe was very likely the home to the greatest teller of tall
tales of them all: Louie Caesar.

One time we were on our way past Farahezen (Black Rock Rim
Around), a fish camp some twenty-five kilometres (15 miles) or
so up the Duhogah, on the west side of the river. We stopped at
Louie and Marie Caesar's camp to drop off a mattress we wanted
the elders to have.

Visitors are usually treated to a nice meal, and while we were
there, we noticed a strange set of uniforms hanging in the back
of their tent with an Edmonton Trappers baseball cap above.
When we asked about it, the old man began taking out his pipe
and filling it with tobacco from a tin. This is always a Dene sign
that we are about to hear a story, and from this man it was going
to be good!

"Well, that was quite a while ago when I left here," he began. "I
ended up in Charles Camsell Hospital in Edmonton, *Mola Neneh*
[White man's country]. I was flat on my back for a whole year and
got to know my doctor quite well in that time. One day he asked
me if I wanted to do something besides just being in the hospital . . .

"'Of course,' I said. 'The nurses are treating me well here, but it
does get tiring.'

"The doctor told his nurses to let me put on my clothes, and
we left. After a while we were in a big bowl, with so many people
in there we sounded like the geese and ducks up around Miller's
Cabin, down the river in the spring!

"I had my cup of beer and a small flat like everyone else, but I
was also looking at a small clearing way down in the middle. There
was a man standing way down there, waving his finger up at the
crowd, and saying something—

"Knowing how to read lips and even at that distance I could

make him out saying, 'One more, one more, we need one more player! Someone didn't show up. One more, one more—'

"Before I knew it, the doctor on my one side raised my hand, and the nurse smiled and nodded her head 'yes.'

"The man in the clearing far below pointed at me, saying, 'Okay, you up there, you come down here and play!'

"Before I knew what was going on, two RCMP officers took me by each side and walked me down. I was brought to a little house underground, where a man waited.

"'Louie,' he said, 'do you know what's going on around here?'

"'No,' I told him. 'I don't know you, and I don't speak English anyway.'

"Pointing to a set of fine clothes he asked me what I thought of them. 'Well, I like the pants and the shirt, of course,' I replied, 'but I really must have the hat!'

"'I'll tell you what, Louie,' the boss man explained, 'if you do a good job for me today, you can keep all these nice clothes, and the hat!'

"I also pointed out to him that the clothes I had on were the only set I had from home and I asked him if it was okay for me to put on his nice fancy ones over the ones I was wearing.'

"'Good, fine, Louie, whatever you want. As long as you do me a good job today.'

"I was taken to a plate on the open field, with all of them people watching, including my doctor and nurse high above.

"I was also given a stick, which I did not know what to do with. So I just stood there for the time being. In the distance a man began some kind of a dance and threw an object at me but missed. The person behind me caught whatever it was and the fat man behind him put up one finger. This happened again and out ran my boss from the little house underground. He dragged me back inside and again asked me if I knew what was going on around here.

"'No,' I told him, 'I don't know you and I do not know what you are talking about.'

"'Well, let me tell you something, Louie. We didn't give you that there stick for nothing. And that man in front of you is not trying to hit you! You've got to hit the ball and run around. Otherwise, no clothes and no hat for you!'

"This time I knew what was going on. I strutted to the plate and started squeezing the piece of wood I was given. Wood shavings were just coming down, let me tell you! I hit that ball as it came at me, but only with about three-quarters of my strength. I started running around them bases . . .

"The first time around wasn't so bad, but the second time around people started throwing their beers at me, which I caught, drained, and kept going right around that circle of bases. The fourth and last time around women were throwing their babies at me to kiss and gently put down.

"Well, when all that was done the man from the little house underground came running up, telling me that I had earned the set of clothes and the nice hat fair and square.

"My doctor even said that I was now cured of my tuberculosis and that I could return home.

"Several years went by, and about a week ago, I heard the mention of the word 'baseball' on the news. My wife knows how to speak seven languages, including English and French, so I asked her to translate for me.

"She listened to the radio for a while and asked me, 'Husband of mine, exactly how hard did you hit that baseball?'

"When I told her I didn't really use all my strength, she told me that what she heard was that a Dene man from faraway Radelie Koe in the Northwest Territories hit a baseball from the Edmonton stadium that was finally found, after eight years of searching! She said that they had ten people working during the day and another set of ten at night, trying to find the ball.

"'And when they did find the ball,' she said, 'they built a small little monument, with your name, Louie Caesar, on it!'"

Where the Wild Geese Roam

That old man sure got himself busy!

Back home in the Radelie Koe area, we have our favourite places to go. One that comes right to mind is *Ga Doeh* (Rabbit Island)— and just about any other island when the time is right. On Rabbit Island when you show up on a late summer's evening, those hoppers will be all standing up, one after the other. You can walk along just like in a Western and blast all you want and take them home to clean and cook.

Another place is all along the Duhogah all spring long, just about.

Which is what this one old Dene man was doing there with his grandson, who'd never been out with his grandpa like this before.

The old man told it to him like this:

"*Se Sieh* [Grandson], it's real easy to do now right here. All you see here are these little *Kha-ehsoo* [goslings], which are not real ready to fly yet, but can run like the dickens and maybe swim some, too.

"So, you are lucky to be with a real expert here on this sandy island today, and the best thing is we don't even have to waste a single shot on 'em. You just watch me close and follow right behind, that is if you can keep up with this ol' gent. I'm just going to run these here little geese down, grab 'em by the neck and twist 'em, two by two! All you have to do is follow close behind with your packsack and fill it up with this good stuff!"

With that, the young fellow's grandfather took off like a man possessed, in and out among the crazed goslings, picking them up and wildly swinging and twisting their necks in one fell swoop. He was doing all of this so fast that every time a pair of goslings landed at his grandson's feet, they would stand up again, dazed, but with their little long necks unwinding, and take off going every which way again!

By the time the old man got himself all tuckered, he suddenly stopped on a small rise in the island, all bent over with arms akimbo, chest a-heavin', hands gripped to trembling knees, gasping.

"Okay, Se Sieh, that should be enough for now. How many did we get? I bet we are goose-rich now, huh? They are going to sing some songs about us back home tonight for sure!"

When he could kind of catch himself without laughing out loud the young man replied, "Er, none of them, Ehseh. None, they all took off again. Must have real tough necks, this bunch!" He didn't have the heart to let his grandfather know that he had already been through the entire batch of Kha-ehsoo on the island a time or two.

And with a sheepish look they slowly walked over and took off in their boat again, not even bothering to try to catch the gaggle-o-goslings swimming desperately away all around them!

Down Home for Spring Hunt

He was always singing our Dene songs.

Lawrence Manuel and the elderly drummers back in town would always be singing our Dene songs, just breaking into one of our old chants as a way of keeping in touch with our ancestors.

One of the best times I ever had was going out in the late seventies when I was twenty-seven for the spring hunt with my uncle Charlie Tobac and his wife, Laura. *Seh Leh* (my friend) John T'Seleie says it best: "Going out on the land this time of year, for we the Dene, is to do as all other life does, being reborn back into our traditional ways."

The main reason we were there was for the geese.

Uncle Charlie was glad to have me around because, as quick as he shot down the geese, I would load them up to ten at a time in a big ol' packsack and haul them on into camp. Auntie Laura was busy singeing and plucking them, with a big pot of goose stew always on the go, that flavourful grease riding on top.

One of the best parts of living on the land is that you get to eat just about anything you want. There were all kinds of ducks, from mallards to swans. There were muskrat or beaver with their delicious tails to be roasted or boiled and the occasional loche from the Duhogah for their rich and tasty livers.

When we got settled, I had the idea to remake my big ol' four-star eiderdown quilt into a real Dene Sho T'serih. I asked Auntie Laura for some goose down, and she told me to just go ahead and help myself, probably thinking I only wanted a couple of handfuls. I ended up using a total of five large black trash bags! She was not pleased with that at all, as I dozed off with the lightest blanket in the world.

Somebody found a bear den, and the old-timers demonstrated how they used to harvest them way back when. They set fire to some birch bark tied to the end of a long pole and poked it in the big animal's quarters until they woke it up and it came out where they could shoot it right at the entrance.

A good part of camp life in warmer weather is that the hours are long, making for time to spend just talking. Uncle Charlie always told me that he just wished he had the kind of education me, my cousin Barney, and Steve Kakfwi had. Yet again, he was brought up in the old way, which I shared a bit of, but with frequent trips out for school, work, and such.

He also told me, "People get jealous when you stand out a bit and do good for yourself. They use bad medicine, *Edst'ineh* [the crooked way], to harm or even kill you."

He could see that this was going on with me right then, or about to, and also knew how to stop these bad people from doing me wrong.

I always did appreciate that about my Uncle Charlie, risking himself in that way, just for me. I knew so little of these old ways that I would've been seriously injured without even knowing why, much less how.

Camp life was mostly work, but the fun kind, and we came back to town in late June with a good supply of dried geese, a specialty.

You simply skin it and dry the entire body, minus the feathers, of course. You wouldn't wanna be spittin' out down like a pillow a-munchin' fluffy midnight delights! All you need is a bit of salt for the best country food around!

"You Don't Say!"

There was a time when we used to be able to speak with our animal relatives. Even today there is no doubt that different species still communicate with one another.

You especially see different species communicate just before the change in seasons, in spring and fall. Larger groups of birds like eagles and ravens will meet, no doubt to discuss who is planning to go where for the coming summer or fall and when. Here the mighty grizzly bear puts his grouchy nature aside for a moment to find out from chatty raven what he might need to know.

With its ability to fly, raven knows the changed lay of the land and can even warn bear of dangers just ahead, of a hidden cave-in, for example.

Bear will, in turn, provide fish, later.

Thus, life goes on smoothly for the benefit of all.

Trapping and the Dene Nation

I finally spent a winter with my parents on the land.

After many, many years apart, we went out on the land as a family, two of my brothers, Robert and Fred John, my parents, and one of the elders, George Abalon. I have never been one to enjoy the act of killing animals for a living, so I spent most of my time in camp just cutting wood, which I truly enjoyed.

Upon our return to town, I was selected to go to Déline, then known as Fort Franklin, for a Dene National Assembly, in the winter of 1978.

I had been to quite a number of meetings like this, but the reason this one stands out is because it was where we renamed our organization, then called the Indian Brotherhood of the NWT. The intense discussion went on all day, and finally François Paulette and I sparred about it. No matter what, I wanted the name "Dene Nation" to be used, and it turned out to be so.

There was also talk of whether or not we wanted our Dene Nation to be involved with the government of the NWT.

With mixed results, we decided to do so.

PART III

Rough Waters, Tippy Canoe

1978-92

CHAPTER 11

From Six Hundred to Six Million!

At first, this Dene country bumpkin just stood there at a busy big city street corner, transfixed. The heart goes where no man will.

I had been living on the land for several years, cutting wood for the elders at home, when I thought again about an artist, John Turo, who was already down south. I also thought to reconnect with Anne Turner, who had left her home in Little Current, near Wikwemikong, a bit before.

It was the late 1970s and, one way or another, I made my way from tiny Radelie Koe to Toronto, the biggest city in Canada. I had been to some places nearly as big—Montreal and Vancouver—but the sheer size, hustle, and bustle of Toronto got my small-town head to spinning!

After getting my bearings I also found out that *this* kind of action was just what I needed in my life. Without any new and different cultural input, I must have been just kind of vegetating, art-wise, in the North. Also, thanks to the efforts of Norval Morrisseau, Daphne Odjig, and the Indigenous Group of Seven, there was a real need for Indigenous art.

Alternate schools of art had sprung up around the city, and I liked what I saw at Art's Sake on Queen and Peter Streets, downtown. It took a while and some doing, but I stayed in touch with James Ross, with the Dene National Office in Yellowknife, and thanks to his efforts, I was formally admitted as a student at Art's Sake.

Anne and I did try to get together a bit, but I believe the rift between us was the result of my earliest times at residential schools rearing its head up again to haunt and torment. She was the love of my life, but I simply did not know how to respond to that kind of affection.

> Like a single drop of tear in sleep
> our love clung... and dried
>   got washed off
> for another day.
>
> With tears unbidden
> in wash of soul
> gratitude
>
> Her loving touch
> bade my aching heart
> to open of its own in time
>   a trust not there since memory.

Given this chance at being with someone, though, I have always been more goal-oriented and my single-minded bent for the arts did not leave a lot of room for human connection to take hold and sprout, much less bloom and grow.

From the very first, I felt like a kindred spirit within Art's Sake. It was an alternate school set up to allow for the latent talent of its students to shine. There, I met my lifetime mentor, Diane Pugen, one of the founding members of the institution, on the third floor of a factory in Toronto's Queen Street Garment District. John Turo was already a student there, so I joined him.

Although the place could be viewed as relaxed, there was no doubt that we were there to learn. To the great credit of our instructors, who were themselves professionals, for the first year we were not allowed to touch any brushes or paints.

Of course, we did so on our own, and the presence of the Indigenous Group of Seven helped to see the familiar world in a very different way.

The teachers I was most influenced by at Art's Sake were, of course, Ms. Pugen in anatomy, Gord Rainer, Ken Lywood, and a fellow First Nations artist from the Six Nations, Bob Markle, who passed away too soon.

That first year, being a real keener, I made it a point to spend every lunch hour with ol' Dem Bones, a real-life skeleton I would pull out of the closet and just draw, draw, draw, trying to get the proportions right, the ghastly face grinning all the while.

One person in the crowd who spent a good deal of time at the Black Bull Tavern on the corner of Queen and John was Zbigniew "Ziggy" Blazeje, a very gentle soul. The tavern surely was our northern version of the Eagle's "Sad Café," where we made big plans for our art careers, over beers we could hardly afford.

John Turo and I were the exceptions, though, riding a growing wave of a popular interest in First Nations art. The others took to calling us The Bank!

It was Bob Markle, though, who kindly advised the class, "If you want to do this, drink in the Black Bull or the Wheat Sheaf further west, you have to do the other, that is work hard and sell your paintings."

Another popular spot was the Beverley Hotel, which featured different kinds of music on each floor: blues in the basement, rock on the first, and folk, I believe, at the top of the stairs.

On Spadina Avenue, there were always some laid-back beats at Grossman's and, of course, the notorious Silver Dollar, your average Indian bar. You came in, lost your seat in five minutes, and just boogied on!

When we formally started working with colour at Art's Sake, I recall that it was Graham Coughtry who really drilled it into me that I simply needed to relax my brushstroke, to make full use of a wider, looser range of expression, and to vary my images.

Other well-known artists associated with Art's Sake were Dennis Burton, Deni Cliff, Ross Mendes, Robert Hedrick, Joan Van Damme, and Paul Slogett.

From time to time, other artists joined in, like David Ruben, an Inuit carver from Paulatuk and my residential school days.

To this day, I believe it was the insistence of Art's Sake on fundamentals that allowed me to realize so much potential in the four years I was there.

I don't recall anyone ever having made it big on the art scene from Art's Sake, but then again, that would've defeated the purpose of the place. We definitely did not want to have the same kind of commercial drive as OCAD, the Ontario College of Art and Design, just around the corner. In its very own way, Art's Sake was like that ray of brilliant sunlight you come across after a rain shower on the lake, your boat somehow suspended for a seemingly endless moment in mid-air somewhere between grim reality and the real world!

I had been given a glimpse of a different artistic way sometime before, through the works of Cary Ray, but not in any concerted way. With the combination of that experience and my formal studies at Art's Sake in Toronto in the late seventies, I soon came under the influence of the Indigenous Group of Seven.

John Turo was already firmly entrenched with the Nishnawbe Woodland School of Art, even being lauded as the new Benjamin Chee Chee, with his graceful and flowing lines. We were invited to group showings with Norval Morrisseau, Goyce and Josh Kakegamic, Art Shilling, and the rest of these innovators, absorbing a new way of depicting what was latent in our young souls. There was no doubt this was the balm we needed from still-fresh scars of residential schools. Others in this famous and groundbreaking group included Daphne Odjig and a Dene, Alex Janvier of Cold Lake, Alberta.

For a time, I was taken under the wing of one of the older artists in the group, Eddy Cobiness, who took great pains to take me step by step through what I needed to unlearn to open up these channels in my native being. Another, Eleanor Kanasawe, was a classmate at Art's Sake. We even worked on a hand-printed series of the Dene Nation logo for the office in Yellowknife.

To my mind, though, the best of these was Saul Williams, whose tortured soul I well identified with. He was a technical drafting virtuoso, who could effortlessly paint lines as fine as human hair. The lines were new and vibrant, reawakening the Indian me, before I had only been conscious of a European view of the world.

He could also compose brilliant stream-of-consciousness poetry that I got into the habit of writing down. He continues with his poetry, mind you, but how I wish the ones he composed on the spot survived the wild times.

Marriage and Home

A dream can also wake you up. While at art school in
Toronto, I met and married Ruth Ann.

Ruth Ann was the daughter of a German soldier and a Russian mother. When her father asked me why I wanted to marry her, I simply said, "Both our People lost our wars," and that was enough for him to bang his fist down on the table and shout, "Permission granted!"

Thanks to the efforts of the famous Inuvialuit carving brothers, David and Abe Ruben, and our artistic friends, we had a ceremony at City Hall, followed by a grand reception on the roof of the Bond Hotel.

After I was done with my four years at Art's Sake, the alternate school, we flew all the way from the big city of Toronto back to my home of less than a thousand. This surely must have been a cultural shock for Ruth, being in a completely foreign culture far from home.

When we got to Radelie Koe, there was no place for us to live. The only place we could find was in a tent we set up just on the outside of town. Them were some cold winter nights. Mercifully Aurora College saw to allowing us to stay at the local community college building.

For a time, we lived in the band housing. The last place we had was our own small log home, next door to Edward and Pauline Gardebois, with the Orlias family on the other side, on a side road to the Duhogah.

The first week in May 1983 saw the arrival of my oldest son, Luke, who was born at the hospital in Inuvik, some 322 kilometres to the north. The new love of my life! One of the best experiences of my life was seeing him for the very first time. And while he was asleep he gave the sweetest smile, as if knowing Daddy was there.

I brought him to his great-grandparents, who gave him his Dene name, Fieh Bah, and boasted to the little fellow that they would "go hunting together."

As any proud father would, I spent hours carrying him around and even making a game of changing his diapers so he would not throw a fit. I must confess to really spoiling the little fellow, although there did come a time when he simply insisted on walking all the way to and from my rabbit snares all by himself. He would grow to show that real Mountain Dene stubbornness.

Two years later, Victor Lorne put his mom through an excruciating birth, finally coming forth at high noon on Father's Day! I told all who would listen that I was a "pretty good shot!" He, too, received his Dene name from Grandpa Peter Mountain Sr.: K'ihnah Hihndareweh, his Dene self.

With these two new arrivals in my life, I came to think of change, like the residential schools, in a new way. In order for there to be a future, there has to be a new way of living. But like entering a new and strange dwelling, it takes time for one to adjust. I had everything going for me then, but I was haunted by devilish and pesky ghosts from the past.

Although I did provide as the head of the household, I was yet a slave to the infernal bottle.

Dene Museum/Library

This non-lending First Nations research centre was the first of its kind in the North.

An initiative of our Dene Language Group was to help revive our dying native language on a community level. With the help of Cynthia Chambers, my sister Dora, and a number of other community members, I put together the Dene Museum/Library, the first of its kind in the North, to gather and preserve our history. I worked with Cynthia, along with local consultants who would eventually put together curriculum material in the school. One of our goals was to have the first three grades taught in our Dene language, to help ensure its survival.

However, even after a couple of years, it became apparent that we were spinning our collective wheels. Any kind of a government plan, by its nature, is a bureaucratic one. Most of our administrative arm became tied up with writing reports and proposals for funding, so just staying afloat as a group took up the bulk of our time, leaving very little for community-related activities.

As for the Dene Museum/Library, I had no problem doing what needed to be done. At first it was simply looking at material which had already been written, and following up to gather more in-depth background for the community. However, anything made available to a First Nations community invariably becomes public property, so we lost most of what we had with disorganized central control.

When I left to study library and information sciences at Lakehead University in Thunder Bay in the late eighties, I came back to find that all of these precious records and photographs had been stored next to a Band Council furnace, reeked of oil, and were ruined.

So much for First Nations initiative.

A Family Tradition

They always wanted that Dene Gold!

When the moosehide is just the right shade of Dene gold, our ladies know their tanning work is done.

I grew up around these ways and well recall the round holes in the ground at our fish camps, with the sticks still standing that marked the spots where hides were smoked. You still see these markers now and then, certainly by the houses of those that still work the hides.

It all starts out on the land, hunting the moose or caribou and making sure you don't damage the hides by hitting the wrong spot when you shoot. Even before that, you have to learn to pick out the healthiest-looking animal, the one with the sleekest, shiniest, and darkest coat, a tall bull, for instance. Then you have to be careful the way you skin the animal, so there won't be any weak spots or holes in the hide.

Although many of the old-timers also knew how to tan hides, there was a clear line, a cultural division, marking what was expected of a boy or girl. All of my sisters were taught from an early age how to fix leather. My sister Judy proudly gave me the very first pair of moccasins she ever made at the tender age of six!

Although they all became recognized for their mastery of these traditional arts, my sisters also found out at some point that the women of Radelie Koe, and very likely elsewhere, had a kind of a best-tanners club, which only a select few could join, making one a proud member of an elite. I do know that most of my closest female relatives belonged to this exclusive club, but will not divulge any names, for fear of mayhem.

Suffice it to say that the tanning process is not an easy task.

A few years ago, on one of my frequent visits to Judy and brother-in-law Michel's home, my sister casually mentioned that she was "really busy." Thinking that she was talking about cutting their daily catch of the big coney fish, I asked her how it was going.

"Well, one will keep you busy, but today I am working on *six* moosehides, all at once."

Remembering the few times I tried even scraping one hide and walked away shaking my head at the aches and pains you immediately build up in your fingers, arms, and back, I simply had to marvel that my own sister is a Dene Wonder Woman!

A completed hide is made into a hollow and hung up in a tripod with a smoldering fire of *shingerih* (old rotten wood) below to eventually bestow that prized golden colour. After fleshing, the hides are repeatedly soaked in a natural brain solution, saved from different animals, stretched on a pole, and smoked to get every bit of blood out. The brain solution is kept stored in a cloth bag in a cool, dark place.

The Dene Gold adds a golden hue and lovely aroma that people treasure so much, some, like me, to the point of sleeping with a piece of hide under my pillow.

"Daddy's baaad!"

More heartbreaking words have never been felt.

Right from the start, our two little guys got along famously, as if somehow breathing in the fact that they were in for a rougher than normal ride.

For a time, married life was about as regular as we could make it, although we were in a small town, which my wife found unnerving. At the time, people still took to drinking and misbehaving without much notice. This kind of communal dysfunction was a part of our official stance. In fact, when I told the social worker in the band hall that I needed counselling for my drinking, she just laughed at me! This kind of dysfunctional intergenerational residential school trauma was the norm, and even lasts today. We have taken over from the priests and nuns in playing down to even our own children.

One of my closest friends outright laughed in my face, on my way to treatment, after I had put forth a challenge in my column in the Native press to have our leaders sober up.

When I finished a month of treatment at Edmonton's Poundmaker Lodge, I came back to a marked lack of support for my sobriety from my own People, and was back to the bottle in no time. Because a smaller place like this is so dependent on people helping each other out, any kind of alienation eventually leaves its mark, with people often dying as a result of social neglect.

That demon alcohol, and the memories of residential schools it served, still had its evil grip on me. Like a puppet on a string, all it took was the mention of a party and I would be gone. Poor wife and children back in the little one-room house, like the one I grew up in, with temperatures going to minus thirty on a winter night.

Only now, the entirely self-sufficient Dene village we grew up in had somehow become a very scary version of itself, as if the only ones expecting any sleep were six feet under at the south end of town. (Some of those graves were so hard to dig, taking all of a frozen night to pick at solid ground, as if the suddenly departed had the door to Hell jammed shut to honest labour.)

A babysitting Roman Catholic Church next door echoed, with an outdated and archaic Latin dirge, the voice of a pedophilic priest Émile Petitot still rising in hypocritical pride.

Hills that once rang with the calls, laughter, and joy-filled shrieks of sliding parties were now haunted in yellow streetlamps, dogs forlornly baying at passing drunks.

The rayuka, northern lights, to us were the spirits of people who had died too young and danced like inviting maniacs, swooping into windows, leaving trails open for their next vacant spot in a mad conga.

One evening, after yet another days-on-end drinking binge, I came home to my beloved son Luke at the door, his usual smile and open arms finally turned by my sallow skin and sunken eyes, he was wailing, "Daddy's baaad!"

Being of the headstrong sort, he wouldn't let up, his little heart smashing against our log home's walls, rending new holes in the fabric of my already fragile soul.

That one image, like the first crack across the river that starts the spring flood, stayed with me for the next decade it took to start seeing him and his younger brother again.

End of the Line

He had asked me what I wanted to do about the Olympics.

Back in 1968, my cousin Fred Kelly and I were at the very top of our game, as part of the NWT Territorial Experimental Ski Training (TEST) Ski Program, a cross-country racing team just beginning to put the North on the sports map. I told him that my education was more important for me and that the team would do well, no matter who was on it.

I had already won the Tom Longboat Award, and that was good enough for me as far as sports went, like a gold medal in the Indian world. He was always so jealous of that.

Yet at the back of my mind, I always remembered the way I was simply given the award, by a school official, in the hallway of Joseph Burr Tyrrell High in Fort Smith, like a library book I had dropped. Even way back then, I knew the entire team was just being used in one way or other. Truth of the matter is, when you live in a world of Mola privilege, you don't get to see all the strings being pulled, every which way, to make the magic happen.

But when you have been living in freefall, from being yanked away from friends and family pretty well from birth, it's a whole different world. The only question is, do you go along with the program or wake up and live?

As expected, the team did well enough in the Winter Olympics held in Sapporo, Japan, in 1972. Some continued to represent the North many times over.

The times, too, for me were more about
the movement away from such as medals
about change and life on Ground Zero
the streets...

One little-known fact is that the level we trained at was so high above normal everyday life that any fall, when it happens, was too great a distance for the normal person to handle.

From residential schools, I also knew in my heart
we Indians were expendable
to be simply tossed away
when done with...

We buried Fred, "the Kelly Express," in a cold, ordinary grave at home. He had a sudden brain aneurism at the alcohol treatment centre in Inuvik, after finally going for treatment. It happened so fast, he didn't even make it to the general hospital there.

This was the end result. It began when the coach and staff of the TEST Ski Program knew Fred had a problem with the drink, suddenly cut loose from residential school, without backing, even in the workplace. He was the Kelly Express, that's for sure, but only as long as he was on skis doing what the Man wanted.

After he could no longer race
he was on his own, end of story.

And in a very real way we were
all MIA, missing in action
while the combat raged
mostly within.

More than less,   just waiting,
    biding our time.

His story, like this sad chapter
fit as well as any epithet
on stone.

A Poisoned Cloak

The cloak, given to Hercules by his wife, in Greek mythol-
ogy, was to ensure his faithfulness. Donning it, he sweated.
The deadly poison clung to his flesh, corroding him. In
extreme agony, he threw himself into a funeral pyre and
was burned to death.

All some Jews had
on board the trains
taking them to death
was hidden gold or diamonds.
They offered to pay for water with these precious gems.

Payment made, no water arrived.

Frenchman Claude Lanzmann's *Shoah* is a harrowing and
controversial nine-and-a-half-hour film of the Nazi death camps,
from the voices of survivors: Jews, Poles, Hungarians, and other
"kapos" forced to work there.

It was quiet then
    and still is
after all of these years, over seventy years later
As if the ghosts were always just there, waiting . . .

perhaps yet.

Two thousand Jews were buried
    at first

and then burned
the remains were dug out, by forced Polish hands
with no tools allowed.

The sheer length of the film, like the long endless trains, carrying their thousands . . . millions of moving dead, simply does not
make sense in any logical way.

Only a format
like final words on stone
will do, somehow
to have us at least

return to our human selves
in collected pieces.

The German efficiency, cold-hearted
carry out a devilish, insatiable hatred
animistic self-loathing.

The only way the train drivers could do their job
was drunk, on vodka rations
to drown out the screams from cattle cars they pulled
into Treblinka, Sobibór, Auschwitz, Birkenau . . .
Belzec . . .   Buchenwald . . .
Dachau
even the names, metallic, unforgiving

the drivers ghoulish tour guides
on a one-way line
to Hell

And always the cars
coming back empty.

A hand coldly gestured
slicing across the throat
from wayside citizens
to Jews on board the trains
meant certain death
waited
a short distance down the track.

"We were told that Auschwitz
is where they were burning people
      and we didn't believe."

After selections
      some taken for work

all went quiet.

From "where the People went"

"An hour or two later
everything was Death
. . . like magic, everything disappeared"

". . . the only thing
they were guilty of
was that they were Jewish People."

All of their wealth was taken from them
      perhaps the real target
to fuel hard times
and in the end
their lives
by a nation blinded.

Thousands were stacked
"like wood," right off the trains
many having slashed their wrists

mothers their own daughters
before themselves.

Just off the train's ramp, the dread "Infirmary"
the sick, elderly, and children
immediately shot
    falling into an open pit
ten to twelve feet deep
full of corpses.

Kapo slaves could expect the Infirmary, too
for disobedience.

Some things human eyes were never meant to see
Now through rain-veiling
solemn tombstones in vacant lots . . .
an empty horizon far off
bleak sun
living for this day
    with hearts just warm enough
to beat out
a grim tale or two.

"Disinfestation Squads," arriving in Red Cross trucks
to move people along
in an orderly fashion.
Only there
with Zyklon B canisters.

Ironically, everything had to be done
in an organized way
so the Nazi's would "not lose time."
On the other hand, the Jews
were down to their last minutes, literally.

"People fell out of the gas chambers
like potatoes"
Jews would rather be shot
than help clean up their own People
piled up
in front of the gas chambers.

At peak periods
the numbers alone
were staggering.
In Treblinka, twelve to eighteen thousand a day, every day!

It was a
"Production line of death"
but a primitive one

    mountains of bodies

screams and silence
the language of death.

"There was a total silence,
Nothing moved in the camp
And we wondered;
'Where did they put all these Jews
Who had just come in?'

"... but none of them had the faintest of notions
that in three or four hours
they would be reduced to ashes."

At first, in Chelmno
eighty packed in specially equipped trucks
with the exhaust pumping carbon monoxide
and the dead driven off to the woods
to be burned ... some still moving

History proves that this practice
of systematic genocide had been
in the works for a good thousand years before
by Christians and governments
     so, nothing was new
except, except for the Final Solution
which was a turning point
in history.

Right from the third century
Jews were told:
"You may not live amongst us."
Now the Nazis said,
"You may not live!"

It really was a Final Solution
"People who are dead
will not reappear."

Some villagers, now living in former Jewish houses
dared to say it was God's will
to kill the Jews
for the death of the saviour Jesus Christ

... but was it this same God who gave Hitler
the orders and detailed plans for the death camps
all drawn up and ready to go
like some kind of a uniformed Moses
with a funny moustache?

One underlying and undeniable fact
like a deep underground lava flow   to the very gates
of Hades
     Regardless of the war itself
the Jews were to be completely
and utterly exterminated.

This had never happened before
in the entire history of the world.

"We are human!
Don't you understand that?!"

As one survivor said,
Today you either smile
. . . or cry

And yes, this is brutal.
It slams into your senses
making a mockery of reason.
Yet, beyond
the soul quietly
    achingly   insistently begs
at least
for these survivors
to bear witness
like a dead heart yet beating
from a distant universe
coming back
in moonlit waves.

"It wasn't this world.
It wasn't humanity."

A man just standing
staring vacant.
"Look at him. He is dying."

One Jewish official
in the doomed Warsaw ghetto
talks of himself wearing
"a poisoned cloak,"
as Hercules once did.

... and wrote "they even want me to kill the children
with my own hands."
Just hours before he committed suicide
a day after his Jewish charges
were taken to their death.

"I will give them an everlasting name"
(Isaiah 56:5).

In doing so God Jehovah
made to test the faith of his Jews
releasing an ultimate hatred to their very core
leading them to their fiery end
to begin again
out of the ashes.

Making *Shoah*, Claude Lanzmann from the first resolved not to
ask the why the Jews were killed ...

The obscenity "instantly glaring"

"There is no why."

Rather, to uncover the untouchable
the simple words
to help recreate our own vision
in a visual mirror.
Investigative journalism with a touch
of ethical grounding.

In the end, the challenge
to connect the dots
in living testament
back to ourselves

as human beings
to an opulent and faithful idyll

with glimpses
of ultimate virtue:

The woman who
failing to save her lover
methodically dug him back out of a mass grave
and reburied him herself.

A Jewish freedom fighter
survivor of the three-day Warsaw ghetto uprising
April 19, 1943:　　"If you could lick my heart
it would poison you
... I thought I was the last Jew."

And on the German side
this ever-present sense of denial
"What could I do?
... I had to follow orders!"

Some poignant and definitely lesser known, non-Jewish German citizens were cast into prison for daring to stand up against the all-encompassing Third Reich. We learn about some of them in Erich Friedrich and Renate Vanegas's *Hitler's Prisoners: Seven Cell Mates Tell Their Stories.*

In the chapter "Richard Welder: The 'Good German,'" this German soldier recalls:

"I also saw quite a few Jews, who—as in Germany—
had to wear the Star of David on their chests.
Although I'd never thought much of the Jews, I
couldn't help but feel sorry for these men, women

and children who walked about the city streets like ghosts.

"I wondered now what Hitler's real reason was for his intense hatred of these people. These poor souls with their hollow cheekbones were starving to death. They weren't even allowed to beg or to approach anyone who was not Jewish. They had to step down off the sidewalk when passing a gentile.

"One afternoon as I walked through a side street, I noticed a young Jewish boy leaning against a wall of a house. With his glassy eyes, he didn't have to say a word. I saw hunger written all over his face. I thought of my son back home who was about the same age. I approached the boy and told him to stay where he was, and I would come back. Apparently he understood. I went back to my quarters and took half a loaf of bread from the mess hall. I hid it under my jacket and walked back to the side street. The boy was still there where I had left him. I handed him the bread. He looked at me and quickly disappeared into the courtyard."[11]

The soldier was first given four weeks for this simple act of human kindness, beginning months locked away.

The real story in the moment's pauses
behind blind eyes
    as if we do not want to know
our real lives
in our waking hours . . .

"Lord, judge me not
by cruel light of day
but let me slip back
in amongst these fair ghosts
of another..."

There is no way to return to this without clouding over, like the mists of the missing, through which passed the trains carrying all the people on their last journeys, returning as empty as eyes newly opened, forever awaiting...

SHOAH
This kind of festered memory
tethered to reach
just close enough
to keep
an eternity
at bay
in that forbidding pause.

A question lingers:
Was this simply an evil against the Jews
or a fatal human flaw?

When you now consider
Israel's treatment
of Palestine

are we fated
to an endless cycle
of meaningless violence

even beyond

some greater light?

Lakehead University
This was one very confused time for me.

I took our little Dene Museum/Library as far as I could at home in Radelie Koe, but I now needed to learn how to set up a proper library. My application was approved to take Library and Information Sciences at Thunder Bay's Lakehead University, so there I went.

Having been in Thunder Bay some years before at Confederation College, I was somewhat familiar with the place, and I took up residence at student housing. The atmosphere was just too lax, with the other students more or less in party mode like me, although I was definitely more.

Without the anchor of a family life, my drinking was by then completely out of control, and even when I moved out to a room in one of the staff's homes, it didn't improve things much with my studies. It didn't help that a lot of what I needed to know was technical and downright bureaucratic, something I never did have much of a bent toward at all. Some of it, though, like political science, I found fascinating and would have eagerly pursued had my mind been with it at the time.

One day, I called home as usual to find out how things were there, and my grandfather Peter Mountain Sr. made a request: would I just come on home and spend some time with them?

In our world, this carries about the same authority as a papal edict, so I put in for my travel home, which was processed.

"If You Have a Dream"
Each visit like sitting at the feet of royalty.

Although he must surely have known that I was physically falling off the edge, my grandfather Peter Mountain Sr. spoke to me with thoughts that these were times like a slow-moving cloud passing.

He and Grandma had requested that I spend their last years with them, and right from then, I was taught many of the things I had been missing out on for years.

Grandpa knew that I was the kind of person to make plans, and he would put his lessons to me in such a way that he knew I could not fail to understand what he meant: "If you have a dream, you must work on it every day to make it come true, Grandson... Once this dream comes true, no one can ever take it away from you, for you are the only one who worked to make it come true."

He told me of his time working in the silver mines of the Yukon during the Gold Rush years and said that if I ever met a Frenchman all I would hear them say all day would be "*Bon, bon, bon* . . . Good, good, good*," and that I should always watch the Western movies, with horses, and his favourites, wrestling shows, with the "*Mola, k'ehnawh yawh ehkedehshįh!* [White people throwing each other around!]"

> . . . Looking back now
> he already knew
> I would recover
>
> and would
> one day sit
> in the Alberta/Montana Badlands
> cowboy hat on
> and a Mountain Dene
> moosehide jacket.
>
> His kind of vision
> hard to find
> these days

During those troubled years, I even made it a point to spend as much time as I could right on the land, living in a tent, and doing what I loved to do, cutting wood for the elders, which was then brought to them in town. I would also come into town every once in a while for a shower and to buy supplies.

Ak'et'sech'ih

One chaotic life, scourge oneself!

Life in any small town has its ways. In the case of our Radelie Koe, as in every traditional Dene place in the North most likely, many of the older ways are still being practiced to some degree.

Being a gravedigger definitely ranks right up there in terms of an odd way to carry on. The ones who help out in this way are somewhat apart from the normal goings-on in town.

In exchange for food and other considerations, the small group goes around cutting wood for people as a kind of public service, although they are traditionally regarded with genuine fear, very likely from their being close to the concept of death, which most Dene, our Navajo Dineh relatives to the south in particular, want nothing to do with, in any form.

When you are allowed any respite from this life of constant activity, you can go ahead and rest, yes, by all means, but with a block of wood for a pillow. The ones who are doing this, *ak'et'sech'ih*, for the first time cannot even get to sleep for three days. And neither can that person cut up a caribou head, nor cut along that animal's back, when skinning.

Even as a part of normal public life, some of the more ardent and traditional gravediggers add cold water to all of your meals for a year, as part of the dread ak'et'sech'ih, and in all ways find other means to humble and do without the normal needs of life.

The rewards are great though, a long and healthy life being one.

Being Indian is just not easy, except for the ones already dead and buried. Then again, we believe in reincarnation, so life itself does carry on.

In Company of the Dead

The most picturesque view in town belies what is just underground.

The year 1928 was probably the most devastating for the North, with an influenza epidemic sweeping like the grim reaper's scythe through a sheaf of wheat. Now with most of the town of Radelie Koe moved up to higher ground, I have many of these ghosts for company only a few yards from my log home. The house itself is something of a historical site, having been the home of the original Chief T'Seleie, who signed Treaty 11 on behalf of our People in 1921.

Records are scant and the number of elders who might recall that far back are few, but there were so many people simply dying off that the chief at the time ordered the young men to gather all the corpses so they could to be interred in a common grave.

What makes it all so sad is that, with global warming, the soft gravel banks all along the Duhogah are now giving way and caving in. One side of the rail for the mass gravesite has been moved in.

For all of their potential unrest, though, I never had a problem getting good sleep when our family lived there.

CHAPTER 12

The Man on the Moon

Of an evening's balm you may see him yet, waving.

One of the places I would go to get out of the mainstream was the little fishing village of Tsiigehtchic, which sits snugly where the Arctic Red River meets the Duhogah. When there I usually stayed with musician and teacher Bob "Tootz" Mumford and his wife, Margaret Nazon.

I would take the time to go and see my father's ol' time buddy Billy Cardinal too. He told me of some hilarious times they had fish guiding at Plumber's Lodge on the Sahtú, Great Bear Lake.

Tsiigehtchic was home to many good storytellers, like Noel Andre, who was also known for his way with a fiddle and for being a fisherman par excellence.

But the one place I felt most at home was with Alestine Andre and her father, Chief Hyacinth Andre.

One Friday night, the old man was home alone, and we were standing on their porch, looking up at a full moon. "You know what happened up there?" he asked me.

Not knowing what to say, I just asked him to let me know.

"Well, Grandson, it was a long, long time ago, way before all *this* came along." He waved at the row of houses down the old dirt road. "There were these two young brothers who were laying on their backs on the alleh, spruce bough floor, in their teepee, just spending some time in the late winter evening, looking up at the stars.

"The younger of the two had been given a pair of mink fur pants for being of a special kind. They were counting their girlfriends, and one would go: 'I love my darling there, that really shiny one ...'

"The other would go, 'Nawh, not even as pretty as my sweetheart, way over there, up in my heavens ...'

"Time was going by as it does in the Forever Land of the Far North, and the elder of the two boys said that it was now time to go to sleep. They were burning up too much firewood laying up talking anyway.

"'No, *Ondieh* [older brother], this is fun, let's keep choosing!' cried the younger.

"Just as he said so, the big ol' full moon popped out in clear view of their teepee smoke flaps.

"'Now *there* is my favourite of all, my future wife!' exclaimed the young lad. 'I am going to marry her!'

"'Now you are really talking silly,' he was told. 'Our parents are really going to be cross with us for staying up late and burning all this wood.'

"'I guess you don't know why they gave me these pants, huh?' his younger brother demanded. 'Here, I'll show ya. We can go up there to meet my wife right now.'

"'Now I know you are really being silly and stupid!' the elder scolded him.

"He was just going to put out the fire at the centre of their teepee when his younger brother strode over, saying, 'Well, let me just prove it to you here. Take my hand.'

"Wanting to humour him, his brother took his hand, and before they knew it, they were actually rising, up, up, and right to where the teepee poles join. When they got there, the elder of the two was too heavy and dropped back to the ground. The younger one still higher up there yelled in a fading voice, 'Ondieh, brother, just look for us under a full moon!'

"To this day, when there is this kind of a shiny moon, you can see the younger of the two as the Man on the Moon, standing there waving, with one leg shorter than the other, from where his mink fur pants tore off at the place where the poles join in the teepee."

When he got done with this lovely story, Hyacinth Andre pointed out that, "The White man claimed to have been the first to the moon in the late sixties, but it was a young Dene child who made it there long before, when the world was new."

Duhoyieah Gorigudih!
(It's more beautiful on the islands!)

One day, I thought spending time in the islands of Manitou would be a good way for me to get away from the cares of town life. I asked my good friend Charlie Kochon for some help. We got a Ski-Doo and went across the frozen Duhogah, picked a good sheltered spot, and put up a tent. We also cut a good supply of spruce boughs for the floor and some wood, had tea, something to eat. He left, that was it.

I was now as close to heaven on Earth as I wanted to be, with only the rayuka, northern lights, and stars for company.

> Standing out there most nights
> in the faint glow
> of a tent's gaslamp
>   rayuka, northern lights
> playing just above
> must have surely brought me here
> to whatever I find myself doing now.

When the Band Council got wind of what I was doing, it got a crew to cut a proper trail through the ice ridges across the Duhogah River and got different crews with machines to haul the wood into town for the old people. One person I did a lot of work with was my old Grandin College schoolmate Peter Silastiak, of the super-quick reflexes and majestic basketball moves! This time around, he was an expert with the ol' coffee pot and would take a break at the drop of a mitt, and so would I!

Back at my camp on the island, I would get the occasional visitor, one being my childhood friend and relative Archie Rabisca. He loved to take his dogs out for a run and would drop by just to have some bush tea, rabbit if I had it, and haul a load of wood back.

Like another person I know, Archie had polio as a child and walked with an awkward amble, but he was strong in his arms and could do everything else needed as far as work went.

A few other people took to coming by, usually to get away from abuses at home during weekends. Sad to say, but I had to host my own mother quite a number of times like that.

My days and nights out there, as at Bluefish Creek and some other places I stayed for extended periods of time, went by in a kind of idyll. At the time, in fact, I really thought that was all I would ever want to do with my life: work in the service of the elderly.

Seh Leh Beyah
Busy squirrel was he.

The famous storyteller and elder Louie Caesar had this name for me: *Seh Leh Beyah*, which translates to My Friend's Son.

When I was out on the land across the river from town at Manitou Island, I would spend all of my days cutting wood. At night I would love to stand outside, looking at all the brilliant stars, thinking how small I was in the universe.

One time I was in town and visiting with Louie. He wanted to thank me for being out there and asked me if I was doing this all by myself. When I said I was, I started to tell him about this one squirrel that would make a noise to wake me up in the morning.

I would work all morning until that one squirrel made another and different call at about noon, sort of marking my time to have something to eat. At the end of the day he would make one more closing time sound, when I would pick up my chainsaw, axe, and tools and head back to camp.

I told Louie that squirrel was my only company.

"Well, Grandson," the elder told me, "that's me out there keeping you company."

Only then did I realize I was still in the presence of the good old Indian magic!

Never in Anger
The young man goes through a kind of hypnosis.

Right from my first contact with Inuit students in grade school, I longed to have been born Inuit.

Residential schools being what they were, restrictive to the nth degree, my simple wish was met with scoffs of derision. These places, after all, had little to do with wish fulfillment, nor even wanting to make a better life for us Dene students. Rather, we were to follow archaic orders, with a repressed and outdated religious zeal brought over to virgin First Nations lands.

Yet I have continued to be personally amazed by a people living even farther north than my home on the Arctic Circle. In a country so flat you see mirages of crêpes, the Inuit thrive, with almost all their food reserves under seven metres of solid ice!

Every time there is something on TV about the Inuit, I put all else aside to watch and maybe learn something. They would start with a pile of frozen fish, for instance, lining them up in a row just long enough for the purpose, and cover them in caribou hide. They secured a rope along two rows of these fish, with caribou antlers lashed between. Then they squirted water on the bottom runners and smoothed it with moss in hand, making a super-slippery surface for the new sled!

When a young man is ready for his first hunt out on the frozen tundra, an elder, usually father or uncle, will sit him down and put the guy through a sort of hypnosis, to ensure success in a land where the difference between bringing back food or not is often starvation—simple as that.

One of the main lessons taught to the hunter is that there will be no doubt in his mind, from start to finish, about the outcome of this venture.

And to never, never do anything in anger.

With lessons learned, and overeager emotions kept at bay, it always spells a successful hunt.

Stella's Road On Home

Twilight shadows on the soul.

Our local Band Council was now really beginning to flex its muscles with companies wanting our resources. One of the major projects had to do with seismic work on our traditional lands. One winter in the late eighties, I signed on to try my hand at this kind of work, in preparation for further oil drilling.

Our crew rode out on cutlines and laid down line that would be used to find out the potential for oil reserves below. It wasn't danger-ous work, but the hours were long, and a good worker could often expect to do overtime and receive good money, if dressed for it.

My sister Bella and I made arrangements to meet our younger sister Stella, who was planning to get married after a whirlwind tour around the world. Rather than simply chartering back home from Norman Wells, we decided to rent a truck and ended up with a number of passengers, some riding in the truck bed. There wasn't a lot of planning involved in this, and over the new winter road, we broke down some ways in from Apache Pass, about 130 kilometres from town.

We had no tools, and not being mechanics, we could either just stay there or try to make it to town on foot. There wasn't any good dry wood on hand to make a big fire, stay warm, and just wait for rescue. My main worry was for a young boy who was with us, so I told the rest I would start walking to town. We were still in party mode, and my two sisters, Bella and Stella, chose to set off with me. Never having been this way overland before, we misjudged how long it would take. That and the fact of poor judgment, with alcohol involved, made for some poor decisions.

Knowing I could make better time alone, I encouraged them to go back to the car, and left the two behind and set off on a run.

After going on all night, a vehicle driven by our uncle John Louison Sr. finally came along and I told him what had happened. We went back to get everyone, but by that time, Stella had hypothermia from exposure. We didn't make it all the way back to the nursing station in time to save her.

It was like when you look at a picture you took that comes back fuzzy, you think, "Did I really take this picture?" not knowing that the camera, like the alcohol we had at the time, was as much at fault. We often end up living on, blaming ourselves for the entire blurred times.

Knowing that Stella was very close to our grandparents, I went to their home to let them know what had happened. Without a word my grandfather took me outside to bathe my ears in snow, to save what was left from the frostbite.

Through all of the traumatic night, I hadn't even noticed that Mother Nature had left me with a grim reminder of having lost respect for the cold. A good part of my left ear would be further payment for this serious error in judgment. To my mind, though, Bella, who was entirely helpless to do anything for her sister had the hardest of memories to live with.

In traditional Dene manner, dear Stella lay in state in our home for four complete days before her funeral. Even through our deepest grief, everyone remarked on this angelic wisp of a smile on her face, as if she had already known of her coming and further journey home. Her usual long black hair glistened like raven wings in flight. Moonlight just highlighting its inner depth.

Elders who knew said that in her few short years, Stella lived more of a lifetime than most do.

> Again . . . we were caught in mid-operatic stance
> actors in sudden spotlight
> having forgotten our lines
> magnetic elements slowly turned to negative force
> yet somehow mercurial
>
> Japanese Noh players
> forever mimed in place
> waiting in vain   for even that glim *goba*
> some far-off dawn
>
> to match in this pitch
> of ours.

Rayuka, Aurora Raven

There are many stories told of Tahsoh, God's merry
prankster, the North's perennial raven.

Besides being beloved of these old-time legends, raven is much beloved for many other reasons. My grandfather Peter Mountain Sr. said that this is the one "real boss of the land," more so than even Wageh (eagle), Sah (bear), or Beleh (wolf).

"Whenever you see Tahsoh's feather laying on the ground, pick it up right away and put it away under a tree or a bush nearby. Tahsoh, raven, does the best job of all, cleaning up our land all year 'round and does not like to see its own feather just a-lyin' around like that."

The Last Mile

Having been born right on the land, I have always been attracted to people who live the traditional life. Jean-Marie (Gene) and Camilla Rabesca were like that. Gene's mom, Martha, was about as down to earth as you are ever going to get. She was of a previous generation and never went to residential school. As with most Dene elders, she was full of good advice. She always reminded us that when you are with a group of people, especially while travelling, you should make it a point to just be kind and make sure to say only good words to each other. "You don't know what kind of day the person is having. What you say may be taken the wrong way or make it worse," was Martha's reasoning.

Gene and Cam spent almost all of their time in the country, and I was always going to their home in town, mainly to joke around with Gene and see what they were doing. They had a kind of down-to-earth country humour, full of implied good advice on how not to live.

One time, Gene asked me to go with them to their cabin way out in the Loon Lake area, about 130 kilometres northeast of Radelie Koe. It was really cold that winter day, about −62°C, with a powerful wind blowing, but we went anyway because his family was out there, in need of supplies.

It's always colder travelling by Ski-Doo; because of the speed, you are moving right into the cold and wind. It took longer than usual as we stopped to check his traps for marten. The idea with cold is to just keep moving. Each stop makes more of a chance for freezing to set in, often dangerously so.

At this one stop on the way, we made a fire to warm up. Gene always liked to cut and put more spruce down to sit on than anyone else I have ever been with, and when we finally got settled in with our tea, he started talking about what he called The Last Mile.

"Y'know, Tony, we've got a long way to go . . . but we will
get there.
Once you start something, it's always best to just keep
going until you've got it all done.
And not any ol' way, either.
Do a good job, so you don't have to do it over again
    and don't get onto a side road to something else . . .
just stay the way you are going, and never, never say die .

Don't give up.
There's something after every one of us, y'know . . .
gonna catch up with you someday.

You can always tell a person by that last mile . . .
when you have nothing left in you to make your
way forward
    not even the strength to lift your leg for another step
and that cold north wind coming
right into your face.

If you keep on going, past that last mile you really
have something.

You are somebody
this land will remember,

and love."

Great Northern Arts Festival

A brilliant light shining to art

Just at this very low point in my dismal life, the arts came to the
North. Charlene Alexander and Sue Rose started up this creative
initiative in 1989 to showcase our cultural expressions for the rest

of the world. I was glad to get the call to go to Inuvik for the very first of these festivals.

The group was relatively small, so we did everything together, from sitting someplace drinking coffee or beer, to listening to someone on the guitar, to going out on a boat hired for a cookout at Airport Lake. This was what I needed to stretch tired artistic muscles.

Life in a small Northern town is such that just keeping the home fires going and hunting for something to eat can take up all of every day. But at least now I could start thinking of doing some artwork for a specific event or buyer. Just knowing there were other talented people out there made it all worthwhile.

But here, once again, in the one delta place, Inuvik, which had held me and other residential school survivors virtual prisoners some thirty years before, it would take some doing for me to express myself artistically! A kind of invisible wall of shame loomed large every time I passed the Grollier Hall building. Many sex-related court cases and convictions came out of the dreaded place, after all.

That sting from the strap just for speaking our God-given language is something that stains you forever. Especially after having learned to walk like a Dene man again.

> If a building could laugh
> felt to me like the place
> mocked all whoever lived to tell the tale
> or just learned to keep it all well hidden.

> Some bridges are more like mountains to climb, though.

> For the time being
> a ready bottle would have to do
> to keep them ghosts from rising up

> once too often.

Over the years, the saddest part was simply being an artist among those local survivors, having gone through the same pain and cultural degradation, or worse, still trying to get by in this one of all Northern towns.

> The July midnight sun holds many secret
> unshed tears.

"I Will Never Be Rich!"

Our elders always led by example.

In a small town where everyone knows each other, you can't get away with much. People who talked for no reason, without backing it up with action, were looked down upon and knew it. Your relatives and, in fact, every adult in the place were just as much your teachers as those at the local school, and in many ways, more so.

In fact, the Mola kind of education, which focused on knowing things from the mind, was seen as inferior to being able to do all the things you needed to know to survive in the coldest region in the world. That was someone who was said to be "smart." Life up north, especially in winter, is unforgiving. But I have always noticed that the farther north you go, the friendlier and warmer the people are.

We could also choose our own teachers, and one of the best in Radelie Koe was Jim Pierrot. Our elders knew that people who came to see them weren't there just to pass the time of day, although a lesson in life could easily be taught while working on a boat, for instance. Life during the season of the midnight sun, pretty well all summer, was definitely more laid back than during a dark, freezing winter. One of these times, with his usual small group of eager listeners around him, Jim started talking about money, or the lack of. "Grandsons, I will never be rich, and this is why. I love my people too much, so I can't keep anything away from them. If I put some money away, what good will it do me to get rich and watch my relatives starve or do without?"

Over the years, Jim Pierrot was pleased to see that his listeners learned. He said, "All the young guys I talked to many years ago are doing good now. They have their own jobs, married a kind-hearted woman. Got their own trucks and house and can help people out too, when they need it."

He had his fans in other places, too. One, Chief Hyacinth Andre of Tsiigehtchic, always called him Good News brother-in-law—Good News because that is all he ever heard about him.

Later, every time I asked Jim to make a blessing for an art project I was working on with the youth, he was glad to do so and made the time. To this day, those murals are still in as good shape as the day Jim Pierrot prayed over them. Others I did later started wearing away, even over a single winter, a testament to his powers.

When I took to travelling as cultural ambassador for the North or Canada, I couldn't help but notice that wherever I was in the world, his son Ronald always reminded me to "Pay respects to the land or the water," to show respect for these new places. And he, in turn, always placed himself in the service of our community.

CHAPTER 13

Through a Jagged Edge

It felt like I had no past.

When my grandparents asked me to spend their last four remaining years with them, I didn't bother to ask why. These elders had already proven that they had a firm grip on our Dene past.

One of the things my grandpa talked to me about at some length was our very old ways, and how not even our present Dene know of our past that far back.

Grandma was the first to go, at well over a hundred years of age.

In between turned out to be my sister Stella, who passed after our rented truck broke down between Norman Wells and town.

The last time I saw him at the hospital in Inuvik, my grandfather thanked me for spending the time with them and assured me that in exchange, "I will always be with you in times of need."

I knew that he was familiar with *Edst'ineh* (bad medicine). But right at the time they were all dead and gone, I sure did not feel any kind of presence. In fact, it was more like I was hanging on to the open flaps of the bottom of a box—freefalling, most times with only a half-empty bottle for company.

A few people did try to reach into my empty world, one being Alfred Baillargeon, the drummer and singer from *Dettah* near Yellowknife. He was one of my dad's childhood friends and got a kick out of me dubbing him in Dene.

Brother-in-law Bob and sister Lucy Ann made their cabin out at Tibbit Lake available, but even out there, immediate memories of close relatives forever removed dug in for real.

Into this vacuum stepped my lifelong friend Johnny "JC" Catholique of Lutsel K'e. He not only gave me a real home to be a part of as long as I needed, but he had just become part of the Native American Church.

This came along when a group of our Southern Dene relatives, the Navajo, came a-callin'. These were Hanson Ashley and his wife, two other roadmen, Peter Chee and Lorenzo Max, Jerry and Fred Hatathlie, Joe Bedonie, Garrison Yazzie, and one *Bilagáana* everyone just called Sky.

I could already feel the warming, blanketed breeze of reality envelope me . . . in from a cold, cold time.

No Light Left On

Like those who are lost, my road took me in circles, sometimes even seeing my own art on someone's wall through one cold window. When you are an artist, the distance from a place you can afford and the street itself is not all that great, really. And Yellowknife wasn't as welcoming as it used to be.

Yet the people couldn't be faulted in my case. I had literally given up on myself and felt the need to just melt away into some dreamer past, whether it existed or not. Most days I just wandered around aimlessly, not wanting to let people know that I had nowhere to go, although there was no doubt that I was in trouble.

I was more or less a nuisance to the people I did know, and they had no choice but to let me know I was simply not welcome in this condition. Thanks to my athletic past, it wasn't all written on the physical me. Yet inside, I needed any kind of an escape.

With all the grandparents who raised me now gone, and a dear sister too, I was like a canoe someone set adrift, heading anyplace the current went. This was usually into the cheapest bottle of fortified wine, Taster's Choice. Being alcohol, it wouldn't freeze, so if I wanted to save it, all I had to do was leave it somewhere for later.

Thanks to the Baileys, an Anglican couple on Latham Island, I could at least have a bowl of soup and a piece of floor to stretch out on for the night. Or if there was room, I could go to the Salvation Army downtown. Any open doorway would do, or an apartment stairwell.

The strangest part of it is that, in a very real way, I wanted to know what the whole homeless world was all about. In order to understand it, you have to be homeless, and it's very challenging to live this.

I got one hell of a scare once, almost falling off a railing on the top floor of the Explorer Hotel to the cement a good fifteen metres down. Yet an angel or two must have been watching out for me because, one way or another, time just went by with me hanging on.

Thunder Rolling through My Soul
The doctor said he died of a broken heart.

A story with the saddest of ends is that of Chief Joseph *Hinmatoowyalahq'it* (Thunder Rolling across the Mountains) of the Nez Perce. In 1877, haunted by official lies, he led his people in a last-ditch 1,900-kilometre march, retreating from where they had been forcibly removed, in Lapwai, Idaho.

In a miraculous series of pitched battles against no less than five American generals, his courageous small band made it to within sixty-five kilometres of the Canadian border before hunger and hopelessness forced their surrender. Yet his many inspiring words live on, such as, "It does not require many words to tell the truth." And, "An Indian respects a brave man, but he despises a coward."

I was brought up by my grandparents and was taught to take the words of my elders and People literally and to listen the old Indian way, with the intent of putting their words into practice. Even though I have always thought of myself as an anarchist, I could not, in truth nor practice, ever make much of a revolutionary, not in the historical sense anyway.

Among the words of this great leader and First Nations orator were the ones in which he outlined his right to be accorded certain freedoms, to travel and trade as he wanted, and in exchange, he would submit to any penalty for breaking the White man's law.

Living in times of change, of course, means standing up for some fundamental differences in culture, but I also did my share of owning up to momentary lapses where the official rules were concerned. Yet there are times in your life when you have to abide by some very fundamental human principles, no matter the cost.

Even during my most difficult times, when I was missing relatives recently passed, I simply chose to personally take great pains to own up to and pay the penalty for wrongs committed. Not as a hero of any kind, mind you, just as a sensible human being.

There is a certain kind of mis-paganized paralysis
that sets in
when you know you are doing wrong
    trying to somehow push back

especially when it's too damn late.

For those who do somehow pass these gates, not everyone can survive, yet again, the kind of grim reality it mirrors, even with experience. We've all known them, those who come back from that human-made lonesome prison, the human person now gone, a hulking presence too close to ignore, waiting.

Rather it's like that ol' too-scary dream
where you go through the motions
arms a-pumpin'
    all out of breath!
just rooted to the spot

an ancient immovable.

At the same time, because of some lopsided reasoning for being granted life, we want to get caught and will keep it up until this strange other world clamps down, starting within, for good.

To their credit, the people of Yellowknife didn't outright condemn me for having gone AWOL but chose to bide their good ol' Northern time. What also became clear was that, after I finally decided to turn my life around, I could see that, like the wise words of the Nez Perce Chief Joseph, these people were with me, on my side, all along. For that I shall always be grateful.

Without knowing it then, I was learning that we all make mistakes, and that as human beings, no one stands alone. There is no way to bring back certain times of history, but in one way or another, fate has chosen the path we are always on.

Beaver Pond Bridge

The "wilds" are full of home-friendly ways.

What we like to call the untamed land is the place where nature lives, and we are the strangers. When you are born right on the land, you grow up with an affinity for the way life goes on out there. There really is nothing to fear once you become familiar with it all. To a greater extent, it is we humans who are causing the most damage to the world around us, with our carbon emissions and outright industrial rape of Mother Earth.

Our traditional Northern way of life was surely a revelation to visiting officials, like Judge Thomas Berger, in the seventies, who heard from the likes of George Barnaby of Radelie Koe who reported that we of the First Nations never did have the idea of our country being "wild" in any way, nor did we feel compelled to tame or claim her to our own tastes.

Over the many years I spent out travelling or hunting, I got to know some of nature's secrets, for example, that you could take a shortcut by walking over dams the beavers built, as a natural bridge. Beavers, for their part, make use of muskrats to babysit their young while they busy themselves getting ready for the winter. I have seen smaller birds hitch a ride over rivers on the backs of eagles.

There is a vast and interwoven kind of interconnected dependence going on all the time and in each season, becoming clearer as you spend more time away from what we like to call "civilization." Nature comes awake in spring, blossoms in summer, harvests in fall, and goes back to rest in winter and old age, exactly like the cycles of a person's life.

Even as hunters, when we went out, we never had the idea that we had to kill everything we saw. There is a given time when an animal will be fat enough to serve as food. Most fur-bearing animals will not be bothered at all during the summer, when the sun tends to bleach their fur, which becomes thicker and more suitable for pelts in the winter.

The idea is to become more used to the concept of being a guest in the natural world, to blend in rather than become a problem for our animal relatives.

Oka Wake-Up Call

When the Mola's world is threatened, it becomes a "crisis."

In the summer of 1990, the Oka "crisis," a seventy-eight-day standoff between the Mohawk and federal troops, held Canada in its grasp. It began as a routine protest over a golf course extension on traditional burial grounds and quickly escalated when men, women, and children dug in to emphasize the seriousness of their case in the face of impossible odds.

Over the following two months of intense drama, documented in filmmaker Alanis Obomsawin's *Kanehsatake: 270 Years of Resistance*, we came to learn that what we were witnessing was actually the end result of a very long struggle by the Mohawk Peoples to hold on to their lands.

There was no doubt that this event affected every one of us First Nations people within this country. Even from as far away as the Dene Nation, the RCMP were calling my relatives to ask questions and warn them of my possible actions. I couldn't have been much help, regardless, still mired in a seemingly hopeless alcohol addiction. To his credit, my landlord, Ian Henderson, was of great help right at this time, no doubt knowing what I was going through.

Some two decades after a similar situation at Wounded Knee, South Dakota, Oka served to point out to mainstream society that there continue to be outstanding land disputes and human rights violations right in our midst.

In fact, the drastic and draconian lengths that Canada took to end this particular Six Nations dispute, in a very real way, served to prove one of the main points the Mohawks were making: each of our First Nations has to make its own stand to end our everyday and long-standing colonial oppression.

The one person who could have seen to a timely solution to Oka, Prime Minister Brian Mulroney, was nowhere to be found. Regardless, and in typical government fashion, a Royal Commission on Aboriginal Peoples was struck, and former Assembly of First Nations Grand Chief Georges Erasmus was appointed to head it up, virtually guaranteeing a tacit acceptance of an "end" to the volatile situation.

Yes, of course, our leaders were concerned about what was

going on in far-off Six Nations, but these same ones, once as steadfast as the rising sun, on the front lines 24/7, now somehow came
to look with favour on a decidedly warming secured future. After
all, we were warriors once upon a time.

High Country Magic

The Dempster Highway runs from Whitehorse, Yukon, north
to Dawson City, all the way to Inuvik in the western NWT, and
extends to Tuktoyaktuk on the Arctic Coast. Many tourists use
this route, especially in summer to enjoy the season of the midnight sun, when one day goes on for a total of sixty, all of July and
halfway into August. Either coming or going, this trip is an artistic
feast, with a new and spectacular view around every turn. Along
the way, one can see grizzly bear or porcupine caribou and plenty
of *t'selih* (ground squirrels).

Early September is easily the best time to be in the Richardson
Mountain Range, with the bright orange ground bearberries,
magenta-coloured hills, and dwarf birch to dazzle every eye. The
ever-changing light adds rare drama, as brilliant shafts of sunlight
play along distant ridges and vales in a visual concert of colour.

There is a history in the region, too, going back all the way to
Beringia, when giant mammoths roamed these high, arid lands,
bridging the Americas with Siberian Russia.

"Read THAT Button!"
Some mysteries bear scant evidence.

There was definitely more of a down-home touch to the way things
were with our early Great Northern Arts Festival. The group, from
all over the North's tiniest places, was small enough so we could
go around together, guitars in hand, and just sit and chat at the
outdoor café or on someone's back porch with beer and snacks.

Events like the Northern Games were held at the same time, so you got to be involved with more traditional doings.

But for the artists, food, of course, was the big draw. For a time, you could at least have someone else cook your meals, and regular ones at that, and all you had to do for the ten days was create a body of work, or at least make like Jesus was coming and look busy!

We could always count on good ol' Martina Cardinal to come up with yet another masterpiece of choice fish, caribou, moose meat, musk ox, or even beluga *muktuk* when the whalers came back from their annual run to the Arctic Coast, down the Duhogah River a ways, toward Tuktoyaktuk.

With a bellyful of tasty duck soup, for instance, it made sense to just follow up one of my great inspirations, go up to this head chef, grouchy as she was at times, and volunteer my services. My father being chief made sure our home was always open to the public, so I was always around food. I thought for sure this would qualify for my chance at flipping some jacks or something.

So, up I got, straightened my rumpled paint-splattered shirt, glanced around for any suspicious looks, and casually strolled over to Martina, who was busy cleaning up our usual mess. I had this to say:

"Well, Martina, Ma'am, this here is your lucky day!"

"What you talking about, boy?"

"I am going to put myself at yer services. Am volunteering to do some cookin' back there, next meal or two."

She sizes me up and down her sneery nose, tilting her head this way and that, like really sizing up a silly goose loose at yer House of the Holy Spatula. "What makes you think you can do anything good back here? All I ever see you artists do is eat it up and leave a mess like this here for me to clean up!"

"Well, see here. Y'know I've done my share of creating a masterpiece or two."

"Not from where I'm standing, you're not," she smirks, just kinda itching to flick her cruel dishtowel at my behind.

"What you talking about? This might just be your one and only chance of a lifetime yer talkin' 'bout."

And then she came in for the kill shot. "You ever read your own buttons?"

"What buttons?" I ask.

"The one right on yer black *jieket*

"Oh, this one, you mean? I don't know what it says."

"There's a whole bunch of 'em on ya, boy!"

"Well, people given 'em to me, y'know, and I just put 'em on. Besides the one you're talking about is settin' upside down."

"Well, you stupid bag-a-lazy-spuds, I'll tell you what it says. It says, 'Never Trust a Skinny Chef!'"

And there went a real good chance to impress the ladies as a bone fide Cordon Bleu Chef, thanks to Ms. Cardinal's sharp eye and rapier tongue.

And just to add insult to injury, every time I ran into Martina Cardinal after that choice encounter, she would give me a big "O" with one hand and point to my thin and chastened chest with the other, mouthing, "Read . . . Your . . . Buttons!"

Living as MIA

After a time we simply learned to exist outside the world of humans: missing in action.

My sister Lucy Ann Yakeleya had her share of people coming to visit in the town of Somba K'e for a few days, just wanting a friendly person to spend some time with there. Others, more personal, would take the time away from an otherwise heavy work schedule just to unwind and maybe tell their side of the story.

One of these, Velma Illasiak, was in town to receive some major recognition for special projects she had initiated as principal of the Moose Kerr School in Aklavik, farther north, close to the Arctic Coast.

Velma mentioned that she had never really thought much of all that went with getting any kind of an award, for the simple reason that it was never there when she really needed it—on her way to where she eventually got to on her own. She simply spoke of our heart's yearnings.

This brought to mind a way of thinking that is all too often familiar to any survivor of these kinds of traumatic places and experiences.

My own parents and close relatives never did say a word of encouragement for what I was doing at any one time, and in fact, made me feel like an outsider in my home and family. They were not really to blame, either, having been part of the overtly manipulative colonialist experience themselves. Their generation was never taught to be supportive of the future generation, or even to expect any good in their own lives. Partly, too, to draw attention to oneself in the Dene world is seen to be a sign of poor character.

For my part, I am more in support of the Muhammad Ali "I am the Greatest" school of thought, that is, we should try in every way to rebuild the glory of our First Nations' past. It was very much part of some tribal approach to doing your best, in that warriors would perform these "kill talks," intentionally boasting of their prowess in battle and even outsmarting the enemy for horses. When I was yet a lad, it was a part of our hunting culture for the man who came back with a major kill to tell every step of his great accomplishments.

Overall, our Northern First Nations world did not allow for a lot of artistic expression in the way we think of it now until quite recently. Although we are naturally very artistic people, a professional artist has always been the last to get any recognition, but less any say-so about life. Even our official organizations, like the Dene Nation, have been made to struggle just to stay afloat, leaving artists out in the cold, professionally.

TOP Elder Maurice Mendo, my great uncle, in front of the mural we created for Tulita's new swimming pool in 2012, *How Muskrat Created the World.*

BOTTOM Detail from a mural I painted, with young Sonny Ellton, of a dog team pulling a mother and child. You could say the Dene were born to travel! The mural was inspired by some of my earliest memories; it is on display at the local band office complex at Fort Good Hope.

ABOVE Our old log home (second house on the left) on the main street in Radelie Koe in the early 1960s. These typical Dene dwellings of the time had tarpaper fronts. The English translation for the Dene name of this main road was "where the cattle run." *Photo by Jan March.*

LEFT Looking down from the famous ramparts over the fishing camp, K'ohoyieh (Under the Clouds). A Dene idyll. *Photo by Jan March.*

BELOW A grandmother deep in thought, Elder Pazanne Manuel, sewing the top of a tanned moosehide to prepare it for smoking. *Photo by Jan March.*

ABOVE LEFT My painting of a young woman checking a traditional rabbit snare. *Photo courtesy of NWT Archives (N-1995-002: 9665). Photo by Rene Fumoleau.*

ABOVE RIGHT Ahso Vitaline cutting fish to dry in the sun. *Photo by Jan March.*

BELOW The moosehide boat mural, now on the band office building in Tulita, took form over the summer of 2011. Over that July, I had frequent visits from some of the elders, usually my grand-uncle Maurice Mendo, who told me stories of his own lifetime. The mural was also inspired by my own memories of life in the mountains.

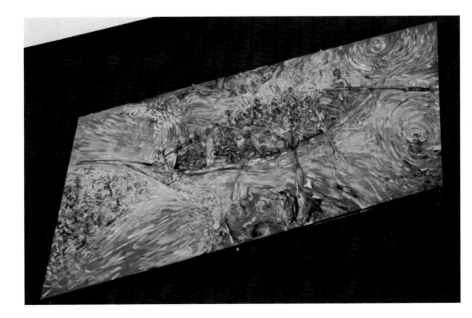

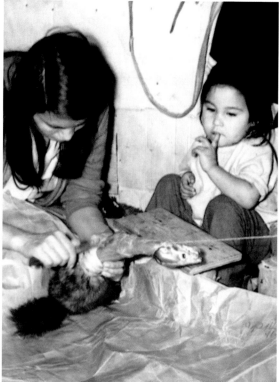

ABOVE My painting of a young woman snowshoeing with her *ahso* (grandmother), who is deep in thought. *Photo courtesy of NWT Archives (N-1995-002: 9674). Photo by Rene Fumoleau.*

LEFT My younger sister, Lucy Ann, picked up all of our traditional Dene skills from our mother. *Photo by Bern Will Brown.*

ABOVE My godfather and namesake, Antoine Kelly, was a supreme bushman, amongst many. Here he's shown making stretchers for marten skins in Radelie Koe while his grandchildren look on. *Photo by Jan March.*

LEFT Me with my younger sister Judy. Note the big ol' red bugs on her dress, and the muddy smears. She always wanted to tag along and play with the boys!

BELOW This one-room schoolhouse in Fort Good Hope brought us kids together. This was one of the first of the old federal day schools. I went to school here from about 1955 to 1959 before I was taken away to Grollier Hall. *Photo by Jan March.*

ABOVE Sports Day in Town. Turns out I always took top place at any of the games we played on sports days. *Photo by Jan March.*

BELOW I have heartbreaking memories of watching my grandmother standing by the water's edge, getting smaller as we would be taken away in the RCMP boat to residential school after every break. That first heartrending parting stayed with me for life.

ABOVE September 19, 1959 is the date I was taken from my home and family. It is and will forever be branded in my mind, as are the numbers they assigned us at residential school. In my painting, *Free Floating, Fallen Leaves*, the birch leaves are suspended on the water like we survivors.

LEFT *Child in a Cage*, a painting of mine that depicts the feelings of being as far away from the world as you can possibly be.

ABOVE LEFT Every few weeks, Judy and I were allowed to leave Grollier Hall to visit our Uncle Joe and Aunt Edith Gully, where we would enjoy real country food, like this Coney fish caught on the East 3 River. It was a far cry from the chalky porridge and dried fish we were fed at the soul-stifling residential school. It was the only access we had to any traditional food.

ABOVE RIGHT At the first-ever 1968 Canada Winter Games in Quebec City, where we cross-country skied. Big airplanes, hotels and TV were all new for us. Here I am (left) with friends John Turo (middle) and Fred "the Kelly Express" (right).

BELOW My painting of my cousin, the famous Fred "the Kelly Express" in full stride in the long glide.

My grandparents on my mother's side in the late 60s. Peter Mountain Sr. and Marie-Adele Mountain. Note that they are both wearing her newly sewn wraparound moccasins. *Photo by Bern Will Brown.*

ABOVE One of my daily sketches, which I've been doing for almost ten years. A child with a pensive stare. Long into the night, at residential school, I would hear sustained whimpering that sounded like wolf pups in an arctic den.

LEFT A photo of me from the yearbook during my days in the Territorial Experimental Ski Training (TEST) program in 1968, the same year I won the Tom Longboat Award. A long, even stride with the "swift kick" was the ideal racing technique.

TOP *Wolf Ghost.* This style of art (sometimes called "peek-a-boo" art) is meant to contain multiple images. Just to the right of the wolf's right eye is a caribou; a raven is just to the left of the wolf's left eye. There's more to the image than first appears.

BOTTOM A session of Hand Games (traditional pre-Vegas gambling) at a gathering of the Dene Nation at Fort Good Hope, 1987. I am in standing the middle wearing a light blue hat and sunglasses, and my late mother is standing at the left wearing a red kerchief. *Photo courtesy of NWT Archives (N-1995-002: 7111). Photo by Rene Fumoleau.*

TOP My painting *Starlight Cutter*. Often the only sound in the still air of the Barrenlands was the *zzzziiiing* from the Swede saw.

BOTTOM *Return of the Moose hunters.* Memories of Mountain River depicted in one of my paintings. The flat-bottomed scows were best for shallow high-country rivers. *Photo courtesy of NWT Archives (N-1995-002: 9673). Photo by Rene Fumoleau.*

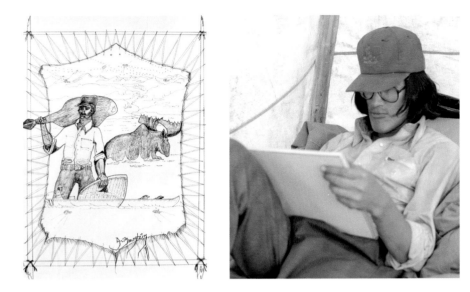

ABOVE LEFT Former Dene Nation president George Erasmus was a great supporter of the arts. In the early 1970s, he fundraised a calendar in which some of my early sketches appeared. *Photo courtesy of the NWT Archives (N-1998-051: 1400). Photo by Rene Fumoleau.*

ABOVE RIGHT I lived in a teepee for many years, often cutting wood for elders; this photo of me sketching was taken around that time. *Photo courtesy of the NWT Archives (N-1998-051-1991). Photo by Rene Fumoleau.*

BELOW Voting in favour of the name "Dene Nation" around 1978 in Deline. Note my stocking feet! My family and I had just come from trapping, and I took my boots off to cool down. (I'm in a red shirt, seated at the table, facing the camera.) *Photo by Rene Fumoleau.*

TOP Trying my hand at paddling a handmade birchbark canoe made on campus at Trent University.

BOTTOM LEFT My sister Judy with one of her prized tanned moosehides. I breathed in a lot of that hide-tanning smoke! The really good tanners had a club of their own, and it took our younger sister Lucy Ann some years to gain admission to that exclusive club.

BOTTOM RIGHT My painting, *Family Traditions,* shows Judy and Lucy Ann in (in the middle, and to the right) busy teasing Mom about some silly deal going on in their lives. Mom would have her turn at them, though.

ABOVE *Rayuka Dog Team.* My painting of the traditional story of an elder who used the northern lights to travel long distance. He can be seen driving a dog team within the lights.

BELOW LEFT This brings us back to a time *When the World Was New. (The Man on the Moon).* My painting depicts the old-time story that Chief Hyacinth Andre told me about the two brothers who picked their girlfriends from the stars; one of the brothers turned into the Man on the Moon.

BELOW RIGHT *Aurora's Raven.* The northern lights are called *Rayuka* in Dene. *Rayuka* literally translated means stabbing around, which refers to how the northern lights dart around in the sky and around the moon. The northern lights can also represent the spirits of people who died young or before their time.

TOP The artists and participants in the inaugural Great Northern Arts Festival in 1989, which came along just when I most needed to express myself. I am in the back row, wearing a hat, fourth from the right. *Photo courtesy of the Great Northern Arts Society.*

BOTTOM A delegation of Navajo Dineh friends were invited up by Johnny J.C. Catholique on a ten-day annual sacred pilgrimage to the waterfall, T'seku Dawedah, and along the shores of Tu Nedhe (Great Slave Lake). I acted as the guide on this trip (I am on the right). *Photo courtesy of NWT Archives (N-1995-002-10091). Photo by Rene Fumoleau.*

ABOVE LEFT The simple act of prayer that is from the heart, not by rote, came the hardest because we were always discouraged from expressing our real Dene selves. This painting is about my return to Indigeneity.

ABOVE RIGHT My late sister Stella is pictured here at the top. It was said that she had the soul of an elder from an early age. I painted this scene after my experience with the bluebird (see "Bluebird Tracks" on page 248).

BELOW After my first experiences in Arizona with the Native American Church, I painted this to reflect my mindset during that time. I experienced a place of spirit, a place so divine, I dared not even breathe.

Meeting *Saho Diyineh*, Bear Spirit, who is spoon-feeding a wounded me in this painting. I had an experience with this being during my first ceremony in the Native American Church. *Photo by Bonnie Devine.*

A portrait of my sister, Lucy Ann Yakeleya. I painted this during the most creative period of my life.
Photo by Stephan Folkers.

TOP Ol' Joe Martin (left) and I (right) on our way to Fort Reliance. "You don't have to go far to find your life," he always said. *Photo by Diane Pugen.*

BOTTOM LEFT My painting of the magenta hills of Kananaskis. The name Kananaskis alone means magic for many photographer and artists.

BOTTOM RIGHT I handed my son a camera, and he took this photo. I have found that my two sons, to whom this book is dedicated, survived and even flourished without an ideal childhood. The children of survivors will surprise you. *Photo by Luke Mountain.*

TOP Acknowledging the land at the Badlands in Alberta on my way to visit our southern Dineh relatives. *Photo by Dorothy Lethbridge.*

BOTTOM My painting, *First Light of Love,* which shows that most important of moments at an all-night prayer meeting: when the eagle bone whistle signals the entrance of the Water Woman, and she brings in the morning water. Gary and Mary Sondoval have always been great supporters of my art, and I painted this for them.

ABOVE This painting, *Dene Drummer and Dancers*, was the first version of what would become the cover of one of the annual Northwestel phone books.

BOTTOM LEFT *My Brother's Keeper*. In matters of culture, family ties can be difficult to deal with. Often the most beloved are farthest away from your heart.

BOTTOM RIGHT *Falling Into 9/11* - My painting inspired by the iconic photo of the Falling Man during 9/11, which is like 1492 all over again.

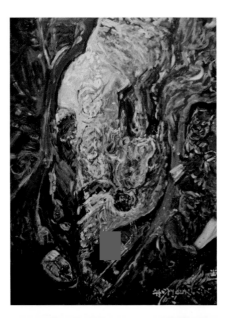

ABOVE LEFT At Lutsel K'e on the Tu Nedhe (Great Slave Lake). I am sitting on the right, and Joseph Catholique is standing on the left. *Photo courtesy NWT Archives (N-1995 002: 10033). Photo by Rene Fumoleau.*

ABOVE RIGHT Taking my art to the world. This coat was made specifically for my first trip overseas. It was made by Mary Adele Chocolate. *Photo by Dorothy Lethbridge.*

BELOW In Siberia, my déjà vu home. I am with the Siberian Russian artist Natalya Yakovleva (left) and the carver son of a famous Siberian shaman (middle).

In the Altai Mountains in Siberia, with my arms outstretched "in Altai wonder."

ABOVE At the Russian/Siberian/Mongolian border in "sublime highlands." *Photo by Svetlana Kazina.*

BELOW With a group of students who participated in the Canada Mongolia Legacy Project at the International School of Ulaanbaatar in Mongolia (with former art school colleague, Sharon Goldhawk on far right).

TOP This painting represents my connection with my good friend Nely Atefi; she was the closest of all to spirit.

BOTTOM LEFT A photo of Nely Atefi.

BOTTOM RIGHT I spent a good deal of my time with my Cree *Shehoyieh* (Anthony Cappo) and Rockridger Kamao Cappo, at Kamao's ranch just outside of Regina, SK. *Photo by Kamao Cappo.*

TOP LEFT Me and my two grown sons having dinner: Lorne (middle) and Luke (right). Making up for lost time.

TOP RIGHT Elder Lucy Jackson, always there for every community event in Radelie Koe. I have yet to see a single baseball game played in this field. *Photo by Antoine Mountain.*

BOTTOM The group of art students from OCAD in Florence, led by famous art history professor Peter Porcal.

ABOVE LEFT Me in Florence standing at the famed Gates of Paradise, the baptistry at the Duomo.

ABOVE RIGHT Two of the original Navajo Code Talkers, Merrill and Samuel Sandoval, the father and uncle of my good friend Gary. *Photo courtesy of Jeannie I. Sandova.*

BELOW A photo in the home of Gary and Mary Sandoval shows Gary's father and uncle, both Navajo Code Talkers who were commemorated by the American government for their service.

TOP LEFT Gary and Mary Sandoval at pre-Christmas Dinner prayer.

TOP RIGHT With Cousin Gordon in our search for a missing young woman. You really have to be aware of both animal behavior and currents when you're searching. We even saw a floating bear's carcass.

BOTTOM My painting, *Tawayatih Got'sehni [Toward Christmas]* captures a time from generations past, when motion, memory, and prayer were enjoined.

ABOVE LEFT One of my ten prayer ceremonies hosted by Johnson and Sarah Tochoney in Arizona. Someone quipped that the two Siberian Russian visitors travelled the farthest anyone ever had for a peyote meeting!

ABOVE RIGHT A woman sets an older-style rabbit snare, the kind that uses the original trip-stick, as done before there were wire snares. Upon being snared, the rabbit is left hanging out of the way of predators. *Photo by Jan March.*

BELOW *My Memory Sleeps with Her.* Impressionism is ideal for multiple interpretations. You'll often find more of life in dreams than in "real" life.

TOP LEFT *Mirrored Light*. The land, too, has a memory, nourished by fallen leaves.

TOP RIGHT *Eagle Arrow*. Only the owner of the name knows the original meaning, which I go into more in the section "Eagle Arrow" on page 317, where I talk about all the different names people have given me.

BOTTOM LEFT You might say that the Dene "spring" starts in the fall, when the air is fresh, travel is easier, it's easier to see animal tracks, and there is no mud. Here I am ready for a Dene "spring" in my sealskin coat. *Photo by Andrew Hammond.*

BOTTOM RIGHT Revisiting childhood memories by the river. *Photo by Evelyn Poitras.*

ABOVE LEFT The drum, like the circle and the sun, is very central to Indigenous culture.

ABOVE RIGHT At the Resurging Dene Youth Conference. Just as previous generations once did, the youth take over! *Photo by Dolphus Taureau.*

LEFT Immersed in thought at The Canada Mongolia Legacy Project mural, Ulaanbaatar. *Photo by Narengerel Bastar.*

BELOW At Bear Rock, looking up at the spot where Yamoria's arrows hit. Towards the future, always, is Bear Rock Mountain and the Legend of Yamoria.

There have been changes, though, with the government, both territorial and federal, lending support when it can.

I still very much believe that we are starving for our own heroes today.

It was not until much later, when our own dreams became a reality, in most part because of our own efforts with the Indian Brotherhood and the Dene Nation, that we came to realize our own worth, and to pass it along to the youth, the future.

For many, though, the real lasting legacy of the residential schools was that it took the one thing most prized in our First Nations culture, that sense of being "a true human being."

Yet somehow, we had worked to develop a good work ethic. In the meantime, we never saw much use in wanting all the fuss that went along with doing things well.

As for the family itself, an eldest like me had to learn to lead in a different way, as in showing the way. In the end, too, this achievement is its own reward, really.

The Procession of Carriages

In a bizarre scene of hopelessness and loss, prisoners in the Nazi death camp at Auschwitz watched as empty baby carriages, looted from them, made their way back to the train station, five in each row.

It took an agonizingly suspended hour for the macabre procession of strollers to make their way to the platforms to be sent where and for what purpose no one could guess.

Auschwitz: The Nazis and the "Final Solution" by Laurence Rees, creative director of history programs for the BBC, is a history of one of the concentration camps in Adolph Hitler's maniacal plan to exterminate all Jews. The book is dedicated to the two hundred thousand children killed in that place of human depravity. To his credit, Rees notes that these innocents, along with the 1.1 million voices forever silenced at that one camp alone, could never be a part of the testimony included. Much of this historical record comes from survivors of places like Auschwitz.

With the child in mind, perhaps English poet John Betjeman says it best:

> Childhood is measured out by sounds and smells
> and sights before the dark hour of reason grows

—JOHN BETJEMAN, *Summoned by Bells*

Meaning, very likely, that we each in our own way learn to act, or not, in those dark realities.

In her psychological study *Into That Darkness: An Examination of Conscience*, author and Holocaust scholar Gitta Sereny focuses on Theresa, wife of Franz Stangl, commandant of the very same death camp alluded to by the Polish prisoner. Sereny quotes Stangl's wife confronting him:

"I know what you are doing in Sobibór. My God how can they? What are you doing in there?"

Theresa held out for several days but eventually gave in to what the Nazi's expected of their women, wives in particular: loyalty, submissiveness, and comfort.

For our part, in the residential schools, the underlying fear we went through began long before we came along, as if we were born into the plans for hellfire and brimstone wrought in the name of Jesus by the earliest Christian missionary zealots to our country. There were, of course, decent priests and nuns, but for the most part, they were given a program to follow and did, with the idea of killing the Indian in us.

Betjeman also reflected on what we have absorbed from the baptismal waters from these religious hypocrites:

But most of us turn slow to see
The figure hanging on a tree
And stumble on and blindly grope
Upheld by intermittent hope
God grant before we die we all
May see the light as did St. Paul.

—JOHN BETJEMAN, "THE CONVERSION OF ST. PAUL"

The resultant cultural genocide served the same purpose as the plans to exterminate the Jews in Auschwitz.

To forever silence the human heart
only our Procession of Carriages went on for much longer
...
to a just-as-undetermined destination

like little brown kites in the hands
of future Mola children

we remain aloft
many mercifully let loose
for the empty

Only the historical procession of carriages has its way of coming back around, this particular one idly pushed back into the market by a Hitler fan by the name of Donald Trump.

Replace the Jews with Native Americans, Mexicans, and Muslims, and it's the same day again, isn't it?

"Throw the Stove out!"

"This went on ALL summer," Billy Cardinal said.

In my travels to different towns I took to visiting people who had been to Radelie Koe or knew my relatives there. Some of them came from Tsiigehtchic, just north of us down the Duhogah. Chief Hyacinth Andre, of course, would be at the very top of my list of those to see, others being Dale Clark, Noel Andre, and Peter Ross.

Once I was at Billy Cardinal's home, and he was in a talkative and friendly mood, as usual. He goes, "Yeah, your dad, they sure don't make 'em like that anymore. Them summers we were at Plumber's Lodge, on Great Bear Lake, we had our little tent set up on a hill off the shore, with a good hard plywood floor, it was good for dancing anyway, and I had my fiddle with me.

"Them Mola, tourist men, weren't used to that bright midnight sun all day and night, so they just went straight to bed after being out in the hot sun with us, fishing all day. But it wasn't the same at all for their wives, let me tell you, son.

"Your dad knew this and every evening, after we had something to eat, he would go and get them and coming back up that hill I would hear him yelling for me to 'Throw the stove out!' meaning he had some serious dancing on his mind.

"That's all it took, and I would rosin up my bow, and away we would go. All night, raising hell and really swingin' 'em ladies around in that ol' tent of ours there! And every day would be the same, even with all the different tourists coming along.

"Busy all day, and come evening, here he is again, coming up that hill, just yelling, 'Throw the stove out!'"

My Bedside Mola Angel

"There is nothing physically wrong with you, Antoine . . . but there is no doubt you are an alcoholic."

We must surely have presented a curious sight. She a Mola nurse tending to a strung-out Dene man. But, then again, maybe it wasn't such a curious sight for the Stanton Yellowknife General Hospital's Intensive Care Ward.

I had joined in a pick-up game of hockey, and we were just fooling around out there on the ice in Yellowknife Bay. After that a friend and I put a caribou head in the oven, and as we waited for it to cook, I suddenly just ran out of air to breathe . I asked my friend to call an ambulance and was rushed off to the hospital.

A number of days later, I came to and woke up in post-op with a physiotherapy nurse by my bed. I was yet quite groggy, with each thankful breath of air a veritable godsend, and she in turn appeared as a divine being come to my side. What she had to say, though, painted not as rosy a picture.

She began by saying there was "nothing wrong with you physically, Antoine. You are a very likeable person, with a good sense of humour. But there is no doubt that you have a severe drinking problem. The next time an ambulance comes for you, it may not make it to the hospital in time to save you. Just think for a minute, seriously, about what this is doing to your mom and your family."

As she spoke these words, I realized that this complete stranger had hit home in making me finally want to quit my drinking forever, and so it is that her words have remained with me to this day. She was like a dutiful and duty-bound soldier of love, sweeping up after the madness, and taking extra care to pick up pieces of a forgotten puzzle. Putting the odd puzzle back together would have to be my job

Nats'ejee K'eh

This place had more of a Northern feel.

I was first sent to the Poundmaker's Lodge in Edmonton for help with my problems with *kotweh* (alcohol) some years before, but the Nats'ejee K'eh centre in Hay River was more geared to Dene needs.

Of course, I could relate to the idea of a First Nations approach to healing at the Edmonton centre, but there were prisoners from the penitentiaries there who had a habit of taking personal offence to even an unkind look, which didn't help an outspoken drunk like me!

One place in Yellowknife, the Tree of Peace, which I had helped set up almost twenty years before, referred me to Nats'ejee K'eh—proof that karma does come around. So, Nats'ejee K'eh, coupled with my resolve never to return to a deadly lifestyle, set my feet firmly on the Good Red Road.

A God for the Absent-Minded

There is a light that shines even on this faraway corner.

I have always had a mind that tends to wander off base, one that busies itself painting outside of our communal human box. But every time I actually lose something, it has this habit of coming on back to me, usually later the same day or soon enough after. My thought is it probably comes from either a spirit above who just wants some balance here, or from one of the grandparents.

Grandfather Peter Mountain Sr., for instance, was a traditional medicine man who could do both good and bad. He let me know not to worry after he was gone, that he would make it a point to watch out for me as thanks for honouring my grandparents' wish of spending their last years near them.

This might also have to do with the power of some sort.

For instance, I will prefer that an eagle feather I've received that is a "man's feather" (that is from the right wing) will somehow shape-shift or go through a powerful transformation.

> Which may go to explain, enduring
>> an earliest life, in the frozen, wintry north
>> and emerging as a superior athlete
>> after tuberculosis
> surviving a number of suicide attempts
> being accorded a second chance at love
> and another try at schooling and
>> finally
> an entire third chance at childhood
> as an elder.

Little matters like these make it all right, and even a blessing of some kind, to be on the forgetful side of life. Don't you think, eh?

PART IV

A New Drum Shines Forth

CHAPTER 14

T'seku Dawedah (Woman Sitting Up There)

Making Raidi Sho, Grandmother sits in watery splendour,
watching over our Peoples.

It's a place people in the North go to every year for a sacred pil-
grimage: Desnedhe Che, a traditional caribou crossing near Fort
Reliance. It is across the lake from Somba K'e, on the east arm of
Tu Nedhe.

Many years ago, there was an old man of over eighty winters,
from the Dene Peoples of Lutsel K'e. He said that his time of dying
was getting near, but that he wanted to do something before he
passed on to *Not'sin Nene* (the Spirit World). He told his relatives
that when he was just a child, there was an old woman in camp
who was very kind to him.

But one day she was refused a special dish of beaver blood
soup, and she got angry, saying, "I don't want to live with people
who do not want to share with an elder. I will leave here."

The rest of the People did not take her seriously and said that
no one could survive on the land in the dead of winter anyway.

One day she was gone.

They couldn't do much about it and, over the winter, simply
forgot her—until the old man told his people that he wanted to
find out whatever had happened to this kindly old lady. He put
his birch bark canoe in the water and paddled for quite some time,
going north and east toward the forbidding Barren Lands, finally
making it to the place they had camped at so many years before.

There he sat, looking around at the shore, thinking, *Where would anyone go and still live from here, on the very edge of these forsaken Barren Lands? Certainly not on the lake itself. There would have been too many wolves that cold winter. And certainly not out in the Barren Lands themselves. Again, too many dangers, and no trees for firewood.*

He finally decided that the best place for her to have gone would be up the Lockhart River, which drains into the east arm of the Tu Nedhe.

He beached his canoe and walked along the shore of the winding river, up, up for about thirty kilometres. He stopped on a high ridge overlooking a set of waterfalls he had never seen before.

Behold! It looked just like a commanding woman sitting down, with the cascading waterfall itself being her dress. Using his sacred medicine, he turned himself into a bumblebee. Flying all around, he finally found a way into the falling wall of water. He was now in a huge dark cave and very afraid. Trembling, he heard out of the dark the echoing of a strong woman's voice:

"Dene, what are you doing here?"

"It's okay," he replied, "I was just leaving anyway—"

"Oh, I know who you are! My little friend from so, so long ago. Here, let me help you."

She then told him of the troubles to come to their People with the modern world and that they could come to use her sacred holy water to help them.

The old man had left at the very end of his life and returned a young man again of twenty years. This was T'seku Dawedah's gift to him.

As Dene youth, these were the kinds of places that now attracted us to help relearn our own culture.

In the early 1990s, at the first of many ceremonies with the Native American Church, we spent ten days on a spiritual pilgrimage to Desnedhe Che, where the caribou come out to the big lake and return in the spring, about thirty kilometres south of *T'seku Dawedah* (Woman Sitting Up There).

A small group of our Navajo Dineh relatives were invited to visit the sacred place, including a Roadman of the Native American Church, Hanson Ashley, and his wife, another Roadman, Peter Chee, and Lorenzo Max, Joe Bedonie, Garrison Yazzie, Jerry and Hatathlie, and a White man named Sky.

After setting up a teepee for the Education Meeting, Hanson Ashley, as the Roadman, determined that we began at sundown. As hunters, we were more used to sitting up at night in summer, waiting for a beaver to surface, so everything about this was new to us. So was the peyote, which I actually had before, but not as a part of spiritual cleansing. When it came to midnight, the Roadman asked if anyone had any questions, or just something to say.

Not ever to be one to sit back and stay quiet, I mentioned feeling bad about my grandparents on my mother's side who had passed away recently, along with one of my sisters.

"Well, whether you know it or not, they are right there in front of you," answered Hanson. "They are right in the fire there, keeping you warm, keeping you company . . . and if you want, I can put some cedar in there for you, for the way you are feeling about them."

Of course, I wanted this, but I was not prepared for the flood of emotion that came with it, as, sobbing, I suddenly realized that, yes, they had been with me in my grief all along.

I made a mental note to find out more about this.

Re-Joining the Circle

I had to relearn how to talk to Nehwehsineh, the Creator.

One of the things I had the most problems with as a survivor of residential schools was to simply pray, as my elder Joe Martin said, "From the heart, without the fancy talk." So far, all I had ever known was to do this by rote, repeating old Roman Catholic bits of doctrine, many in the original Latin, as far from Dene culture as a spider is from the moon.

When I sat beside other First Nations people in the sweat lodge ceremony, for instance, I noticed that the Cree, especially, really knew how to do this, from being born that way, with our traditional teachings yet intact.

It took me a while, but I also realized that the answers I needed were already there for the bidding. The first step, of course, was to accept our own ways of knowing and go along with them. Of course, putting this all into practice was another matter. I had to use our Dene language in a more spiritual way. Luckily, all of those natural and forgiving elements already exist in there.

It was going back to the land and finding all you need to survive and thrive already there to be used. It was also a matter of setting aside the guilt built into the Roman Catholic religion, rejoining the Circle of Life.

In the words of Sitting Bull:

> When a man has lost an item on the trail, if he goes
> back and carefully looks for it, surely, he will find it.

To this day, I will stand before the mirror of a morning and say, "I love you," to myself, while braiding the hair of Spirit Stone Child, a name bestowed to me, and reminding that person that all of those bad things that happened in the past are best left back there, and to pray for a good future.

> ... again, simple as that.

> No matter how long away
> the circle slowly turns ...

> waiting.

Bluebird Tracks

Behold, I stood still, held aloft on a wide, sparkling silvery circular sheen.

One fine day I began feeling all of this pain in my hips, making every step very difficult. There were times it was so painful I couldn't even get up off the bed of a morning. Doctors couldn't figure on the cause, only prescribing Motrin. I did not like to take pills, and besides, my grandfather Peter Mountain Sr. always told me to walk everywhere I had to go. "Your Mother, the Earth, wants to feel your step every day."

For some reason, I thought for sure this was about to change, and for the worse. On a trip back to my second home, Lutsel K'e, I took the time to pick and dry some of that ol' time Dene medicine, the prickly leaves of the ground-hugging vine from crowberry bushes. With that, I went back all the way home to spend a bit of time alone at our hunting lodge up the Duhogah, at the Hume River.

My father looked at me kinda odd when I told him I wanted to bead an eagle feather for my late sister Stella's grave, but he left me with it at our log house.

There wasn't much for company, except for plenty of bears—who were not harmful, just hungry and more or less a nuisance—and the occasional visitor, the odd hunter or ones who had broken down or run out of gas, but it being too early for serious moose hunting, they were soon on their way.

It took me all of a long night to do the beadwork for Stella's feather. Toward morning, with a new light streaming in the open doorway, some very unusual things started happening in my lonesome cabin.

A pretty bluebird flew right through the closed window on the far side where I sat finishing up, staggering around dazed and confused on the wooden floor, then it stood back up, wobbled and hopped a bit, and flew out the door! Totally startled out of my meditative reverie, I got up and walked over to see my little visitor had alighted in some bushes a few paces to the left and then flew off again into the hills beyond.

Just then, I heard some distant thunder rumbling from somewhere way up the Duhogah, toward the imposing San Sault Rapids. Like a single shaft of sunlight through a maze of trees, a fleeting memory of Chief Joseph's Nez Perce name, Hinmatoowyalahq'it, Thunder Rolling Across the Mountains, crossed my mind.

I faltered a few steps over to get a better look and just stood, rooted to the spot. I was now lit from below and felt like I was standing on some kind of a soft cushion, with this wonderful and spellbinding silvery light all around! Like Black Elk and his Great Vision, I had no idea how long I was there, but when I came to my earthly senses, I distinctly thought, for some reason, that something bad was about to happen, that thunder coming from all up that way maybe a warning.

I quickly made my way back to the log house and, once inside, thought that with Stella's feather now done, I should just offer some cedar for it in the stove.

When I reached into my little bag to do so, I could feel something small and hard in there. For some reason *this*, though I did not know what, made me feel very happy at that moment. When I lifted it to see, there was a perfectly round and very unusual purplish-brown pebble in my hand.

No one in town had a clue what this all could mean.

It took me a while, but when I had spent some time among our southern Dineh relatives in Arizona, I was told by different people that my late sister Stella was so pleased someone would go to such lengths for her that she had sent the unusual little pebble to me from wherever it was she now was, away off where our People go.

After being adopted into the Zahne Family on the Big Navajo Reservation, I had one of my younger brothers make it all into a dreamcatcher, which went with me all over the world, and still does to this day, the downy feather attached, quietly catching every wayward breeze.

> Every time I would return home
> and over the years
> a new breath of hope
> from distant thunders upriver
> would always
> just hint among
>
> them dreamcatcher
>
> feathers

Ko Firehyieh Sah

My bears, with shimmering eyes, in the coals.

T'sinaginne, the old Navajo man we called chief, and I looked at the bears glowing in the early evening cabin light, their eyes twinkling each time he went and fanned with his eagle centre-tail feather. It had been a long enough road just getting there to his home on the Big Navajo Reservation.

The first step started with the pains in my hips, at about the time I decided to leave that ol' demon alcohol to its place back in the hell it had dragged me down to on the streets of Yellowknife.

It took me several years, but one way or another, here I was in the Navajo Dineh rancher and medicine man's home, he trying to figure out what these images in the coals all laid out on a tin sheet meant.

"So, *Se Chieh* [Grandson]. Where you come from, are there many bears?" he asked.

"Yes, there are."

"And, when you see them, what do you do?"

"The elders at home tell us not to kill them if we don't have to, but they bother our camps on the land. They just say to use a light-gauge shell, like a .22, to send them back to the bush. They are fat enough it won't hurt them."

"Well, that might be, but this one here is plenty mad at you, tracking you. Them pains in your hips and left leg, that's where you got him. Lucky you came to me just now. Any later and you could very well be crippled for life."

We talked and smoked on it for a while more, and he got me to promise to never again do any harm to this our relative from the Bear Nation.

He also suggested that I needed to have a major healing ceremony done for me and that the Zahne family would take care of it. I was also to spend the next four days "close to the *hogan* [traditional Dineh hut] and think about what you have done and how you are going to fix it all back up in future."

He was talking big ol' time Indian medicine

At the very least this got me to some good and much-needed peace of mind.

Meeting *Saho Diyineh* (Bear Spirit)

I was taken way, way back, beyond Mola time.

Through the haze from the burning coals in the centre of my first all-night teepee ceremony, I could hear the medicine man's chant . . . sending me back . . . back. He had told me that these last four songs would be from a place I was *really* from, a hunting camp up in my mountain home some thousands of years ago, before all of *this* came here. And Billy Arizona, the Bear Medicine Man of our Navajo Dineh Nation, was right.

That Saho Diyineh, Bear Clan Spirit, had me in its firm grip right from the start, just after the sun set the evening before. Through the Cedar Man just to my right, he asked me what I was afraid of.

I told him any kind of "loud or sudden noises" and that I "wasn't sleeping proper."

It turned out this Saho Diyeneh had stalked me for the last few years for trying to harm it. Every little sound got me to jumpin'— even a sudden noise of my own making.

> Living like a shadow . . .
> just waiting for that axe
> I didn't know
>
> > to fall

The evening before, though, I was rather worried about how the teepee for the prayer meeting of the Native American Church would be filled at all. The teepee usually held up to thirty. I was new to this part of the United States, the Southwest, after all, and had come by myself, some months before, complaining about my painful legs.

But this elder brought everyone who needed to be there to help me out with a problem I had created with his Bear Nation.

> . . . Something looking for me
> something,
> didn't know how to die
>
> Can't be outrun
>
> > but knew
> me
> all too well . . .

When we finally got to the midnight water and the break, I went outside, noticing the stars so bright and night air so brisk, familiar to the North, my distant home.

For the first time ever at the growing number of these "meetings" I had learned to go to, I kind of staggered to one side and really threw all of that bitter peyote medicine all up, through tears remembering the words I'd been told:

"That bad feeling we have, y'know, it don't ever go away, unless we do something about it, something from our ol' time Indian medicine ways . . . That bad stuff, it just sits there, in the pit of your stomach, like a cancer, making you feel bad and do foolish, harmful things."

Now, and just after I had heaved up all of them bitter years of pain and outright neglect, I felt a light cloud descend in the blessed night air, alighting its warming blanketed embrace and a nice, soft cushion to walk on from here on in. The rest of the veterans of these spiritual ways in the teepee, they all knew this look I now had and knew that everything would be okay for me from now on . . . and, of course, they were right.

The elderly Cedar Man pointed out the new way the fire was now burning, with a new life, in lively colours, even blues and greens, lively sparks popping. Before, it was smouldering and smoking, causing people to cover their mouths and noses.

Through it, a gruff voice, barely whispering, tired said:

"When that light
shines off your soul
   it leaves an echo
   like a shine
long into lonesome days

A prism

full of rainbows

in the begging bowl
of your life
    reflected all around
    and that's my wish

for you."

It took a number of years more, but Saho Diyineh, Bear Spirit, took pity on me and made it right for me to walk the Good Red Road again.

The Place of S-P-I-R-I-T

It all slowed down and almost stopped, or went on in a very different, holy way. Away from the smoky teepee, I was now sitting on a soft feathery cloud of some kind. Not even wanting to move. A. Single. Nerve.

One of the people I spent a lot of time with when I first arrived in Arizona was an elderly man, Frank Tsosie. His English was not all that great, halting at best, but like two strangers who have somehow known each other some time, this made no difference at all.

I always got the feeling he was very concerned about me being there, if I was enjoying my stay or not. He would always ask me if I was eating okay.

We went to a number of prayer meetings of the Native American Church conducted by Garrison Yazzie, one of the Navajo Dineh relatives from there in Page, Arizona, who had come all the way north with a group to visit our country. A feature of this one ceremony is that a person can request a special prayer, and time is made available. Which is what this elder did toward the early morning of our all-night event.

He let it be known that he wanted the communal tobacco brought over to him so he could roll a smoke and pray on my behalf. He got to talking a bit as he prepared his offering, saying that the people should be aware that this one long-distance trav- eller and tribal relative came a world away to be there. He went on at some length in his own Dineh language, which is related to our northern Dene tongue.

I could only catch a word or two as elder Frank Tsosie went on, but what I did notice for sure was that we were all somehow removed for a time, or maybe we were now in the *real* version of the place we usually knew as the world, what Black Elk called the Shadow World, which goes on the same time as this one.

When the Water drum began sounding
and four songs of the Native American Church
voices were raised in songs only God would know.

In my turn I was, let's just say ... taken
to a wondrous and peaceful, yes, even sublime place
high up along a murmuring mountain stream

water of life sparkling, earthly stars
echoing these sacred tones
off of our daily cares and woes

... I just wanted to stay there
in that grace of Peyote Spirit

forever.

When I looked around
I could tell
all were sacred beings
somehow lifted from daily cares and woes.

Long after he had finished with his prayer offering and the tobacco smoke made its way to the central fire, my lifelong friend Frank Tsosie calmly turned to me and said: "So now you have met the Peyote Spirit, keep her right there in your heart, *Se Chieh* [Grandson]."

> As if in breaking trail to that mountain vision
> he passed away sometime over the years I kept
> coming back
>
> but remains
>
> in my waking S-P-I-R-I-T

PTSD, Brothers-in-Arms

We have a magnetic bond that pulled us together without a spoken word.

One thing I began to notice when I first went to visit with our relatives the Navajo Dineh in Arizona was that almost all the people I spent any time with were veterans of various wars and conflicts.

From the late sixties on, our little band of rebels from the Far North was like a branch of a great tree rooted in the past, trying to right some very basic wrongs, especially from our Treaties 8 and 11 not being honoured by the Canadian government. In the way of youth anywhere, we were going through the motions for change, without quite knowing the way.

Through it all, and like these former soldiers I began to befriend in the American Southwest, it took us some time to have a look at ourselves, what actually happened to us on the battlefield of war, and, in our case, the residential schools and after—how far we had been pushed or strayed from the path of life.

Those fields of actions past were somehow always present, carried around in person like the "poisoned cloak" the Jews at

Auschwitz symbolically wore, with its venom seeping in every day, every hour, every minute, silently feeding on our souls.

We always had a lack of trust in anything, even the simplest of everyday things, going well and, worse, were not able to understand it, much less talk it out.

> Days go by as if Missing in Action
> tomorrow a blank screen
>   with no picture in frame . . .
>
> if there at all
> in just black and white

Thankfully, from the medical world, we found there was even a name for it: post-traumatic stress disorder, a condition familiar to both old soldiers and survivors of the residential schools.

In the end, all we could do was turn to the Creator to bind us together and heal our wounds.

To the Gardens
From a distance, the medicine calls.

A run all the way down to the peyote gardens takes some planning, especially when you are coming from a longer distance, like all the way from Canada. After you have accounted for the amount of peyote you are planning to get, most of the rest of the cost goes to fuel for the vehicle, food along the way, and motels if you are staying overnight.

One route we took went from northern Arizona, across the Navajo Reservation to Gallup, New Mexico, on to Albuquerque and then south to El Paso, Texas, on the I-25. For the final leg, you can turn south on I-35 down to Laredo and Miranda City, to the peyote gardens proper.

All the way, the preferred music is Native American Church peyote music, a good deal of the time the deeper, dulcet tones of the Yankton Sioux, Volumes 1 or 2. Or Navajo's Guy and Allen, William Yazzie from Tuba City, or even Johnny Mike and Verdell Primeaux in the late evening, with that Texas twilight just giving way to the Arizona stars, a big harvest moon smiling on.

A well-known Mexican lady, Mrs. Gardinas, used to be the caretaker of the gardens. She was a kindly lady many have fond memories of. After driving for what seemed like forever, you would finally see her smiling face to greet you and an ol' pot of coffee on the stove.

Navajo Dineh Roadman Lorenzo Max and the Tuba City Chapter of the Native American Church brought all of the materials and built a hogan right there on her property, so future travellers on this sacred pilgrimage for the medicine could have a place to go to worship. The idea, too, is to time your trip for the full moon and have a teepee already set up back at home for the prayer meeting, just for the medicine.

One time a group of us were crossing the bridge into Mexico at Laredo, Texas, and after a time, noticing my puzzled look, my Navajo bro turned to me and asked me if I knew why the Mexicans appeared to be scared of me. When I confessed to not knowing why he told me.

"It's your moccasins, bro. The way the fur comes on out at the bottom of yer jeans looks like you are some kind of a sasquatch monster, with all that hair growin' out of yer ankles!"

Oh, the onerous trials and tribulations of a modern-day holy man! But *Sasquatch*? Always thought that gamey feller preferred the West Coast jungle country!

CHAPTER 15

Painting in Somba K'e

I never thought the city of Yellowknife would end up being
an artistic inspiration.

One day, I just walked into the Northern Images Art Gallery in
Somba K'e and asked the manager, Glenn Wadsworth, if I could set
up and start painting on site there.

Over the following decade, my regular routine became to go
the American Southwest in mid-October and return to Somba K'e
four months later and stay for the spring and summer, creating a
body of artwork.

One of the reasons I did so well was on account of photographer Tessa MacIntosh, whom I knew from my earliest times
there. She provided me with many spectacular images to draw
inspiration from, including one of her daughter Oree (which
means Spruce Boughs in Tlicho Dene). I should also mention that
Robert Alexie Jr. of Fort McPherson was also an invaluable source
of images.

Ol' Joe Martin

He was my personal safe harbour.

One of the features of Dene life is that once you get to know how
to do the basics, you can also choose your teachers. That's what I
had in mind when I asked Dene elder Joe Martin if he could take

me out on the land with him sometime from his home in Dettah, just across the bay from Yellowknife.

Summers we went out in his boat, and in winter we took his truck and he taught me a lot about the old ways of doing things. Each time we landed the boat somewhere, he would ask me to try to explain what I thought of the place, like what to expect in the way of animals to hunt. Over the years, he must have surely known that we would only have so much time together because he made it a point to make each one of our trips simpler and more elemental as we went along.

Toward the end, he took to calling me his favourite Dene, which was a real compliment coming from such a respected man.

He also told me a funny story about another young man who went out moose hunting with him. As they stood up on top of a small hill, his young companion loudly exclaimed, "Boy! I haven't seen moose in a long time!" . . . just as a nice fat cow took off from just below them.

And Joe Martin was always extending his help on into the world, too. We made a plan to have my old-time friend and southern mentor, Diane Pugen, come up from Toronto to go on the spiritual pilgrimage to see T'seku Dawedah, the spirit woman said to live up the Lockhart River from Fort Reliance.

Diane and another lady arrived by vehicle, and she was so excited to meet this genuine Dene elder that she went on and on upon being introduced. Typical of our elders, Joe took a long time to get on back to her, with Diane standing there ready for an extended and in-depth conversation about all things life. Finally, Joe replied with a slow and extended, "Ooooooooooh-ooooH!"

My friend from the south even ended up picking up this all-purpose phrase and used it often during her visit!

Of course, being something of a holy man himself, Joe Martin taught us how to approach this traditional spirit woman at the falls, for the best results to our pleas for help. He carefully explained that spirits like this one were not interested in prayer the way it is done in church, repeating words you have learned to say.

"One should speak to this holy woman from the heart. Make the story your own, the way you would beg your mother for something, with real tears running down your face. Do not be ashamed and she will hear you."

In practice, his advice made the most sense of all, with T'seku Dawedah's mists of holy water streaming down your cheek it took little else to think of yourself:

> In the presence of a rare divine . . .
>> many among us
>> knowing this could be their only chance for a healing
> we all broke down
> and pitifully asked for forgiveness
> and another chance.

Magenta Hills

That high country was an artistic Valhalla.

On my way south from Yellowknife each late fall, I would make it a point to visit Sharon Lennox. She had a magnificent two-storey log home at Bragg Creek, outside of Calgary going west toward Banff. We took frequent road trips to the stupendous Kananaskis Country to take photos for later use.

From the first I saw of Kananaskis Country way back in the early seventies, I knew it would be a dream to capture on canvas. So when it turned out that I knew someone who lived there, I was eager to spend some time in the place.

I had met Sharon Lennox some time before. We shared an interest in all things First Nations—she was involved with the Sun Dance, and I with the Native American Church. I took to dropping in on my way to and from Arizona. Morley First Nation was close to her place, and we would drive there just to spend a bit of time.

The aura from the fields of wild sage took me all the way back two decades, from when we would travel south from Somba K'e to the Indian Ecumenical Conference with its thousands of visitors from every tribe in Canada and the United States. Hearing again the powwow drum on the Stoney Reserve, sleeping in my own sweetgrass-scented teepee.

One memorable work I did there, *Magenta Hills*, captures that certain pink hue you sometimes got in the hills and valleys of those picturesque lands.

As with all of these memories, Sharon passed too soon a few years later, of cancer.

Price of a Soul

A Roman Catholic soul was worth a total of $285!

Now living a sober lifestyle, I had more time to check into my residential school past, finding comments in church records from high school at Grandin College: "A serious student, but adversely affected by friendship with Michael Beaulieu" (!) and to get a few things straightened out with the Roman Catholic Church, of which I no longer considered myself a member in any standing, good or bad.

First off, I brought up the matter of divorce at Yellowknife's local St. Pat's Diocese. I was a member of the Native American Church, and I wanted to make a clean break of my marriage. In a matter-of-fact tone I was told, "This should not be a problem, unless you plan to remarry."

"Well, what about just leaving the Roman Catholic Church?"

Again, normal sotto voce, like I was ordering a ham and cheese on rye or a Fudgsicle: "Well, that is another matter altogether, Mr. Mountain. If that is what you want, we can arrange that, yes, but you will have to pay in the amount of $285."

The simple matter that my newborn soul had no idea I was being signed on to such a lifelong contract at birth held no bearing on the matter at all. After all the pain and suffering of a failed cultural genocide, this is what it all came down to. From my age at the time, the total of $285 worked out to just over what I was expected to receive per year from the Canadian government for being a Treaty Indian: $5!

Sure seemed like some kind of a conspiracy to me.

It may well be that no less than ten thousand angels rejoice when a single soul is saved, but that same soul comes with a price tag on an earthly plane, less than three hundred dollars, preferably in cold cash. Presumably this price goes up with inflation.

Immediately repelled by the idea of any further dealings with this bunch of reptilian crooks, I simply left, never again to grace such idiocy with my marketable presence! As the saying goes, some things are just better left in the hands of God, and not his supposed earthly "servants."

When you think that this is the reality religious bodies hide from their honest churchgoers, it's no wonder many survivors of residential schools intentionally shield themselves with the bottle, as I had done for a good quarter-century.

On the other hand, as a member of the Native American Church, all that was required of me was not to drink nor use drugs and to at least have a way to support myself.

Meanwhile, the priest holds a chalice, no less, of wine to the heavens, and preaches sobriety.

Not hard to see the logic of clear thinking, is it?

Mr. Tochoney's Visions

The glowing coals told him what was going on.

Johnson Tochoney and his wife, Sarah, saw to conducting a total of six ceremonies in Arizona for me over the years. The first was when I first arrived there. Good and kind people that they are, they just volunteered to do this for me, and in no time, the teepee was up and the special oak firewood all prepared and ready to go.

Each prayer meeting of the Native American Church comes in sets of two, one for the original problem itself and another, usually the following year, as a thank-you meeting.

The final set of four meetings I requested was actually a part of my healing from residential schools. I took the Canadian federal government to court for severe trauma and abuses suffered during my time at these dread places of cultural genocide. As a part of the opening, I had a Nishnawbe elder come and do a sweetgrass ceremony, meaning that I could not tell a word of lie about my experiences all day. In conclusion, the federal government head of the hearing simply said, "This is the best testimony we have ever heard about this one subject."

They ruled in my favour and said that I could add to my compensation an additional program meant for recovery. When they suggested one someplace in Alberta, I right off halted the proceedings and told them that these kinds of programs were what started the problem in the first place and that I could come up with something better.

Eventually, we agreed on this series of four prayer meetings, the first reconciliation of its kind.

Over the day my hearing took, we went all the way back to when I was continually strapped and punished for daring to speaking my own Dene language, and all the way to being sexually abused. At the very end of the long day, I quoted a First Nations warrior who said: "We were never afraid of your guns, nor your bullets. We have but one life to give. We were most afraid of the one who would not tell the truth."

Ponca statesman Chief Standing Bear uttered, "Good day to die," explaining that every day in the service of the people is a good day to meet one's maker.

Incidentally, this same man was made to suffer through a

degrading civil rights trial to legally determine if he was a "person" or not. Judge Elmer S. Dundy ruled in his favour on April 18, 1879, at Fort Omaha.

> "Neither in its true form is the Good Day to Die a defeatist way of seeing being.
>
> More, it serves to address the very purpose of life itself."

Over the years, I had spent most of my time in Arizona on the Big Navajo Reservation, often with the Tochoney family, near the Western Agency town of Tuba City.

My brother Johnson was sought-after for his ways as a genuine medicine man, and I was always naturally curious to find out from him what this practice was all about. This may have well started when he told me of something funny that happened while he was helping a woman who came to him in great distress.

"She said that she was going to lose her job if she didn't find her office keys," he said. "So I told her we needed to go back to where she last saw them, which was in her hogan home. I set up to burn some cedar, had a look in the coals, and asked them if there was a little pup in the house.

"They brought this funny-looking little rez dog out, and I let them know to just let the little guy on the floor, but to give him something he shouldn't be having and just follow him where he goes. Sure enough that little dog took off and buried whatever it was they gave him under this tree a little way from the hogan, and when they dug in there, she found her keys!"

After one of the ceremonies he conducted for me, he said that 'round about midnight when he took his special feathers and eagle bone whistle out before the time of the midnight water, he saw "a mountain standing there, close enough for me to see that it was open at the top. It was hollow inside, and there were a large number of paintings slowly coming out of it, and way down inside, on the floor of that mountain, were all these animals, walking around in a great circle."

At about this time I was going all around the world as a cultural ambassador for the North and Canada.

In Moscow, when we were in the Kremlin and Red Square, in fact, I requested a brief stop on our tour so I could go ahead and lay down some sacred tobacco in respect for our First Nations ceremonial ways. I did the same in Rome's St. Peter's Basilica, the world's largest church.

First Light of Love

As the eagle bone whistle sounds, she waits to come in.

The eagle bone whistle signals the single most important part of the all-night prayer meeting, when the Water Woman brings in the morning water.

As the sun rises through the teepee doorway, the image of the sacred water bird comes to life, confirming that the medicine is a good, strong one.

Spirits in the Sun

In our little family of Radelie Koe, artists sure got around!

It wasn't only ceremony that helped me to heal, family and art played a role as well. Just about everybody in our family was an artist of one kind or another except for Dad, who only ever knew how to make trouble! Even though we travelled a lot, we met at least once a year in one place or another, usually at the Great Northern Arts Festival at Inuvik in July. It was usually my mom and two of my sisters, Judy and Lucy Ann. They would make it a habit to sit me right down in the middle of them and tell any woman who came along to "Just you move right along, he's already taken!" (I always found a way to seek out the person in question and at least try to right this grievous lover's faux pas.)

So it came as no surprise when we were told that we would be a part of a grand Canadian First Nations art show in Scottsdale, Arizona. Having been going all the way there for quite a number of years by this time, all I had to do was find the Northern group when they got there. Ours turned out to be the only group with four artists from one family: Mom, myself, and my two sisters. Mom fell in love with the horse-drawn carriages that would take her all over that tourist town.

And we were very lucky to have a big, brawny, and genuinely heavyset Navajo man in tow to help drag my sister Judy, no shrinking violet herself, grimly shrieking, out of every jewellery store.

My Dineh relatives took to calling her T'seku Nezhonih (Good Woman)!

My Brother's Keeper
Some things are best left aside.

One of the many times I was in Arizona, one of my younger brothers asked me to make him a pipe. I had told him I was a pipe carrier, one given the sacred duty of handling a traditional pipe, which represents the connection of our Mother Earth and the Great Above.

I was greatly puzzled by this request and thought to take some tobacco to an elder there in Tuba City. This man was Arapaho and married into the Navajo Dineh Nation.

The man carefully listened to my situation and then proceeded to tell me a long story of how the original sacred pipe had been given to his People. He ended by letting me know that I would know what to do and left it at that.

More time went by, and as I thought more of this, I also had to take into consideration that one of our brothers had passed away under a questionable situation in prison.

This sacred pipe is used is to follow along the Medicine Wheel, which purposefully includes all the Peoples of this world, including the Mola.

Knowing that someone has a bad heart, that is, some serious resentments, and could do themselves harm by omitting the important part of the ritual when you pray to the northern direction to pray for Northern Europeans or Mola, I decided against passing along a pipe to my brother.

Such is the fate of a brother's keeper.

Falling Into 9/11

There is a sense of inertia here, to the point of a certain lack of meaning . . . a vague rankling at the psyche.

When the iconic image of the Falling Man, a photograph of a man who jumped to his death from the north tower during 9/11, first ran in the *Baltimore Star* and other newspapers, it created a media uproar, especially among American officials who did not want the world to know that about two hundred people died in this way.

Associated Press photojournalist Richard Drew took the photograph. There is no definite identity of the person, but it is very likely Norberto Hernandez, a pastry chef at a 106th-floor restaurant.

Whoever is in the image, all who witness it agree that there is very likely no other single image that so encapsulates our times today—that our world is now so mockingly defined by this overwhelming sense of despair, and how we humans are surely destined for suffering.

In my painting *Falling into 9/11*, which was inspired by the iconic photo by Richard Drew, I use the paradigm of the colour of the traditional Medicine Wheel.

When you take into account the basic colour scheme for this work of art, you will note that the progression of colours in this rock cave include the yellow for the East, or our Asian relatives.

Next is the red for our First Nations of the Americas.

Moving on, we have the blues, often used in this wheel to represent the Black Nations. Within this area appears the image of a seated bear holding a fan of eagle feathers in ceremony. We believe this one animal/relative to be a doctor, able to dig for medicinal roots in the ground to heal. Immediately above in totemic order are the eagle and the trickster coyote.

Finally, in the barely visible sky, is the white for our European Peoples, or the direction of the North, and spirituality. Seeming to magically appear from this lofty haze are some warrior figures, including that of a conquistador, one of the first to pillage our native lands. Worked in is a polar bear with a seated white buffalo calf just below.

There are, of course, as with my style of painting, a good number of other images to symbolize a multitude of meanings, as with life itself.

Ehkoleh

"Sedidileh hagoht'elih"

One of the things our Mola friends can never get used to is our First Nations' seeming abruptness and what they like to call "stoicism." This is mostly based on our cultural belief in non-interference, that is, a belief in the mystery of life itself, letting events unfold as they may.

My grandfather Peter Mountain Sr. told me a number of times that whatever you come upon is fine the way it is, and that you are the stranger to the situation, and that you especially need to know what *not* to say or do.

Over my years of travel, one thing I can never get used to, especially with city folk, is their way of wanting to know absolutely everything about everything, right down to personal details, even upon having just met. In our Dene way, for instance, it is considered rude .to ask personal questions unless something is specifically brought up. This, of course, leads to some rather comical situations.

In matters of romance, for instance, ladies will always want me to take my dark shades off, so they can see my eyes. After pointing out that we find it offensive to look directly at a person, the lady will take some time to avert her eyes, making for more discomfort!

This matter of *ehkoleh* (non-interference) includes a good part of life, too, in that we make it a practice to only take what we need from nature and make an effort to leave it without any sign of our having been there.

Dr. O'Connor's Brave Stand

At root were rare forms of cancer four hundred times over expected rates from a tiny community like Fort Chipewyan.

Dr. John O'Connor arrived in Canada from Ireland in 1984, little knowing that he would change the face of medical history.

After ten years as a family physician in Nova Scotia, he moved his family west to Alberta for better opportunities. Working close to Syncrude Oil's operation at Fort Mackay, he became familiar with bitumen, oil with the consistency of peanut butter, which needs tremendous amounts of energy to extract, process, and upgrade to lighter fuels. With new processing methods, the industry soon boomed, far surpassing Syncrude's goal of one million barrels per day in 2004.

Increased production did not, however, come without cost. In 2000, the doctor began noticing some rather serious pathology, very high concentrations of cancer on the shores of Lake Athabasca, downriver from the Alberta tar sands.

At the time, eighty percent of the community lived directly off the land in one way or another. The elders noticed changes, especially to the water, which now had an oily sheen to it. The fish were strangely deformed, with missing or extra parts. Muskrats and many of the traditional plants either disappeared completely or were harder to find.

When these alarming cancer rates, including cholangiocarcinoma, a cancer of the bile duct, were reported, the province recommended a study in 2003 but never followed up. There was never a response from Health Canada.

Totally taken aback with this one case, and his own father's death from cholangiocarcinoma, Dr. O'Connor knew then that this was his reason for being in Fort Chipewyan.

In 2006, CBC reporter Eric Denison did a story on Dr. O'Connor's findings and things have never been the same.

Over the past decades, Dr. O'Connor's personal and professional ordeal has been a long and costly one; he lost his job over the issue of the Alberta tar sands. Yet he has continued to stand by his findings.

In February of 2014, he was invited by officials of the American government to Washington, DC, where he told senators in no uncertain terms that the "Governments of Alberta and Canada have been lying to cover up health implications of Canada's tar sands industry on northern Alberta communities," and that "Government needs to stand up and take actions to prove or disprove there is a problem."

These senators then called on Secretary of State John Kerry and President Obama to conduct "an immediate and comprehensive study" of public health risks to communities from the proposed Keystone XL pipeline, which would carry bitumen from Alberta across the Canada/US border to refineries in the Texas Gulf Coast.

The US Senate voted down plans for the XL pipeline on November 19, 2014. Dr. O'Connor noted that "When pressure outside Canada is exerted the government reacts."

In January 2017, President Donald Trump issued an executive order to approve the XL pipeline.

§§§

My family has been no stranger to cancer. Mum died of it in the summer of 2011, one sister overcame hers, and Dad was diagnosed with it in the spring of 2014, soon after I began writing this book, and then one more sister, quite recently.

I have written quite a number of articles about this for my column, A. Mountain View, in *News/North* out of Yellowknife, making note of the involvement of such notables as Chief François Paulette of the Fitz/Smith Band on the NWT/Alberta border.

Failing to get any concerted response from an overseas trip on the matter, Dr. O'Connor got in touch with filmmaker James Cameron, of *Avatar* fame, who expressed an interest in doing a documentary on the Alberta tar sands. When environmentalists in California started to speak up publicly on the matter, the federal government in Ottawa finally saw wise to order the testing of industry emissions and tailing ponds.

Hunting with the Chief

Whenever we took a break, he would tell me some history.

If Chief Fred Sangris and I were out in the Simpson Islands hunting ducks, the stories would have to do with how these were created from the rocks that our ancient cultural hero Yamoria threw at the giant beavers as they swam to escape. Or, elsewhere in the area, how the famous Akaitcho himself was buried close by.

Over the years, Chief Fred Sangris gave me the kind of education you just don't get from the Mola books. He grew up and lived at one time or another everywhere we went, whether it was a few miles from Ndilo or way out near Gordon Lakes. In fact, were we to keep travelling to his former trapping grounds in the Barren Lands hundreds of miles away, he would still be right at home.

There were a number of fierce storms that only happen in the rock hard, granite world of the Tu Nedhe, Great Slave Lake area; I was mighty glad to be in the company of a regular Dene Rambo, let me tell ya.

We had our lighter moments, too. Like the time we were out duck hunting, and he told me that I would get a break as camp cook this time around. All I needed to do was pluck the ducks we did get, and he would get some vittles goin' on the campfire. I was indeed curious what he might have in mind, so got to the ducks and was done in an hour or so.

When I got back to where we had tied my boat, he pointed at the fire with the knife in his hand.

"Check it out, jes' have yerself a looksee."

I strode over and lifted the cover off this big pot he had on the grill, and sticking out of the boiling water was what appeared to be some kind of huge claw! Turned out he got hold of a lobster, no less, from somewhere. Over that strange but tasty lunch, he told me that he had gotten a taste for seafood some time ago while firefighting, but also noted, "The elders wouldn't go near it. They said it was some kind of big BUG!"

When I let him know I was going to Russian Siberia, his parting words were that I would "meet someone I knew." Sure enough, I pointed out in a presentation I made at the Siberfest event in Siberia that I had "never seen my Uncle Peter Mountain Jr. in a suit before," pointing to a man seated a couple of rows in. It turned out that he was the director of a museum, and in reply to my comment bought one of my paintings for his collection.

Another person, a hunter, gave me a homemade skinning knife that I passed along to my chief, Fred Sangris.

Could be he used it later to pick at his lobster dinner!

CHAPTER 16

Taking the Arts to the World

Now that I had my own life back in order, I began to be
noticed for the arts.

First there came a trip overseas, to Germany, to showcase the
arts of the North, in 2002. My sister Lucy Ann Yakeleya later said
that she made it a point to follow on behind, to watch all these
Europeans suddenly take notice of the man in the moosehide
jacket calmly riding on an airport escalator. This jacket, made by
Gameti's Mary Adele Chocolate served me well for many years
to come.

For me, this trip to Germany was a continuation of school
and art-related travel that began when I was yet in grade school,
first "outside" to Edmonton, then to Quebec for cross-country
ski racing, and now listening to Beethoven on an international
flight. As my grandfather Peter Mountain Sr. said, "Dreams do
come true!"

A few years later, there was Siberfest, a combination cultural
conference and art show, in Novosibirsk, one of the largest cities
in Russia. One of the funnier events there started innocently
enough, with a panel discussion involving a number of represent-
atives in different fields, including the Russian cultural director.

Each person at the table was asked to explain their field of
expertise. The person to my immediate right rolled up his sleeves
and launched into the role of diamond mines in our North.

When it came to my turn, I explained that we of the First

Nations world made it a practice to tell a story before a crowd of people at events like this one. I started talking about a personal challenge I made to myself the night before: to order my breakfast for the following morning only in Russian. I asked the lady at the front desk not to interrupt me, but to send up exactly what I was listing for her.

When the appointed time for breakfast came in the morning, I went to answer the knock at the door, there stood a lady holding a silver covered silver tray. When she lifted the cover there was a blow-dryer there! She even asked me if I wanted it plugged in.

A few years later, a smaller group of us from the North attended Expo 2005 in Japan.

When I told my uncle Thomas Manuel at home in Radelie Koe that I would be going to Japan, he told me that there shouldn't be any real reason to do so. Smiling to himself he told me that the last time he heard there were only twenty-six people there! Our elders will stretch the truth as far as it will go, to test your judgement.

The group that went to Japan was smaller than the one that had gone to Germany and Russian Siberia. Our journey to the Land of the Rising Sun took a total of thirteen hours. I watched five movies on the way.

When we got to Nagoya, the fourth-largest city in Japan, we were told that the airport we were landing on was specially built just for Expo 2005 and would be taken apart after it was all over in September!

There were quite a number of people who came through our Canadian Pavilion over the time we were there to display our art and the drumming of Michael Cazon of Fort Simpson. Others in our group included Karen Wright-Frazer and Brenda Lynn Trennert and Métis fiddler extraordinaire Lee Mandeville.

We presented to a group of elementary students who were so well behaved. They sat there intently listening to what we had to say while an interpreter translated for them. About an hour after they left, someone came back and told us they wanted to show us what we had inspired them to do, so Michael and I were taken to the Expo's media centre, where they showed us an entire newspaper story, complete with photos, of all we had told them about the Canadian North!

§§§

One night I couldn't quite sleep right, having heard that there was a tornado heading our way.

I told Mr. Cazon I wanted to offer some tobacco in a little park in front of our hotel, on behalf of all the American soldiers who never made it back from the staging grounds in the country during the Vietnam War.

From my time among our Navajo Dineh relatives, I had learned that about four in the morning was the best for a prayer offering, with the morning star at its brightest, way before the dawn.

Toward the end of that spectacular event, we were all in our hotel lobby in the host city of Nagoya. We noticed that everyone in the lobby was dressed in tuxes and evening dresses. When we asked them what the occasion was, we learned that the emperor of Japan's son was just then expected to check out from his stay there.

Just then one of our group, Métis fiddler Lee Mandeville, came strolling in, humming merrily to some tune he was listening to, with earphones on. His wardrobe just then included a Hawaiian print shirt with colourful flowers of all sorts, cut-off shorts displaying his hairy legs, and sandals. Needless to say, a beefy bevy of security guards quickly hustled him out a side door!

A few years later, I was again picked for a trip to the Siberfest in Russian Siberia. I had fallen in love with the place. In tribute to the manner in which the Native American Church had made my way in all of this possible, I asked for a moment to put some tobacco down near the Russian Kremlin and Red Square in Moscow.

Five Councils with Bear

Over a decade, I returned to our ancient homeland a total
of five times.

The first time I returned to our original homeland was in the
summer of 2003 for Siberfest, a circumpolar cultural event held
somewhere in the Far North every three years. As with everyone
else in our Northern delegation, I really had no idea what to
expect but was continually surprised at the rich artistic life in the
Siberian capital of Novosibirsk, itself one of the five biggest cities
in the country.

And what a country! Russia spans almost the entire way
around the very top of the world, from Finland, above Europe
in the West, all the way to almost touching Alaska on its eastern
border, with a total of nine time zones.

Our group of artists and the business delegates who were pro-
moting Canadian diamonds must have presented quite a spectacle
indeed, for our Canadian Pavilion drew a large number of curious
visitors, with the print, radio, and television media seeking our
stories and personal photo ops.

When we left some ten days later, I let it be known that should
this event happen again I would give anything to return to this
wonderful country. What kept pulling me back to Siberia is the
way people live with a sense of the good in life, despite having survived hundreds of years of the roughest times in all of humanity.
One of the reasons I learned to love this country so much was for
the way the people, with grace, survived so brutal a history. They
lost, for instance, some fifteen million in the Second World War
alone, with none of it being recorded anywhere.

At first, I would visit just to be near Novosibirsk and from there
to nearby Berdsk and the *Akademgorodok* (literally: Academic
City) scientific study community just there.

Thanks to the government of the NWT's Industry, Tourism
and Investments Department, which organized the trip, and to

the moosehide jacket Marie-Adele Chocolate fashioned for me, I was included once again a few years later. This time, I made arrangements to make my own travel plans back and took up with a small group of First Nations enthusiasts, who introduced me to their world.

Having fallen in love with the place, I saw to returning a total of three more times on my own, each time living in Berdsk with the family of Russian Army veteran Pasha Maximoff, his wife, Galia, and their two daughters at their home with the large garden, a cow for fresh milk, and chickens for eggs. I got along with the retired Russian army sergeant right away, and his training even came in handy. He treated me for food poisoning from a helping of bog myrtle, a concoction I was served by the gang in their teepee.

Pasha's English was not all that good, but when asked he would demonstrate the right way to do a Russian goosestep-like march, toes pointing high and sharp, and tell us what a real AK-47 looked like. His battered jeep never failed to get us where we needed to go, always at full speed, over the rough, pot-holed roads. Many of our mad dashes were to the local bank, where the bank machine, when working and approving a withdrawal, sounded like an old Elan Ski-Doo motor finally turning over—which somehow sounded like a magical Mozart concerto, with merry ol' cellos trilling a finale of good fortune!

After I got settled in, there was no shortage of special treats, teas, and the famed Russian pastries, which found their way to where I sat in front of their TV. They surely must have found it comical, this Indian guest from who-knows-where, trying to pick up a few words in their language from European soccer games, which they themselves found silly, more like diving meets, with so many "dives" going on every couple of minutes!

Each time we got together with our little group, the Maximoffs lovingly spoke of the Altai Mountains to the south. One day we took Pasha's jeep and went there. The Altai Mountains, of course, stole—and even now keep—my heart of hearts as a lasting treasure. My love for Mother Russia was complete.

A Spiritual Siberian Cradle

The remote and exalted Altai Mountains whisper of myths yet kept alive there. They have long been regarded as second only to the Himalayas in terms of spirituality.

There was no doubt in my mind that I had been away up here in the Altai Mountains some time(s) in the past, toward the Mongolian border from Siberia, for in one day alone I experienced no less than five cases of déjà vu, one right at the majestic gateway to the home of the shaman's son.

The one traditional Siberian shaman's son, Vyacheslav, was also one of the most acknowledged carvers in the entire country. His carvings were almost as finely made as a Swiss watch . . . and kept ancient memories alive.

His family home was designed like a heavenly fortress, with an emblematic eagle standing sentry high aloft, overlooking their mountainous realm.

I bought a total of three of his works of art. They depicted what he called "The Spirit of Fire," which related an ancient tale through conflicts and wars, featuring heroic people, simple family life, and ever-changing times. They also serve a purpose: to protect the home.

Even though you've never been to this essential home before in body, its loving arms leave you another pilgrim in a long line back home.

As if through some kind design, I was beginning to understand what my grandfather, Big Ehseh, Peter Mountain Sr., told me: "You will make many tracks, trails, in this lifetime, and one day you will come upon one you do not recognize. That one will take you home."

Two Seasons in Mongolia

When I was yet again in Siberian Russia, for the fifth and last time, I noticed an event online. The name was a familiar one from way back in the days of my first art school in Toronto. Sharon Goldhawk was married to Greg Goldhawk, the Canadian Ambassador to Mongolia. As it turned out, she was making use of her earlier studies in the arts to help produce a women's film festival.

So the plan became for three of us to take the jeep belonging to my adopted son Sergey—a Russian academic whom I had a deep connection with—on over there, along with the gifted painter Natalya Yakovleva. This proved to be much more arduous than the simple idea of looking at a map and connecting the dots in between where we were in the Altai Mountains and Ulaanbaatar, the capital city of Mongolia.

The land itself was flat enough that we didn't have to use any roads—not that there was one. All the fast-flowing rivers were flooded over and the bridges unusable, so we had to find fording places to make our way. We finally saw a young man on a motorbike coming over from a distance. It turned out to be our official Mongolian welcome.

When we got to the family home, we were greeted with all of the relatives sitting around the biggest spread of home cooking we could imagine, and all for us!

Canada/Mongolia Legacy Project
A venerable Genghis on one side and a powwow dancer on the other.

The International School of Ulaanbaatar, Mongolia, was hosting a cultural week. Through our contact at the Canadian Embassy, Sharon Goldhawk, an interpreter named Nara, and I made arrangements to start work on a mural with the Grade 7 and 8 students, along with a few gifted artists from the lower grades.

I told a few stories to a series of classes during the ten days of the event and told them about an Italian technique for works of art meant for public display. We could work on three 4 × 8 boards with a single image and then secure them all together using hinges, so the mural would be mobile and available for display for future projects.

Thus began our concerted effort, with staff and the many pupils, to eventually produce a grand vision to commemorate the fortieth anniversary of Canada/Mongolia relations. This was a fine conclusion of my three-month stay there among our ancient ancestors.

Down Home Sauna Sweats

Dense hazes of humid steam enveloped our group in the
cramped room, the scent of cedar heavy all around.

When I wasn't travelling for the arts, I often returned to Somba K'e, where a number of us would get together at Stefan Folkers's homemade sweat house in Old Town or at my brother-in-law Bob Overvold's at Pontoon Lake. Before these were made available, we would simply meet at the Ruth Inch Memorial Pool's sauna across Franklin Avenue from the CBC.

As a part of our personal recovery from our former lives of substance abuse, we styled these sauna sweats after traditional sweat lodge ceremonies, complete with four "rounds" and a communal meal after. In time, our little circle of regulars slowly started to include others of the same mind, like William Greenland and Edwin Kolousuk.

We took turns conducting these ceremonies, and I recall one in particular in which JC Catholique enlightened us about the purpose of the "grandfather rocks" the water was poured over to make steam:

"This here is the last duty for us, given by these grandfathers, in all their wisdom. These relatives are the oldest element here on Earth. They were here when the land was formed, and after listening and answering our prayers, we can put them away, back to Mother Earth."

It wasn't always so serious either. There began to be quite a tourist craze all the way from distant Japan, with groups of rayuka, northern lights, enthusiasts coming to the capital city every four days. I got to meet quite a number of them, with my cabin/studio right behind the Allooloo's Narwal Bed and Breakfast over at the end of Peace Willow Flats on the shores of Back Bay.

One young fellow there expressed an interest in going to a genuine First Nations ceremony and came along to Bob and Lucy's cabin. My brother Robert, the carpenter, had added a lounge area, with the sauna on the other side. There we sat, taking it easy before going back in for another session of hot steam. Elvis Presley's "Love Me Tender" came on the stereo and our Japanese guest jumped right on up, singing along. Let's just say his Elvis impersonation wouldn't pass muster on a Vegas stage.

That was quite enough for the gang, as someone quickly suggested we go in for the next round, pronto, between stifled laughs from all and sundry.

A. Mountain View

About this, long-time editor Bruce Valpy, now with News/ North in Yellowknife, called me in.

Bruce Valpy asked me if I would be interested in reviving the column I once had with the *Native Press*. One hesitation I had was how it would affect my art career, such as it was. After he assured me that many artists in the past were known for making their views known to the world, I thought I would give it a try.

It took a few months to get into the habit of making statements about what was going on in the North and elsewhere, but over the years, I became even more known for my writing than for my painting. My column covered social issues, matters of Dene culture, and art-related subjects.

One of the things I did notice was that although some people took personal offence at the devil's advocate approach I often adopted for effect, there was a definite purpose to my attempt to wake up the North and help to change some things.

When you take the risk of taking a stand on a controversial issue, like my suggestion to have only a survivor of the residential schools serve on the Truth and Reconciliation Commission of Canada, you have to also be willing to back up your stand. In this case I lost a close lifelong friend, but that is the cost of change. To want to have everything nice and easy is simply not the way life is.

I was most proud of making a difference for issues like fracking.

Also, it all helped out when I began my research for a Master's of Environmental Studies in Toronto, which took me to the United States and overseas.

Dear Nely Joon

No doubt the single greatest influence on my life at this time was Nely Atefi.

Nely Atefi was originally from Iran and had to be spirited out of the country for her family's political and religious beliefs. We met as I was getting out of a cab for the Aboriginal Film Festival in Toronto in November of 2007, and she just happened to be waiting at the corner of University and Spadina, to go into a premiere at the Jewish Centre.

We hit it off right from the start, and I found many features of her Baha'i belief interesting, as she in turn did with my beliefs.

After I earned my Bachelor of Fine Arts degree a number of years later from OCAD University, I continued my studies at York

University where she worked as a student liaison, and we continued our friendship where we had left off.

She was supposed to come on down to Arizona in December of 2012, and although she overcame the cancer she was suffering from, the physical complications that followed suddenly snatched away her precious life in late January. She was laid to rest and scores of mourners shared stories of this sainted and so-young person.

In honour of Nely Joon's ("joon" is a Persian term of endearment that essentially means "dear") love for our First Nations, a Cree man, Kamao Cappo, sang an honour song at her cold and windy gravesite in February 2013, and before an array of final florals, I was asked to recite these words of a Baha'i prayer:

> . . . O Lord of glory! I entreat Thee, fervently and tearfully, to cast upon Thy handmaiden who hast ascended unto Thee the glances of the eye of Thy mercy. Robe her in the mantle of Thy grace, bright with the ornaments of the celestial Paradise, and sheltering her face with the lights of Thy mercy and compassion.

§

> In a poorer world, we do what we can
> to carry forth our humble ways
>
> richer though
> in some secret sweet
> these same times
>
> forever.

I have called upon her spirit many times since then.

Rockridger Kamao's Ranch

He stood at the little reception lobby, his Australian rain
slicker marking him as a real cowboy among city folk.

That was the first I saw of Kamao Cappo, a Saulteaux man, at our Nely
Atefi's funeral. What really impressed me was when he said that he
had taken a taxi all the way from Union Station in downtown Toronto
to Mount Pleasant, costing him almost a hundred dollars. That is after
making a last-minute decision to fly all the way for the event.

Later at the gravesite he was asked to sing a song, which he
did, a traditional Saulteaux song, in memory of our dear Nely
Joon, who had done so much for each and every one of us there.
I made a mental note to find out more about him and, when the
chance came, took a flight to meet him at his ranch a little out of
Regina, Saskatchewan. The family land is situated in the peaceful
Qu'Appelle Valley, a long series of First Nations campsites in that
otherwise flat country.

Along with his wife, son, and two daughters, Kamao Cappo
runs a ranch to help inner-city youth learn how to be around
horses. In time, this also teaches them to be independent and able
to fend for themselves in an uncertain world.

One other person I spent a bit of time with was Kamao's
brother Tony, who took the time to show me the grounds of their
annual rain dance. It's essentially the same as the traditional sun
dance, but just altered a bit from when these Indigenous spiritual
practices were outright outlawed.

He also shared some of his superlative drawings with me, ones
that compare with the best of Michelangelo, all based on Cree
beliefs. I was made to feel right at home and spent some time just
continuing with the notes for this book.

One funny incident included the young four-year-old Hadar,
who I was warned would go around "trying to steal people's des-
serts." I didn't think much of this little bit of trivia, but I made sure
to gobble up any sweets I had on hand with him in sight.

So there I was, as usual, typing away at the coffee table, when the curious little tyke, thinking my little flat black USB stick to be a tasty bit of chocolate, grabbed it and stuck in his mouth, fully intending to swallow it whole, until I desperately reached over and quickly popped his cheeks, thus saving my life story!

Otherwise, on the whole, I will always have my fond memories of the occasional horse-drawn chuckwagon rides, with a mass of squealing children enjoying every minute of it, a number of others riding alongside. To my mind, work with the youth could never get any better.

Sahtú in the Arts

An artistic gem fell out of the skies.

When I got done with my first year of art school in Toronto, I got a call from Andy Short in Norman Wells asking me to go and work with his office, the Tourism and Investments Department of the NWT.

The plan for this arts initiative was to help highlight the cultural life of our Great Bear Lake Region and maybe eventually set up co-operatives, as the Inuvialuit and Inuit communities had done. The project was very successful, receiving the coveted Premier's Award for Group Activities after several years.

Our small and mobile staff consisted of Leanne Taneton and a Pakistani man, Nazim Awan, whose habit of carrying his food around with him made quite an impression among us Dene. One person who came forward to help was Tony Grandjambe, a fellow tribesman from our hometown of Radelie Koe. He played host to me in his home there on the shores of the Duhogah

It was good to finally be home, for the summer anyway, after having lived in the southern city of Yellowknife for so many years. The murals we painted ranged from the six-by-sixteen-foot *Dogsled* mural in my hometown of Radelie Koe, to the *Traditional*

Fishcamp mural in Déline, and the eight murals in Tulita, including the *Moosehide Boat* mural, done on the outside of the Band Office building.

Missed Childhood Relived
This was the kind of education I needed.

As I began to move further beyond the boundaries of Radelie Koe and the memories of residential school, life began to open up for me.

For all of their good intentions, both the Canadian government and the churches misdirected our Peoples. In fact, there is little doubt that the residential schools were cultural genocide. But with our resilience and innate strength of character, we eventually received at least an apology from the federal government and some reconciliation.

For my part, this all became a reality when I began my formal art school studies at the Ontario College of Art and Design (now OCAD University) in the fall of 2007.

I had gotten some training years before, in the late seventies, at an alternate school, Art's Sake, but OCAD University now addressed and challenged more of my intellectual needs and abilities, with residential schools a part of the issues involved. We had required studio courses, along with some academic subjects in lecture-type settings.

One added feature of my stay in Toronto was that the eldest of my two sons, Luke, was living there, and we each, in our own way, rekindled a part of our lives that had gone unattended for over two decades.

This in truth was the main reason for all of my prayers in the Native American Church, to somehow be shown and allowed a way to reconnect with my two boys, since my divorce in 1986.

As for the parts missed from being confined in residential schools, what I was missing I now had: some close friends, like

Nely Atefi and Jimmy Dick, the Cree Sundance Man I had met so many years before. In a very real way, we shared our caring warmth in a cold city.

Over the four years of my studies, I at least maintained my grades and coupled it all with some work with the youth back in the North, with Sahtú in the Arts.

That T'siduwe Fork
A real elder sees that marker.

Not everyone who reaches a certain age in the Dene world gets to be an elder. Of course, everyone gets older with age, some much sooner than others. The old saying "thirteen going on thirty" has something to do with this, too, for the ones whose sad life is already written all over their faces at a young age.

Our Navajo Dineh relatives have a saying: You have to challenge your life! One of the main challenges happens when you one day turn a corner and have to make a conscious decision. Are you going to be one who makes an effort to recall all of what makes us Dene, and make that extra effort to pass it all along to the youth? Or do you just quietly resign yourself to everything that comes along with getting on in years and start complaining about all of your physical ailments and generally become a burden to your relatives?

In a small Northern community, we children right away caught on to the idea that every adult was a teacher and that you could actually pick your own, offering to help them out with cutting wood or getting them water, or whatever else they needed. In exchange, you got bits of candy, a piece of frozen bannock. Or best yet, valuable lessons in how to do certain things. How to think and do for yourself as you got older.

One such person who was always thought of with this kind of wisdom was Lucy Jackson. As I carried on with my education to help the youth along, she became an increasing resource, someone I could talk with, to either verify the ways I was being taught to think, or to gain added insight into an older way of understanding life.

An Artistic Paradise

From the airplane coming into Florence, Italy, you see a sea of burnt red, the clay roofs of buildings that are not common in the Western world. But the entire impact of this world of art doesn't really hit you until you start walking the narrow cobblestone streets marvelling at the way all of the sixteenth-century Renaissance buildings make you feel so ... well, *young*!

It is said, and with good reason, that this tiny European country contains some three-quarters of all the art in the world. There is really no doubt that it is simply everywhere. You can, as I did right upon arrival, go as far as you possibly can and then try to find your way home, mine being just off the Piazza della Repubblica, near the famous Duomo.

Knowing naught of the Italian language, it took me some time to find my way to my Via del Inferno, Hell Street, an ancient haunt of artistic types like me. Every corner I turned bespoke some intrigue done in the name of human foibles over the years, things I wanted to take root, deep to soul.

> The long way didn't bother me at all
> I was somehow home. *Home*!

The following day our Florence group met at the OCAD University's classrooms, right downtown on Via Nazionale. Our famous art history professor, Peter Porcal, took us through the basics of the frame of mind we would need to make it through the next eight months of our third school year.

Aside from his truly irreverent, highly individual brand of humour, he had this unique way of instilling a sense of discipline in an entirely *molto gentile*, very kind, Italian way, often with an added gentle brush of your cheek to get the point across. Right away this *molto gentile* soul dubbed me "Maestro," for reasons of his own, no doubt.

We gathered what we called "Porcalisms." For example, he would refer to sculpted angelic cherubs as "those flying little bastards." Once you heard it from Peter Porcal, you would never ever be able to see these relics from the Renaissance past in quite the same revered light. In fact, he had his own way of making history come alive in a very contemporary manner.

One of these very first lessons was at the tiniest of churches in Firenze, the Chiesa del Santi Apostoli, close to the Arno River. After an extended lecture on all the stolen Italian art borne away to places like France by Napoleon, Peter Porcal let us know in a subdued hush that the size of a place of worship very much had to do with its relevance, as far as initial intent.

He said that because of its relatively cramped space, this was better suited for prayer, whereas the world's largest church, St. Peter's Basilica in Rome, able to contain some fifty thousand people indoors and another several million outside, defeated the purpose of worship.

I took this to mean that the more people physically present to the Lord, the less the voice. It also happens to perfectly align with our First Nation's belief that the object(s) of worship is not all that far away. For instance, the Navajo Dineh believe that the spirits much prefer roadside clumps of grass to dwell in and are oft nowhere to be found in grand human structures built to honour—and much humour—the eyes of God.

In a very real way, Peter Porcal instilled in us that a disciplined way of looking at the world would reward us. For instance, when we came to yet another grand house of worship, which on average took some two hundred years to build, through famine and war, he asked what was the one thing the grand edifice encapsulated. "Faith" was his one-word reply.

> Faith, in spirit
> in mankind

His own legend preceded him, in all who spoke of this very unique art history teacher whom we were blessed to know. Little did we know that he would not be long for this world he loved so.

CHAPTER 17

Déline's Summer Sunshine

Of all five communities in the Great Bear Lake Region,
Déline certainly was the best to work in.

When I got to Déline from my art studies in the big city lights of
Toronto, there was still snow on the ground and ice out on the
lake. Housing is always an issue in these small Northern places,
so the solution turned out to be the mission building, which stood
near the local church. Typical of Dene humour, I was there to hear
people's confessions!

After being there for a bit, though, I ended up in the home of
local leader and elder Charlie Neyelly and his wife, Gina. From
them and others, including Joe Blondin Jr., I began to hear more
about a small group of local prophets, including the famous Etseo
Ayha. He foretold many events that came true after he went on to
the spirit world.

The Four Prophets of Déline

God certainly smiled on Déline, a little fishing village on
the shores of the Sahtú.

With its rich store of pristine fresh water, Great Bear Lake is one
of the seven biggest bodies of water in Canada. It was once sorely
endangered when uranium ore was being extracted in nearby Port
Radium. Curiously, it was also home to four great seers into the

future, including Etseo Ayha. When you consider that Déline (Fort Franklin then) only had several hundred people, this was an extraordinary man in their midst. Three others from there also had these spiritual powers, Joe Naedzo, Andre Andre, and Joseph Bayha.

The one person who made all of this fascinating history come to life for me, when I was in Déline in the summer of 2010 with our Sahtú in the Arts, was the elder Joe Blondin Jr. He would come into the Aurora College campus building where I worked with the youth and tell me these stories from the past, often with the supporting written material.

He even knew some of the people involved, as in the one about the time at the height of the Second World War when a worried Canadian government, with an American general, the RCMP, and some interpreters in tow, consulted Etseo Ayha. They wanted to know if Hitler's German war machine would invade the Americas.

When the prophet assured them that "the bullet," meaning the enemy army, would not, they asked him what he wanted in return for this vital and reassuring information.

In response, he humbly requested food for two winters for the people of Déline.

Among My Mountain Dene
All roads lead to Bear Rock Mountain.

One of the perks of working in my Sahtú, was that I got to travel to each and every one of its five communities: Fort Good Hope, Norman Wells, Tulita, Colville Lake, and Déline. One of these in particular, *Tulita* (Where the Waters Meet) was very close to my heart. There, Sahtúdé (Great Bear River) flows into the Duhogah, east from Great Bear Lake.

I had quite a number of relatives there: my grand-uncle Maurice Mendo, the Yakeleyas, and Menichos, and probably others, who made me feel at home once I got there to work with their artists and the youth.

One time in particular comes to mind, late June of 2008. We were all set up in the boardroom of the local hotel, where I was to conduct a workshop to introduce our arts initiative. Just as I was about to start, the federal government's residential schools official apology came on the TV, live. We decided to just watch it and go from there.

Once Prime Minister Stephen Harper got done with saying how sorry Canada was for what had been done to the survivors in the name of colonialism, we turned the set off and just started talking about our own experiences, in our Dene language. It took us a while to go all the way around the big conference table, and the last person to speak was our elder, Maurice Mendo.

He started in on how life was there in the Tulita area when he was growing up, the traditional life of hunting, trapping, and fishing, and how this started to change once the trading post and Roman Catholic Church came along.

Elder Maurice Mendo's words also brought to mind the legend of Yamoria at Bear Rock Mountain, how our cultural hero Yamoria caught up with a number of beaver there. This was at a time when the world was young, with giant animals preying on the People.

"Sacho, giant beaver, would swim right in beside hunters in canoes, tipping them over and eating them."

Yamoria, the One Who Walks Across the Universe, killed and skinned three of these harmful animals right here at Fieh Tehni-ah, Bear Rock Mountain, tacking their hides on the side of the rock face. He then shot an arrow into Duhogah where it meets the Bear River, to mark the spot, made a fire, and cooked some of the meat. Smoke from that fire is still visible today for those lucky enough to have a long life.

Our belief is that, as long as we remember this legend of Yamoria, we will always do well as Dene.

It took the elder a while to lay it all out for us, but we could clearly see that our problems as a People began when we were made to rely on the Mola and their way of life.

As I sat there, I could not help but think that this would be a great summer for our project, Sahtú in the Arts. I was right, for we ended up with a total of eight new murals for the community there. One in particular, the *Legend of Yamoria*, went to the local Chief Albert Wright School.

Another, *How Muskrat Created the World*, as told by Maurice Mendo, made it onto the wall of the new swimming pool, so the children would know their own Dene legends.

> And, of course
>> without really knowing it
>> as dreams will
> the very beginning of
> *From Bear Rock Mountain*

Bobble-headed Me
"She thinks I still care."

The opening refrains of yet another forlorn kill-me-now country song wafted over to my desk from the office radio. And there went my head again, snapping back from the impact of that chugging base and rinky-dink piano, whipping around like one of them inflatable bottom-heavy rubber dolls you get at the county fair. You punch it on the nose, and it sways back to near the floor and comes on back for more!

Such were my summers from 2008 on in the real North, the Sahtú, Great Bear Lake Region. It seemed that the more I loved the place, the sadder the songs on the radio got, as if people for some reason *wanted* to be that one step closer to the musical graveyard of hopes and dreams. Got me to thinking that their dreams couldn't have been all that great to begin with, to have even come this far on a guitar and lonesome voice from down Tennessee way.

One saving grace was that I was actually raised on this kind of music, so there was some kind of comfort to it, if I tried hard enough to stifle the silent tears and grinding of teeth. Made me wonder how I was ever going to dig my *own* way out of this madness.

Short of any grim turns for unknowable depths, one outcome of all of this was a six-by-sixteen-foot *Dene Hand Games* mural for the arena in Tulita.

Truth be told, late August and the time to go back to school in Toronto came just before I went and threw myself mercifully into the arms of Mackenzie River!

Dene in the Arts

Our collective residential school experiences came
in handy.

Even though our original work with Sahtú in the Arts, the cultural lives of the Great Bear Lake Region, came to an abrupt halt during my six university years, all was not lost. When I returned from my first grad school year at York University in Toronto, I was charged with finding a way to continue and expand upon my plan of study in the field, beginning at home in Radelie Koe.

I took a good lesson in not being hasty in just going ahead and starting in on whomever I met and thought might have something for me. First, I took great pains to find out who exactly might best fit the type of questions I wanted answers to. My previous work in the arts of the region had clearly shown that the PTSD evident in our everyday lives could be part of this research and that the elders were the best source for any direction it needed to take.

As for an immediate application, I wanted to, at the very least, do a mural for the new Chief T'Seleie School.

I must say that it took all of the four months I had before returning to my formal Master's of Environmental Studies with some much-needed and relevant material. As part of my studies, I was given the resources from the Prince of Wales Northern Heritage Centre to add to whatever I could get from my annual visits with our southern Dineh Navajo.

Two of the main components, as it turned out, were the parts that each of our separate Dene/Dineh Nations played in the Second World War, whether in the mining of uranium needed for the Manhattan Project, or the heroic Navajo Code Talkers and the use of our language to win back our democratic freedoms.

Each person, in their own way, added their input to what I was doing, often without even being asked to, often not knowing how valuable their say was.

Navajo Code Talkers, the Dineh Kiss of Death

... When b be bear/Shush and r-rabbit/Gah

... Shark/Destroyer and Submarine/Iron Fish

... the staccato Japanese ear must have boggled at snatches of

melodic Navajo sounds over the radio!

After the surprise Japanese Imperial Navy Air Service bombing of Pearl Harbor on December 7, 1941, America simply could not gain a toehold in the Pacific. But just in time, a First World War veteran, Philip Johnson, had an idea based on his fluency of the

Dineh language. As a missionary's son, he grew up among unilingual speakers of the oral Athabaskan tongue.

He knew for sure that with less than fifty *Bilagáana* able to speak it, Navajo would serve as an ideal military code.

The Marine Corps thought it would be worth a try, and twenty-nine Navajo speakers were recruited and trained in this top-secret mission at Camp Pendleton, Oceanside, California, in May 1942.

Early tests revealed that this would work. A half-hour-long transmission was dramatically cut down to a twenty-second message.

After the first marine Navajo Code Talkers got over their sea-sickness on their way to the Pacific Theatre, they were put to an intensive in-field military exercise. As a vital strategic staging area, the Japanese island Iwo Jima had to be taken by the US Armed Forces. The final landing of this largest campaign in the South Pacific followed several months of heavy bombing, which only served to disrupt enemy sleep patterns, the fortifications were so well embedded in volcanic rock.

What followed was five weeks of some of the fiercest and bloodiest fighting in the entire Pacific Theatre during the Second World War, the outnumbered Marine Corps up against thirty thousand Japanese troops firmly dug in, with some eighteen kilometres of underground tunnels, first to face beach defences of twenty-one block houses, ninety-two concrete pillboxes, and thirty-two camouflaged artillery emplacements, ready with machine guns, mortar, and rocket firepower, certainly enough mayhem for the ages!

Between the second and third unanswered amphib-
ious landing
on the forlorn volcanic beachhead at Iwo Jima –

Ere gates to Hades slammed wide open

shimmering scythe-like
samurai blade

soul of sun risen
    poised
in guillotine moments

§

In this magnificent silent sigh
Navajo Holy People
long-called into battle

smiling
ready – Heaven's breath
made supreme weapon

mightier by far
than mere pen or earthly sword

§

From far-off desert sands
faint ... mounting ... echoes

eaglebone whistles

THE ENEMY WAY!

From that "Awful Grace of God," five days of seven kinds of
Hell. This was the only battle in the Pacific in which the marines
lost more men than the enemy, almost nine hundred, including
three Navajo Code Talkers killed in action and one wounded.

Six Code Talkers, at work for two days straight, relayed no less
than eight hundred coded messages without a single error!

This is an astounding achievement, for a group of fresh high-
school recruits from the high desert country of the American

Southwest to the middle of the Pacific Ocean, from dry flatlands to volcanic jungle island, twenty-five square kilometres of rock. These young marines had never been beyond the local trading post and now, fresh off a big transport ship, had to deal with culture shock while huddled on a beach, completely exposed to heavy enemy fire. When they finally advanced farther inland, they had to move every few minutes to avoid radio detection!

Major Howard O'Connor, signal officer for the 5th Marine Division, was moved to say, "Were it not for the Navajos, the marines would have never taken Iwo Jima."

One team the major referred to consisted of Merrill Sandoval, father of my host in Tuba City, Arizona, Gary Sandoval. The other was Thomas Begay, at the time receiving Sandoval's messages aboard a command ship.

High praise, indeed, for a group of high-school sheepherders, one of whom signed on at only seventeen years of age.

The famous Joe Rosenthal photo of the American flag being raised over hard-won Mount Suribachi has Pima Indian war hero Ira Hayes among the soldiers. For all intents, the victory flag at the very southern end of the island of Iwo Jima looked to be an exclamation point!

The last of the original twenty-nine Navajo Code Talkers, Chester Nez, died on June 4, 2014.

Code Talker Home

"You can use anything that's in here. We don't want any stingy people around."

These words, by my host Gary Sandoval, same as my late mum would have said, set the tone for my stays at he and his wife Mary's home, over the twenty plus years I have been going south to our relatives, the Dineh. Especially when my visits were a bit longer, when I was working on this book.

I couldn't have picked a more suitable place to go, either, with much of what I had to say about how Navajo history correlated to our Northern Dene's in terms of uranium and war in general.

His father, Merrill, and Uncle Samuel both served as Code Talkers, marines, in the Second World War, and his son Holyan served overseas in the army.

In terms of family life, what made it especially hard was that the code talkers could not say anything at all about their top-secret mission during their tour of duty. In fact, the military code itself was not officially declassified for almost a quarter of a century after the Second World War ended. With this, President Ronald Reagan pronounced August 14, 1982, "Navajo Code Talkers Day."

Later, Bill Clinton awarded congressional gold medals to the original twenty-nine, and silver medals for all who qualified, for helping save democracy in the West.

If I needed more personal information about the Vietnam War, Gary's next-door neighbours, retired Judge Robert Walters and his wife, Lilly, filled me in on the effects of Agent Orange and the test bombings on Navajo lands.

Medicine Man Abraham Begay, a frequent visitor, and others told of their times in selfless service of the nation.

Tawayatih Got'sehni (Toward Christmas)

> Grandma sits in her little makeshift shelter
> and moosehide tannery
> to all the world in a land of her own making
> as only the elderly can
> She lives in a memory
> of times when her own teachers took her by the hand
> to make her very own first pair of moccasins
> for an older brother now gone.

Lying in peace
in some other part of this vast mountain country
shaded by this very special tin
of a just-lonesome blue.
In a late-September feathery dusting dusk of snow,
every now and again
a light from a distant star
to show the way for a visiting relative ...

Warming their hands
by her special embers of Dene gold
shingh-gireh ...
and older, aromatic willow
like her, on its way
back to *Denendeh,* the Land of the People
but with a final blessing
to clothe the living.

With Cousin Gordon
People at home have always been a People of the land.

Having spent about twenty years away from home in Yellowknife,
it took a while to get back into the rhythm of real Northern life
when I returned to Radelie Koe. One of the things that set our
smaller community apart is the way life is so in tune with the land.
There is a kind of patience you won't find anywhere else.

Most things go by the way of the weather, so there is no need
to rush if things are looking rough outside. At the same time, when
it is too hot in the midday heat, it's best to wait for later, when it
becomes cooler.

What I had in mind to do was continue with my work with the
arts. Aurora College made it a point to allow me the use of their

campus building whenever I found myself in the Sahtú, Great Bear Lake Region, so I got busy once again creating murals with the youth for the community.

Right from the start, my cousin Gordon Kelly and his wife, Clara, got into the habit of dropping in to see what was going on.

Soon after I arrived in the spring of 2012, he suggested a trip on up the Rabbitskin River to its source, near the site of Yamoga Fieh (Yamoga's Rock). This is one of the main traditional landmarks near Radelie Koe.

The story goes all the way back to what an elder and Dene statesman, the late-George Blondin, called "when the world was new." We humans were so much a part of the natural world that we shared a common language with our animal relatives. One of our cultural heroes, Yamoga, "He Who Walks Across the Universe," was also busy making things safe for us. This warrior battled with an evil giant, *Koh Hehdien* (Without Fire), who was so tough he went around, even in winter, without footwear. They fought for half a moon, until Koh Hehdien was turned to the rock that now forms part of Yamoga Fieh.

Our trip up the Rabbitskin was an all-day boat ride, with a good number of musk ox, of all things, along the shore, along with some of your usual bears and ducks, but no moose nor caribou. We don't usually bother those big animals in summer anyway. It's better to wait until they are fatter, in fall.

Times spent with a single person on the land draws you closer together, and it was good to watch a real man of the land in action. He left no sign unnoticed, not an unusual gathering of seagulls nor any strange swirl in the current.

Twilight Mists Tochoney Heights

My very own Navajo teepee sure looked good, just
standing there, her arms reaching for the heavens.

One early evening about four years after I took the Canadian government to court, I was in Arizona for one of the prayer meetings we had agreed to as part of my settlement, my tenth ceremony overall.

We were waiting for more people to come by to sit up with us, the teepee meeting set for Christmas Eve. My Navajo Dineh brother Johnson Tochoney and his wife, Sarah, arranged for the ceremonies and made this teepee, complete with liner and poles all the way from the State of Washington. My very own Navajo teepee sure looked good, just standing there, her arms reaching for the heavens.

As I went out and took down my air-cleaned Siberian-made ribbon shirt from the rack it hung from, I could see that Sarah was still busying herself, as she had been for the past few days, checking on an entire steer cooking in the traditional way, in a pit dug nearby.

Once again, we knelt all night with our sacred Mother Peyote, in solemn prayer for the future. Over the years, I invited a number of people to these ceremonies, including my younger son Lorne, a Dene man, Ronald Antoine, who was having some kind of a problem with his skin, and this time, my adopted son, Sergey Chupin, and another artist, Natalya Yakovleva, all the way from Siberian Russia.

One church member was moved to remark that this was surely the farthest she had ever "seen anyone come for a Native American Church service!" As usual, we had a grand feast, which only my sister Sarah and her daughters knew how to put on, with plenty of food and Christmas gifts for our guests to take with them. Sitting there later, with the grand view of the Western Sacred Mountain, Doko'oosliid, San Francisco Peaks shining in the distance, my thoughts drifted on back, over a seemingly long, long journey, from when I first arrived in Arizona over twenty years before complaining of severe pains in my legs.

Johnson and Sarah Tochoney were some of the first people I met in our southern Dineh homeland on the Great Navajo Reservation. What with a feeling for missing some who were now gone, I knew for sure I would keep returning to this, my second home.

CHAPTER 18

Turning the Page

The shining days . . .

Putting a book together is no simple task, and the writing alone took at least two years, with about the same time to make time for revisions and to add a few extras. There is no doubt that it takes quite a lot to do this, not the least being other people getting involved.

Early on I mentioned to events organizer and my close friend Lynn Feasey that I wanted to check out her artist retreat, Points North, at Mahone Bay, outside of Halifax, Nova Scotia, on the Canadian East Coast. For a number of years before going there, I wanted to start with this book project but could never quite get a handle on how. That is, until I just sat down at her downstairs apartment and started trying to remember my youngest days, way up in the mountains from my home in Radelie Koe.

To this day I don't exactly know what it was, but it must have been that salty air coming in the window from the nearby ocean, ancestral home to us all. The same kind of déjà vu that happens to every artist who finds a muse began to take place within me there and has carried on since.

Lynn also told me of a woman she met named Jan March who told her that she had been at my home so many years ago as a university student way back in the early 1960s! One thing led to another and, as it happened, my mother had been this student's cook when she was doing her research, along with a Japanese linguist named Hiroko Sue Hara, whom many still remember.

Along with various other treasures, including a homemade silk embroidered woman's jacket my mum made, Jan March had quite a collection of old slides, which I had made into digital images. There is one in particular (see photo section) that shows a lady setting an older-style rabbit snare, the kind that uses a trip-stick. Upon being snared, the rabbit is left hanging out of the way of predators.

My Memory Sleeps with Her

"And death's pale flag is not advanced there."

—WILLIAM SHAKESPEARE, *Romeo and Juliet*

When the Sun Dance Man Samuel Shirt first asked me to "make up a feather," I thought it was going to be for him, so I put a special touch to the beaded handle. As it turned out, this item was to be a part of a naming ceremony for me that took place in a sweat lodge we had at the annual spiritual pilgrimage at Desnedhe Che, near Fort Reliance, to visit T'seku Dawedah, Woman Sitting Up There.

He told me that this one white bald eagle tail feather would be my protector over the years, which it was. The "live" tail feather, that is, a feather from a bird still alive and vital, travelled with me all over the world for the following fifteen years or so. Spiritual paraphernalia like this is thought of as a person, and indeed even to the point of the carrier being more like a younger relative, following its guidance.

I made several others like it, one for Dene entertainer Leela Gilday and some others. When I gave one, a special spotted one, to honour my dear friend Nely Atefi at an outdoors ceremony at York University, little did I know that she would pass away in only a few short months from complications of cancer, which she had seemingly conquered at the time.

> How little do we truly know
> of *life's* mysteries.

Back in my second home on the Big Navajo Reservation, I eventually just had the feeling that I needed to replace my old faithful feather, which I now felt to have "tired out." My nephew Thomas helped me.

Back in Toronto in the spring of 2014, three years after her passing, I let dear Nely Joon's aunt know that I wanted to pay my respects at her gravesite. As it turned out, they were going there too for the same purpose, so we made it a part of our prayers there to lay to rest my long-time feather where she slept in peace, close by to a large tree I came to love.

As I was working on this book, my memory wasn't as sharp as it should've been. I was actually thankful that some of it wasn't, to tell you the truth, the rooms not exactly as the Lord would prepare, for *anyone*.

> But others, like looking for that favourite ol' worn-out football T-shirt
> make you feel real human, and nowhere to be found . . .
>
> Leaving you all the way back there
> standing, alone, in a dark closet
> all night long . . .
>   for daring
> to be Dene
>
>   . . . and this PTSD, like a faulty random select . . . simply
> picking other extremes . . . wincing in pain, with each

hand-whack of the dreaded brush, for speaking my
own language.

(And without that changing
without the blocked-out WHY
    in morning light
we are all
still back there.)

Within this enclosing vacuum we are left to wonder: is the not
knowing worth the weight of what we are missing?

Again, I am reminded of having to put down Dee Brown's *Bury
My Heart at Wounded Knee: An Indian History of the American West*,
from painful association, yes, but also with disbelief that I had
been lied to *so* badly.

In our arrogance, we assume that an atheist, for instance, has
no faith, period. We are left with our limited sense of the real,
guided by a flashlight with an ever-dimming battery.

In all of this reverie and confusion, when I asked a Navajo
Vietnam vet and Dineh Medicine Man to do a cedar ceremony
about it, one of the things he found was that the feather I had
dedicated to dear Nely Joon's memory should have been laid to
rest elsewhere, on higher ground, at least.

We all have this tendency to want to change the past
as simply as you would
turn to a favourite
passage
in a book.

Either way I am still one of the very lucky.
My memory sleeps with her
thy
Heavenly handmaiden ...

like Dante's eternal, unrequited allegory...
forever turning
in refracted
lunar light
just below
Earthbound waves
to catch the wayward
adrift...

Ponder ye, sole heir to sombre thought; in life we tend to want for the best parts, that of Romeo and Juliet exchanging longing glances, glowing phrases over moonlit balcony and brambles, little knowing that reality is more like when the true lovers meet in Juliet's supposed tomb, Romeo's soliloquy, Act IV, Scene III:

O my love, my wife! Death, that hath suck'd the honey of thy breath, Hath no power yet upon thy beauty; Thou art not conquer'd; beauty's ensign yet is crimson in thy lips and in thy cheeks. And death's pale flag is not advanced there.

§

... E'en this half-decade later
she still in dreamtime reigns

joyous and oh so resplendent!
in longed-for paradise

Yet not intended
to my own
frail human longings.

How thin, really

some

ties in our minds
to bind.

Yet somehow stronger
for nets
we mend.

How strange, too, that dear Nely Joon's gravesite at Richmond Hills would be all that is left of my rebirth. Well, maybe not *all*. It would truly seem, as the Japanese practice, a broken vessel, once cracked and broken, mended with molten gold, takes on a special sheen hence.

One of Creator's twists of fate is that we are left and led back to the concept and meaning of ceremony, how stripped of all seeming worth, a naked need for a simpler approach fills an emptied spirit.

The way ceremony has always been intended to have its own memory reminds me of when I would always make it a point to stop in Calgary on my way to and from my beloved Arizona. There was a Blood Indian from Standoff, Alberta, by the name of Keith Chiefmoon who worked at the Indian Friendship Centre there. He had this fine-ground flat cedar that he used when he ran sweat lodge ceremonies. Being an appreciator of the finer things, it goes without saying I was very taken by that powdered cedar. I still do my ceremony that same way today, sprinkling that fine powder, mixed in with bear root and that fungus from the diamond willow.

Which was also the essence of the rare ones
    like Nely Atefi
for my wounded spirit

Embracing alchemy.
From simple vessel
to beauty way . . .

Take this memory
an echo . . . your recurring dream

ever closer

warmer
to polished touch.

Mirrored Light

He sat there railing about this and that.

Although it becomes easier to be considered an equal, as an adult
it is still considered impolite to interrupt an elder. As a part of
needing some help with his finances, my father wanted to talk
about things that were going on around town. He knew that, as
a writer for *News/North,* the weekly paper out of Yellowknife, I
could influence change.

And this rare visit was also somewhat personal, with him
maybe wanting to apologize for having been so headstrong about
every single thing in the past, I would suppose, that is without
actually just coming out and saying so.

Our Dene elders are often hard to read, and probably for
their own reasons. Out on the land, for instance, a firm hand can
ensure survival.

But here in town, and as full-grown men, if there was a peril,
we had learned to at least put it off as, well . . . life. He had been
our chief for twenty-five years, several lifetimes, as that one
position went, so he was used to having people hang on to his
every word. Except for the fact that those days were now far in

the past, and, at his age, he was now needy and not in any kind of command.

So for the time being, he would just have to be satisfied that someone was willing to listen to him going on about some meaningless paper problem. And be content to affirm that, yes, "I'm still talking here!"

As for myself, after a lifetime of heartbreak at his hand, I just had to take whatever I could, as a family member, of his being just too proud, even in the face of growing old alone. So the part of him sitting there mouthing words about this and that did have a sense of the comical. You outgrow it, so you can recognize it right off, like watching some old black and white.

This film noir, dark comedy had an ironic twist
stage set, such as it was
behind windows shaded from the glare of the midnight sun
. . .

Anyone yelling "Cut!" would have not hope
of any dimmed lights

All the funny asides
nothing between people, really, ever happens just to one
it has to be me, too . . .

Putting together a book about residential school experiences is like that, trying to describe a foreign land, your own feelings are like that, somewhere you haven't been before, but need to go to, in order to live.

Like anything else
it comes with practice
and will surely follow
with more polished

works
sometime along the way

Besides, that kind of history of personal hurt, the intergenerational residential school trauma, can only be met by compassion, a willingness to admit that we can only do so much at a time, as true human beings.

... and sadly, just too much of it should have happened
decades ago now
when it mattered.

Yet again, through
this dark

the mirror
always there

not able
to show the light
until peace ... settled

within

I have always made it a point to let my two sons, Luke and Lorne, know that, within reason, I will *always* be proud of whatever they choose to do with their lives.

So, without even knowing it, they have already succeeded.

... for we survivors
no matter how
l o n g
it takes

to get
to the light

the faith
in the spectrum
is

always

here
and

trusting
the now

Her Turquoise Smile

Through misted cloud
past summer's blue

her face I see
in glacial mountain pool
distant ... warmly a-beam

§

There with her
all memories mine red

slowly now
blossoming human

back, back, she flows
through wishing moons

§

Followed I
her play-filled light
reflected
off grasslands forever green

to predawn goba

§

In buried chests
of chanced gold

midst emerald greens
where even now

she gently smooths
all jagged pasts

leaving just enough

§

'Til evening again
heralds
sightless DAWNING

Warmth

... from any wood stove

relatives from Spirit World
come back
for company

sometimes urgent   in winter
hunting   ravens falling in play   hinting
   drumming in the future

   glowing coals
in teepee ceremony
gratefully accept offered cedar
   forge me wings

Evenings relaxed
comforting

and once in a lone and wistful moon
like the music of Chopin

forever missing

a past just sometimes

here

and now

Eagle Arrow

It could be anything from an ant to a rock or a bird . . .

The old-time Indians always thought of ways to live with Mother Earth. Being that close to nature had its way of giving the People some good teachings, about how to care for one's self, family, and tribe.

A young man just reaching puberty would be expected to go out on the land, usually to a high hill or mountain, to pray, fast, and hopefully receive a spirit helper to show the way to a long and successful life, much in the same way our Inuit relatives have their familiars.

Tom Crane Bear, elder-in-residence at the Banff Centre for the Arts, was kind enough to honour me with a Blackfoot name, meaning Wolf Pack Leader in English. It was especially meaningful having been granted at a storytelling gathering for the youth of Banff and area, while I was there for a two-month writing and painting residency for this book.

In times past, such an honour would involve an especially treasured horse or bow and quiver of arrows, but Old Tom was happy with the beaded eagle tail feather I passed along to him. Suga Pi (thank you).

Over the years I have been honoured with quite a number of First Nations names, including:

> Beleh Fehwedah: Tom Crane Bear bestowed it at a storytelling session, mentioning that as an artist and writer I was leading my Dene People forward.

> Dene Bezieh Raseh: Given by my sister Lucy Ann, to do with all of my adventurous worldly travels.

> Dene Radegoh: Given by elder Edward Kelly, whom I call the same. Funny how that happened!

> Xai Toreht'eh Godene (Man for All Seasons): Given by fellow K'asho Gotine tribesman Jimmy Caesar for being an all-around guy, I would suppose.

> Adzarewegoh: Bestowed after a famed Déline man of the same name.

> Sheyaho Diyin: Given by Cree Sun Dance Man Samuel Shirt, for being more spirit than man.

> Wahtindeh Wozha [*Tlicho*]: Given by the Dogrib, after my father's leadership ways.

Bebah Dweleh [*Chipewyan*]: By elder Jonas Catholique for my enterprising manner.

Seleh Beyawh: By famed K'asho Gotine storyteller and medicine man Louis Caesar, for his lifetime kinship with my father.

Shehoyieh (Shares My Name): By K'asho Gotine elder Antoine Abelon.

Shizhuu (My Son) [*Gwich'in*]: By elder and my adopted mother, Eunice Mitchell, a term of deep affection.

Fiehk'u Dih (Four Guns): By Siberian Russian relatives in the Altai Mountains, near the Mongolian border.

Waga Fihaht'ih (Slow Eagle): By a Siberian Russian shaman, Wesha.

T'sekugho Ehnst'eh (Moose for Women): From Cree elder Earl Arkinson, for a close manner with the ladies.

Muktuk Inuk (Muktuk Man): By Iqaluit carver Jerry Ell.

Awech'ile Beyah: By Uncle Thomas Manuel.

Fot'ineh Yatih Sheleku and Lesalda T'sareh: By Alfred Bellargeon of Somba Koe.

Afereh Zohileh: By Judy Kochon.

Mahe Beshile: By elders in Radelie Koe.

Shi Yazhi: By my grandmother on the Navajo Reservation.

Ridih Sho (Big Medicine): By Gary Sandoval.

As happened in times past, others find it easier to see who and what you are and just go ahead and bestow you with a good, strong name, like the one from my dearly departed adopted Gwich'in mother, Eunice Mitchell of Fort McPherson, well-known for her insistence on Dene language and culture. With these traditions in mind, I have made it a point to leave out the English translation for some of these, so that you as a reader will at least make an effort to learn of our Dene language.

D'sineh Ek'oneh (Morning Song)

Whilst Mother Moon
sits aloft
her knighted throne

Yahkaleh Weh, Morning Star
in starry crown

§

In suspending still

spirit circle dissolves

dreamy fireflies alight
on gossamer Haydn

Ancestral trees
and rose bushes
trumpet in
this new day

Choral eyes
awaken

CHAPTER 19

Dene Spring!

My buddy Gene Rabisca used to talk about this time of
year, with the air just getting a new bite to it.

"It's that Dene Spring," my buddy Gene would say. "You can't help
but notice how the air is crisper, cleaner, as if them moose are just
starting to wake up, geese coming through. Water at the nets got
that chill. Same way for us Indians, y'know. We have a new spring
in our step, like walking in that mountain moss. Because we were
born for this Northern winter!"

I spent some time with him, his wife Camilla, and their children.
Sadly, he passed away a few years ago.

§§§

Life here in Radelie Koe doesn't seem to be the same, especially
when our people get together for community events down on the
ol' baseball field, where Gene would always have a tent set up the
same perfect way as out on the land and we would get to teasing
each other.

The summer of 2015 saw more than its share of rain in the
Sahtú. That fall, I would finally make good on my bid to do a
Ph.D., this time in faraway Peterborough, Ontario. I started on
this personal road to help encourage our northern youth to stay
in school.

You have to take life in a small northern town the way it happens. With a residential school past, I have to set goals though surrounded by a large dysfunctional family. An uncle who nonchalantly asks where my home is, although it's been right here for quite a number of years now, although I'm away from the North a good part of every year.

An aunt who suggests I should have just stayed farther north, in Inuvik, home to the Great Northern Arts Festival I've gone to for several years now. They know little of the number of artists' choice awards I've won.

> From a healthy, vibrant People
> we have become
> dysfunctional
> in a very nonchalant way
>   or is it just another mask
> to help
>
> us survive?

I let her know she will have to call me doctor when I have my Ph.D., when it becomes the way she also wants it for her grandchildren.

With a home of my own not hooked up for power, I am always scrambling for a place to live. It doesn't help that my place is all but crowded out by original paintings stacked in every corner, fighting for space with all manner of hunting gear and long-forgotten papers, books, and stashes of Italian espresso.

This time, I'm in Band Council housing, a two-storey place, thanks to the kindness of Chief Wilfred McNeely Jr. The water pipes come alive all hours of the night. There's no phone, but there is satellite TV, which cuts out for the bad weather.

In a changing world, it's still possible to have a freezer full of fish and meat, the way we always did, food right from the bounty of Denendeh, our Dene Nation.

Another uncle who's spent the entire summer
building over sixty new cribs
for our relatives sleeping
at the graveyard

Michael and my sister Judy headed out to their fish camp, to make giant coney dry fish.

And somehow, out of the half-forgotten autumn mists arise these comforting memories of Gene from those many centuries past, it seems. I can feel a hint of them freezing Northern eighty-below winds whipping our faces as we bravely travelled back out almost 160 kilometres to check on his traps and family tent.

To rested mind, too, the sudden return of
another glorious
Dene Spring!

Our Missing and Murdered Women

"It isn't really high on our radar, to be honest."[12]

—STEPHEN HARPER

These were the words uttered by Canada's callously apathetic former prime minister, a man who, with a simple executive directive, could have ordered an official inquiry into our missing and murdered First Nations women in Canada. Instead these words reveal him to be both a racist and misogynist.

The RCMP data indicate that almost twelve hundred of our sisters, aunts, and mothers joined in the dismal ranks of those unaccounted for. The Native Women's Association of Canada puts the number much higher: over four thousand between 1980 and 2012.

To simply shunt the issue aside as just a "criminal matter" for the police to investigate is no less than a dereliction of the official duty Harper was elected for, bordering on criminal negligence.

The Medicine Wheel teaches us that the better part of our world, the family and community, is in the direct charge of our women, so when they are affected in any harmful way, the children, men, and grandparents soon feel it.

According to Statistics Canada's 2016 *Household Survey*, Aboriginal people represent 4.9 percent of the Canadian population. However, the RCMP data indicates that Aboriginal women are murdered at roughly four and a half times the rate of non-Aboriginal Canadian women. Yet Harper offered a steadfast zero percent in terms of concern and action on the matter.

What makes this especially offensive and frustrating is that he was the only person who could make any kind of concerted move. Other than to do it ourselves, that is—as with the handful of women who courageously began Idle No More, a movement to bring about awareness.

Women in such acts of defiance are nothing new to our First Nations, although a kind of resignation has set in, mainly for the lack of official response to our needs. Among matriarchal societies, the Navajo and Mohawk, for instance, the grandmothers are the ruling law of order.

> The rayuka represent those of our relatives gone too soon
> before their time . . .
> They are neither to the heavens proper nor here with
> us still.
>   And in this case leaving us no trail
> except a bittersweet memory
> *life* itself, though, always has the last say . . .

As with another painting I did with these rayuka in mind, an image appeared again, in this one, a young girl, very likely the spirit of one of our missing and murdered sisters. Then, almost two years ago now, it was the exact image of one of my nieces, who earlier that very morning was brutally beaten to death with a length of two-by-four right on the main road of Radelie Koe, over two mickeys of vodka.

When these relatives do turn up, they are in the last place you would look to find the younger victims: buried beside their grandparents in a lonely corner of the local cemetery, never to be seen here on Mother Earth again.

> Rest in peace, relatives
> until the real dawning
> of an untroubled forever

Hearts in the Mud

> "It is only when the hearts of the women are in the mud that the People are destroyed."
>
> —CHIEF DULL KNIFE/MORNING STAR (1810–83)

In this day of missing and murdered First Nations women, it is hard to remember a time when we were truly free to live and thrive. Even then, after the famous Battle of the Little Bighorn, the Lakota and their Cheyenne allies were hard-pressed to continue their ancestral lifestyle any longer, if at all.

Morning Star was one of the leaders who signed the Treaty of Fort Laramie in 1868, with the understanding that they were now secure for the future, for "as long as the rivers ran and the grass grew."

The Americans did not uphold the Treaty of Fort Laramie, which led to the totally devastating Dull Knife Fight. The northern Cheyenne were taken all the way down to Indian Territory in Oklahoma where, unaccustomed to the foreign and dry wastes of land, they became easy prey to disease and starvation.

Travelling from September 9 to the end of October through Kansas and Nebraska and caught at the notorious Fort Robinson, Nebraska, Dull Knife and Little Wolf made two valiant attempts to at the very least die in their northern birth land.

It is thanks in no small measure to them that their People now have a home at the Northern Cheyenne Reservation, which is also home to Chief Dull Knife College, named in honour of a great and determined leader.

A Meaning through the Suffering

As Buddha would have it, we are born to suffering.

Jewish author, psychologist, and neurologist Viktor E. Frankl perhaps sheds the clearest light on the quest for life, from his own harrowing experiences surviving three years in the Auschwitz death camp.

Whilst watching all around him die from simple lack of hope, the meaning Frankl held on to was getting back together with his wife.

As a survivor of twelve years of residential school, Canada's failed attempt at cultural genocide, I must confess that there was no real conscious and dramatic decision to someday see home again. We did have our annual respite from the especially hated places like the infamous Grollier Hall in Inuvik. I did, though, choose to shut myself down emotionally at twelve, less a solution and more a personal way of dealing with the madness. For all the immediate comfort this gave, I was to pay for it later by not being able to trust anyone to get close, at all.

Yet I do recall making conscious attempts to at least get out of the place as often as possible, and even going so far as going out in minus-forty-degree wintry cold to practise with the cross-country ski team.

I simply learned to channel all the energy it would've taken to hate the place forever and at least do well in one thing at a time, skiing and other sports now, some writing . . . to eventually find out, for myself, this meaning Frankl alludes to:

> The real meaning, though
> no doubt came from hundreds of years
> of Europe and Western society trying to wipe
> us Indians off the face
> of Mother Earth.
>
> A People
> who are of the Earth itself
> in a real way
> are immortal.
>
> And will not bound
> by mere hope
> a future, like we
>
> still   not going anywhere else soon
> if ever.
>
> Something in that spark, in the glowing ashes
> simply hung on,
> over ancient, unforgiving nights
> into tomorrow.

One sure and misinformed connection was that institutions like the Roman Catholic Church, hired by a genocidal Canadian government to subdue us Indians, outright threatened our People with eternal damnation: an indelible scar borne through generations brainwashed to the point of denial.

The reward?

Some eternal bliss
for a few short years
of pain and loss

at the hands of
social psychopaths.

One Final Evil

There is at least one line not to be crossed at all.

Throughout *From Bear Rock Mountain* I've made parallels between our residential school experiences and those of the victims of the Nazi Holocaust.

The 2012 movie *Hannah Arendt* explores the life of the German-born Jewish philosopher and political theorist and how her writings about the trial of Nazi Adolf Eichmann revealed a then unthought-of human condition: "the banality of evil." *Shoah* is another production, a nine-and-a-half-hour look, in agonizing real time, into the calamity of these mass murders.

Following his 1961 capture in South America, Eichmann was brought to justice to stand trial for his major part in crimes against humanity. Writing for the *New Yorker*, Hannah Arendt stirred up a storm of controversy that had to do with her initial impression of the man on trial, Adolf Eichmann, who in no way impressed her as anything but ordinary, to the point of being mediocre, and was certainly not the devil he was portrayed as.

Facing the Allied Tribunal, Eichmann adamantly averred that he was simply a cog in the machine, just doing his job.

In philosophical terms, Arendt also saw through his official status within the Nazi's Third Reich to reveal how it was the man, the person, and not any system nor ideology that was being brought to justice. Up to then there had been no legal precedence for such a situation.

Her argument for the "banality of evil" led to personal attacks by colleagues and friends, claiming that, as a Jew, she was defending the wrong side.

One would simply have to suspect that, like colonialism, this new and potentially virulent form of banal evil is, by its insidious nature, one that can provide both the perfect practical and legal screen. How, for instance, would one take a robot or other non-human entities, like corporations, or even a church, to task for wrongs done?

Sadly, in such a philosophical vacuum, a lack of belief would be the ideal, if not the ultimate, goal. Which explains the religious order at the core of the residential schools.

For instance, except for the uniform bad breath and smell of human neglect, there was nothing out of the ordinary about the priests and nuns who took knowing and willing part in the cultural genocide of our Indigenous Peoples.

A final and chilling note is that, for the most part, when their lifetime of commitment and unquestioned service to the church was done, they just faded off into obscurity, to retirement homes, like cows to pasture. It should be noticed too that, unlike the war criminal Adolf Eichmann, none but a handful of war criminals were ever brought to justice.

Behind the Midnight Sun

Memory has me retracing the steps Grandpa spoke of
the ones you made so long ago
take you on home.

As children in the summer months of July and August, we travelled to various fish camps along the Duhogah, its sun-baked muddy shores a reminder of humble roots, its lazy waters drifting slowly off to distant Arctic shores, even on past the residential schools.

Whether we were at K'afohun, Willow Point, K'ohoyieh, Under the Clouds, or Warih Daghun, just for those few short weeks away from the clinging madness of Grollier Hall, we were worlds apart from the outside, what we all called everything but Radelie Koe.

Once our chores of hauling wood and water or cutting fish were done, the shoreline world was a big playground, the majestic cliffs of the Ramparts a dramatic backdrop to every kind of adventure. And as Grandpa Peter Mountain wisely knew, the land out there along the river was the only place where I didn't want to be anywhere else. It wasn't until we were living in town that I would just sit on the bank for hours, watching the waters go by.

On the land there was something very different about this time of year, with that *sun* always up there, a yearly reminder that some things, like simple family life, the People, would always be there.

We did
　　of course
miss the times when we were most expected to learn our
Dene ways
The Hunting and Sewing Moons
　　fall and winter

but for now
as now

this book, too
From Bear Rock Mountain
brings us all the way back to try to pick up the pieces

as best we can . . .

from its home
secret home

Life is somehow so full of new beginnings

to find
what's behind

that ol' midnight sun

Teachings of the Medicine Wheel Paradigm

The Medicine Wheel is an all-encompassing circle that can not only explain the world we know but, because of its overall structure and meaning, also gives us a realistic picture of times past, present, and future, so that we might live in a meaningful way.

I/EAST — THEORY/KNOWLEDGE SYSTEMS

"Indians and Indian lands" became a Canadian federal government responsibility under the British North America Act in the year 1867, what Canadians like to call the year of Confederation or the birth of this country. Yet we as First Nations were already here for thirty thousand years or more. In terms of ratios, we were dealing with a civilization who could be compared to a child of five years old.

By 1883, the Department of Indian Affairs policy on First Nations education would focus on the residential schools as the primary vehicle for civilization and assimilation.

All of European society in effect is geared to the needs of the individual, basically meaning property. Even our withering Bill of Rights reflects this divide between rich and poor. On the other hand, our First Nations is all about the group and its survival throughout the ages. Still, as an artist, I often had to leave home in order to make a living, which also meant trying to get by in a world foreign to my nature. This kind of isolation served to challenge both my own nature and a foreign European society, while also putting me at odds with them.

ii/south — historical events

The Massacre of Wounded Knee in 1890 firmly demonstrated the difference between the First Nations and European presence here in America; hundreds of innocent people were mercilessly killed for simply being Indians. Part of our new awareness began with Wounded Knee ii, the takeover of the original site in 1973.

Although the last residential school closed in the mid-nineties, the effects have lingered on by creating an inward kind of loathing among survivors, with many ending up in jail or dead.

Staying alive also meant learning as much of the real history of our Peoples as possible and doing your part to turn some of it around for future generations. Of course, it was not always pretty, but it's our story, nevertheless.

In Canada, the Oka Crisis in the summer of 1990 pointed to some deep and drastic divides, with some notable attempts to work things out.

The Residential Schools Public Apology of 2008 had the potential to ease some of these official wrongs, but for the most part, it was not followed up on.

Idle No More sought, in part, to address the drastic figure of over twelve hundred missing and murdered Aboriginal women.

Canada finally adopted the United Nations Declaration on the Rights of Indigenous Peoples in May 2016. But it hasn't yet been incorporated into law, and we have a long way to go just to be on equal speaking terms, much less find some solutions. Is it too soon to ask why we can't seem to come upon any answers?

The great Lakota leader Chief Sitting Bull, who was killed only two weeks before Wounded Knee, may have said it best:

"Let us put our minds together and see what life we can make for our children."

III/WEST — PERSONAL/COMMUNITY

We each have our own stories to tell, mine as a survivor of the ill-fated residential schools.

Even before that, I was saved from certain death by exposure from being left out in the cold Arctic snows. And were that not enough, I had a serious bout of tuberculosis, which at the time was decimating my Dene People. Life can also be seen as a test of character, and our free will. There are times of crisis, when you as a person have to make a decision whether to stand as a human being or live a lie. Our elders speak of this as the "Parts we don't want anyone to know about; that one single moment we want to forget and just go on with our lives."

Yet we all have to live with ourselves, like it or not. In *Bury My Heart at Wounded Knee* Nez Perce Chief Joseph speaks of the power of a few simple words and how one must commit to living in an honest manner:

> "Let me be a free man;
> Free to travel, free to stop,
> Free to work, free to trade where I choose,
> Free to choose my own teachers,
> Free to follow the religion of my fathers,
> Free to trade and think and act for myself,
> And I will obey every law or submit to the penalty."

Far from stubbornly insisting on an impossible past, he was talking about accepting the present with human dignity intact.

For all of it the doctor said, "This man died of a broken heart."

Out of the puzzle my own life had become, the Native American Church found me (as well as countless other First Nations survivors of a colonialist attempt at cultural genocide), at a critical moment, bringing me back to a place within the sacred circle.

When I finally washed up on the shores of the Great Navajo Reservation in Arizona, I had just quit drinking, and I walked with a painful limp from getting, as it turned out, on the wrong side of Bear Spirit. It took a number of years, but eventually I learned to regain my confidence and started to represent my Dene People throughout the world.

As our First Nations elders are fond of saying, "Everything happens for a reason." Taken in terms of the Medicine Wheel paradigm, I would have to say that all things have their way of coming around. It would, though, be a mistake to blame events as they unfold.

For his part, Christopher Columbus washed up on the shores of this Great Turtle Island. The stage was set for the major conflicts that brought us to where we are now. In its essence, any paradigm involves the inevitable acceptance of change, thus the Medicine Wheel shows more spiritual steps on our journey to a greater cause.

As Black Elk said:

"Everything the Power of the World does is in
a circle.
The sky is round, and I have heard that
the earth is round, like a ball, and so are all the stars.

The wind, in its greatest power whirls.
Birds make their nests in circles for theirs is the
same religion as ours.

The sun comes forth again in a circle.
The moon does the same and both are round.

Even the seasons form a great circle in
their changing,
and always come back again to where they came.
The life of a man is a circle also from childhood
to childhood,
so it is everything where power moves.
Our teepees were round like the nest of birds,
and these were always set in a circle, the
nation's hoop.

There is no power in a square."

I must admit that, when I moved back home to Radelie Koe in 2008, I felt some dismay. Several big buildings, including the old band hall complex and others, were burned down by the youth; we were definitely in the grip of some serious intergenerational residential school trauma. Meetings were held and the adults agreed to make an attempt to include young people in local activities. Over the years, things began to change, and now I have committed to do my Ph.D. in Indigenous studies entirely with this goal of reaching out to the younger generation at the core of its focus.

Among other issues, I am focusing on a central and all-encompassing one: resurgence. In Radelie Koe, none other than firebrand Cara Manuel, who also runs the drop-in centre, is spearheading it. The main idea is to find ways to help the youth reclaim their Dene identity and encourage steps they themselves are taking toward leadership.

With all this I have to keep in mind the words of my grandfather Peter Mountain Sr.:

"Grandson, in this lifetime you will make
many trails,
more than you will ever be able to recall ...
but one day you will come upon a set of footprints
you will not recognize.

Those are the ones you made
when you first set out as a child ...

They will take you the rest of the way home."

Never-Never Land

Spirit Stone Child awakens . . .

I have made specific reference to how each and every return to
the North from my travels left me living feeling like one of those
stand-up inflatable toys, the one with the leaded bottom, which
when punched in the nose, drops, then bounces back, only to offer
itself to another of them punches.

American Indian activist John Trudell talks about how
Christianity makes it a point to keep our Indigenous world in its
lap, just as an adult would a child, with threats of the bogeyman
(Satan) waiting to cast all and sundry into a dreaded hell. A telling
point he makes is that even if we become born-again Christians,
we still remain children, forever in debt to the very people who
take our traditional beliefs away from us.

All of this religious sleight-of-hand is not really all that hard to
see through. The one requirement is that you be a thinking person.
Any church depends on an uneducated mass, preferably one with
land that can be willingly transferred at no cost. It is no wonder
that this Roman Catholic Church is easily one of the single richest
organizations in the world!

In this case, the idea is that the People's reward for believing and following along the dogmatic fairy tale—with a Bible to fill in as *the* word of God—is to be granted entry into the magical kingdom of "heaven" somewhere up there in the clouds, playing a harp and having a jolly ol' time of it!

To get there, you have to suppress all of your Earthly, human desires, and confess your sins to a bachelor priest who also gives marital advice. The idea, too, is that none of this cock and bull story ever changes, as long as you are willing to enslave yourself, blindly following along, and take the time to pass on the "good news" to your neighbours and kill anyone who says any different.

To our credit, though, as Dene, we have resisted the ultimate goal of the church, which has so far failed to produce a single priest or nun in the North. In that one way, at least, we have managed to hold true to the Legend of Yamoria and remained Dene.

Whatever my personal feelings, though, on the community level, I have made it one of my lifelong commitments to always be there for young people; my doctorate research explores ways to help them realize their Dene identity and the value of our culture. One of the things you have to deal with is working in a virtual vacuum, with only a very basic belief in your goals and traditions to draw from. One of the saddest notes of this is a very real and enforced suspended animation from without, which only has one purpose: to keep us from ever again planting our feet back on native land, with self-serving government programs like reconciliation as an opiate.

I had an inkling of this as a child, and it has been verified as a fact of life over my many years, so I can think back now as a full-grown human being with, at the very least, the satisfaction of being able to look myself in the mirror without regret. Yet, I am a part of our Dene family, too, and as such have no choice but to feel our collective pain, if not a groundless guilt.

All emotions aside though
there is hope
no doubt . . .
Life itself,
and the future,
have a mind of their own.

After having completed my first year of a Ph.D. in Indigenous studies, I returned home to Radelie Koe preparing for a genuine Dene Resurging Conference to be led by Cara Manuel. One enduring feature was an address by former Chief Frank T'Seleie, he who called a top oil company president a "modern-day General Custer"!

It could also very well be that even our own parents have a hard time recognizing our new way of life, and as my late uncle Charlie Tobac used to say, "We are living in grief for our life on the land."

Along with it all, a very real barrier remains: we have somehow been made to feel—even embrace—that there will never come a day when we awaken to our own true nature and cast aside the yoke of faith and belief, in a real resurgence, a return to our beloved Denendeh.

So, for the most part, this Never-Never Land has us in
its grip
existing in a kind of vacuum of fear-instilled ignorance
now of our own making.

Yet again, the road, or ride
to Fieh Tehni-ah, Bear Rock Mountain
forever beckons.

Sa Ra-ahyile

The sun that never sets.

These are the dream days of summer, when a good six weeks will go by without any night. One tries to adjust and find the time to sleep, but it also brings back memories.

We were finally let out of residential school after a long, cold winter in a foreign land far to the north, and now had the time of our lives out on the land by our beloved Duhogah, the Big River, at fish camp.

Whoever thought up these residential schools really knew what they were doing in terms of cultural genocide, taking the Dene out of the child, depleting the future generation.

There was a lot of work to do, of course, with fish to clean every day and all of the other chores involved with life on the land. But the real lessons we needed to learn to be Dene began in the fall, when the air became clear and people got ready to be out on the real land, the way our ancestors did.

Missing out on that, we simply were no longer there when the hunting began, when the young men prove themselves as providers. Nor were girls taught the tasks involved in tanning hides and doing everything else, making clothing and other essential items.

Over time, even our parents ended up blaming us, the victims, for not being able to do these things. Many of the youth were no longer even taken out on the land when away from school. In its turn, and according to plan, the government and church simply sat back, smiling.

> When you really start to think of it
> Sa Ra-ahyile, the midnight sun
> was a paradox and a metaphor
> for what was stolen from us, as Dene.

What we now need is a waking dream, to ensure our youth never have to go through these same traumas.

Kintsugi Gold

I went to a talk by Max Eisen, an elderly Holocaust survivor, at Trent University.

Andrew Hammond and I arrived late, so there was no room in the theatre where he was speaking. We found seats in one of the classrooms, with a large video screen. As it turned out, the way this precious man's pain-filled experiences came through—even over an at-times-garbled e-transmission—bridged the traumatic ages.

Andrew's own interest had to do with an aunt who had gone through the same experience.

The presentation from the former Jewish prisoner, full of detailed condemnations, was long and meticulous, rendered with so much compassion that nary a soul made the slightest movement in the entire audience.

In the detailed recollection of times now almost seventy-five years in the past, the scene was set when, at just fifteen, the young forced labourer was viciously hit on the head by a guard with a rifle. He was granted a folk remedy, a torn piece of his clothing, pissed on, and applied to stem the steady flow of blood. He was told that the surgery building he was taken to, Barrack 21, was invariably the "last stop," before almost all patients were summarily hauled off to the gas chambers, joining millions in human smoke, trailing off to Shoah.

Just from the smell of human flesh everywhere, all knew for certain there was no return.

My déjà vu set in as he told us how his job became to keep the operating room spotlessly clean; he was only fifteen at the time. I recalled having won a Best Clean-Up Boy Award in the residential school, for always being so neat and tidy—doing that extra best.

In clearest light, the present room seemed to all but disappear. The Auschwitz prisoner stood before me, prescient, towel in hand. Were we indeed of the same flesh and blood?

The rest of the long evening presentation echoes in a blur. Not forgotten, mind you, but as a mere footnote to the one defining moment, which still stands out, past his seventy-four years and my fifty-four, to when we were right there.

I also specifically remember him making a point to vividly recall the demonic lengths his Nazi captors went to recover even the gold teeth from their human prey, leaving not a trace of value, human nor otherwise, to chance.

Yet this happed destiny is what speaks the loudest of all.

In a parallel universe
you can only hope for half of self

déjà vu reveals the truer
fated road.
where possible meets Moment.

There is a kind of magic happens
where we Live
to reunite human with divine.

The Japanese have a practice, kintsugi, of repairing damaged goods, cups and such, with gold. The idea, much like our Indigenous ceremonials, is not so much to replace but to fix the part of you that has been broken and save some part of its past.

Beauty in the damaged.

This especial reality, even in casual, dreamlike memory, finds its way to mend, yes, and to heal.

Carry-On Song

My younger brother Lawrence is never more at home than at the wheel of a Chevy truck, "jes' rollin'" down the highway, blaring out some country tune in his untrained voice. Then again, there is no one I know who is more in tune with his Navajo ways.

His kind of talk takes you all the way back to a time when our People needed any kind of help just to survive the reservation years, after the Indian Wars. The books say what they will, but ol' Lawrence Curtis knows that the Native American Church, for instance, began with our Dineh People, the Lipan Apache, to be precise.

> "There were always ceremonials, all the way back to the start. One was the blessing way, one of the first and most important of 'em. It had four songs in there."

> [He sings one that turns out to be the same song that starts off each Native American Church all-night prayer service.]

> "Then the Midnight Water Song."

> [He sings again. This song is the same one used by the Roadman to announce a water break in dead of night, when you can go on out to stretch your legs some.]

> "An' in the early morning, just as the sun comes up, Morning Water Song. One sounds like saying 'Johnny Wayne, Johnny Wayne . . . ahaha Hohoho!'"

> "Finally we have that one, Closing Song, or Carry-On Song, the last one us Roadmen sing to close off the ceremony, and there you have it, brother. We Dineh started and ended it all to help the People."

So strange in its own way, travelling with my brother, and even being called "twins" by everyone in the Navajo Nation, thinking back to the twins of our Dene/Dineh legends, in search of their Father Sun.

Just being with Lawrence has always been a transcendent experience, as if he is a living embodiment of what Dene statesman George Barnaby talks about, how it is a leader's job to "remind people of their responsibility." In our case the stories and legends are written right on Bear Rock Mountain, the elders saying that as long as we "Remember these stories, we will have no problem remaining Dene/Dineh." Our very identities are written for us for the future, the land being a direct connection to our real selves.

What better way to close off this book about my life and times, than with a word for the future generation, dedicated to those yet unborn?

Coming to the end of a major statement like this one is like working on a painting, or any work of art, really, planning for a newer or more personal version of what has been set down before, and eventually getting to the end—the most fun part—adding what you want, making the words first sparkle and gleam in divine light, like Michelangelo's *Pietà*, then *sing* right off the page, without the added weight, mind you, of posturing or embellishment. Well, maybe a bit of forgivable indulgence, but short of primping at yon "mirror of prose," as the saying goes.

> One way or another,
> the words
>   just the right ones
> in service
> of a moment's classic
> caught somewhere 'tween
> Chopin's throat and poised, lingering finger.

As in life, though, it all goes on in one way or another. I am halfway into a four-year Indigenous studies Ph.D. at Trent University in Peterborough, Ontario, which will no doubt help in adding to whatever else awaits us down the road.

One constant is what we assume is change, but it may very well be this circle turning just slow enough for our memories to be jogged in a different way, the same deceptive page being turned by mocking hands. The real value, though, is to trust in a traditional format, in this case the Medicine Wheel, which has proven to work for over thirty thousand years and counting.

As for the inner workings, as it were, of my writing, I have never been the kind to overdo anything once it is set down. Perhaps it can be improved in certain technical aspects, but the inner life of any kind of art is what makes it real to another—not the minutia of punctuation, spelling, and the like.

Given all of it, though, *From Bear Rock Mountain* has proven to be something of a self-imposed confinement of its own, years of living with a nightmarish ghostly past, and, worse, learning first-hand its language and ways, following its mysterious light over a thousand haunted sunsets.

> Sentinelled   with spirit homes
> in little trailside clumps
>   until
> the dance.

> Knowing that someday
> hopefully soon
> it'll all just go "poof"
> and live on in some glorious infamy
> we like to call success ...

Which is what it all really is, isn't it? Any worthwhile work of art has to begin with some kind of a challenge, in this case it was setting down my own experiences, a failed attempt at cultural genocide, and making it a part of a broader human experience to give it scope or hope. And then the real measure:

> Coming upon it again
> like the tracks my late grandfather
> Peter Mountain Sr. talked about...
>
> "Those you yourself made
> as a child,
>
> and that will take you
> the rest of the way home."

One other note is that this is in no way a "definitive" statement on residential schools per se, if ever such a thing were possible. Pain is just not measurable that way.

Throughout the hundred-odd years these horrid places operated, there are very likely well over a hundred and fifty thousand personal stories of survival, pain, torture, and outright neglect, with countless additional ones of close relatives and our Indigenous nations in general left to somehow make it through an intentionally oppressive systemic genocide.

Most times what makes all of this at least bearable is knowing that someone out there, at some time in the distant future will go, "Hey, I know what this is about! I'm going through *this*, right now!"

Lord only knows it might even be someone with power to change things for the better, someone who's just lost someone to PTSD.

I've drawn a number of parallels here between Nazi Germany and residential schools, with good reason. One further step along this path began with the birth of ethics as a separate field of study. It was born from the 1947 Nuremberg Trials, which failed to actually convict a just number of truly guilty.

In an unending litany of outright oppression, the single most glaring and telling omission is that though American conquerors saw to looking into the balancing matter of ethics—after threatening foreign countries like Germany and Japan were brought to bear and given their due to rebuild—we, the original citizens of America, are still waiting for our sense of justice. This is long after the damage was done, right here at home on our ancestral Great Turtle Island, well over a century after grisly events like the Massacre at Wounded Knee paved the way for foreign occupation on our ancestral lands!

There really is no question, then, that after all the broken promises and treaties, it's always come down to the land and the power to keep us away from any real say over our own lives.

§§§

The matter of picking up the pieces of the Jewish and Indigenous American Holocausts still remains. And though I have somehow found the strength to revisit my times in residential school, I have yet to summon it yet again to go to the site of Auschwitz itself.

Starting out, and too close to the start, being stripped of all Indigenous dignity. Losing almost everyone close for this kind of a statement . . .

> . . . somehow, eventually
> just satisfied to remain human.

Would it then be that the human heart has no other will than to enjoin itself to return home?

> . . . Standing forth . . . lost
> in that thousand-yard stare
> with just enough

Focusing...
from an unknowable
and mirage
past

§

That distance
with power
over all
in its epochal
ancient
sheltering, shading

great speckled tree
in eternally dappled sun

§§§

I began *From Bear Rock Mountain* with Hercules, brought down in expectations of faith. Like this mightiest of men, we, the once-magnificent Indigenous nations of Great Turtle Island, donned the poisonous cloak of the Americas, the disease-infested blankets of broken treaties, various well-meaning government programs, and yes, even education, in the form of residential schools, only to eventually lose our sense of direction.

And yet, this need to carry on, in the words of my grandfather Peter Mountain Sr.:

Ehseh, grandson, do not ever call yourself strong
for there will come a day
when you will realize just how strong
you really are
when no one comes to visit

to check on you bring meat
call you Segot'ineh, relative.

Only then
will you know
just how strong
you really are.

    I began this book simply wanting to put these words of hidden
strength together for the children of the future—for years of not
being able to do so.

    Until close to Mother Ocean...

        and now, nearing *From Bear Rock Mountain*'s end
in El Paso, Texas
right at the Mexican border
to the very outer edge
of our Dene Dream

with these final thoughts...

We are only human and utter our voices for reconciliation
the more binding version being
the resurgence our First Nations have always been a
part of
like an echoing drum.

§

This future
    insistent
takes less natural effort, really.

Could it be that
the real meaning
of carrying on

a mirrored present
like multi-prismed arrows
cast back
to our starry home

from Bear Rock Mountain.

Impossible
in so many ways
to read . . .

yet, recognizably

HOME.

EPILOGUE

Yamoria's Two Arrows

They pointed to it all along.

An old Dene legend tells of the hero Yamoria, the One Who Walks Across the Universe, shooting two arrows to mark the spot where he slew three harmful giant beaver at Fieh Tehni-ah, Bear Rock Mountain.

Early in July 2012, there was a search for a young woman who had gone missing right at the foot of this historic landmark where the Bear River joins the Duhogah. After some time went by with no sign of Nicole Horassi, age seventeen, people from all over answered a call by our Sahtú MLA, Norman Yekeleya, to search. My cousin Gordon Kelly asked me to go with him, and we set off in his boat, carefully inspecting each and every sign: seagulls gathered on sandbars, any groupings of ravens for the same, backwater eddies, the head of sandbars. We even came across an old bear's carcass held up on some shoreline trees. There is no doubt that every boatload of searchers did exactly the same thing, looking with the practised eyes of born hunters and trappers.

The missing woman's body was finally found about three weeks later and not where it might've been expected, all the way past our hometown of Radelie Koe. Rather, the elders of Tulita were right when they said it wouldn't go far.

The poor teen's remains came back out of the Bear River

almost right at the spot where Yamoria shot his two arrows to mark his legend, to remind us to always strive to simply remain Dene.

> Seems his message is as good today as when the world
> was new
> as if wanting to keep this one young woman close
> in our name . . .
> the underlying message, too,
> undeniable.

Like Hercules in his poisoned cloak, the more we survivors of the residential schools struggled to free ourselves of our fate, that of showing faith to a foreign crown and church, the more we were doomed—our very flesh becoming fatally infected with each move to life!

In a very real way, we will have to recognize Yamoria's vision and practice our own identity as Dene to be granted a future at all.

> For the time being
> our ancestors wanted the young Dene lady
> back to Denendeh, the Land.

> And just maybe
> to remind us, again, of our missing
> and murdered Aboriginal women.

And, as any good story or legend does, this has meaning in a broader, universal sense.

I was having lunch with my friend, Cree Sundance Man, Jimmy Dick.

He told me about how he connected with some kids on suicide watch. "When I started to speak to them in Cree they caught on right away. I asked them what they thought they were doing, trying to kill themselves, when all around there are people fighting for their lives with cancer and all."

It could surely be seen that whatever final return we Indigenous Peoples are eventually granted, despite our stumbling blocks, these kinds of individual walls need hitting.

And as for my own version of *From Bear Rock Mountain*, this began as a life and times story, more or less, but finds itself, as with life, carrying on, with probably quite a number of songs yet unsung.

Through it all, my Navajo Dineh brother Johnson Tochoney probably says it best, when after my tenth ceremony of the Native American Church, four of which he officiated at, he said: "Brother, you are still a very young man!"

This one medicine man's simple and yet unfathomable wisdom also points to the way our paths always have a way of meeting up. Bear Rock Mountain may well have been there right from the time when our first Dene ancestors beheld their majesty, thirty millennia ago. So the idea of each of us reaching back at the very most a hundred years to stay connected to our youth is really not a lot to ask, is it?

> As with one of our main teachings
> the person, Yamoria, did all of it
> like every man of the land would
> as ritual
> CEREMONY
> hunting, killing the evil beaver
> skinning, tacking the hides up, cooking some
> and marking the spot
> at the very centre of Denendeh
> our Dene World

to simply teach us
how to live.

Like every single person born to live out their version of life, mine at first had to do with a certain feeling of dread, which over time began to reveal *hope*. Could be we only go by the trail we either make . . . or want to.

And, for what it's worth, the ultimate meaning, or direction, of the two arrows our cultural hero Yamoria shot into the site at Bear Rock Mountain are yet lodged

. . . deep into our human souls.
And like the one the angel of God used
on a willing Saint Teresa

through unspeakable pain
frees us.

ACKNOWLEDGMENTS

Mahsi to Bruce Valpy from *News/North*

My fellow writers: Kathy Fisher, Richard Van Camp,
Danielle Metcalfe-Chenail

Halifax: Lynn Feasey of Points North, Allison Simmie,
Susan Miller

Ontario: Mary Ann and Kirk Alberga, Nishnawbe Homes, Maggie
Quirt, Philip Cote and Rebecca Baird, Chris Mah, Luke & Lorne
Mountain, Andrew Hammond and Bart H. Krebs

Regina: Kamao Cappo and family

Radelie Koe, Fort Good Hope: Doug Louison, John T'Seleie,
Lucy Jackson, Judy Lafferty, Betty Barnaby, Bill DeYoung,
Yamoga Land Corporation

Southwest: Gary and Mary Sandoval and family, Judge Robert
Walter and Lilly, Johnson and Sarah Tochoney, Marty Borhauer,
Lawrence Curtis, Mary Barnard

Yellowknife: Bob Overvold, NWT Arts Council (and Bolshoi
Yeoman Boris Atamanenko), Denendeh Development
Corporation, Kirby Marshall

Banff Centre for the Arts

Canada Council for the Arts

Truth and Reconciliation Commission of Canada

Yamoga Land Corporation

Firenze, Italia: Andrea and Patrizia Nibbio, Giulia Scarpa

Tori Elliott, publicist, and Taryn Boyd, publisher

Kate Kennedy, Rhonda Kronyk, Warren Layberry,
Mary Metcalfe, and Claire Philipson, editors

Colin Parks, designer

Lucy Ann Yakeleya, for the SheetaoT'ineh Mountain
Dene translations

and countless others, in one way or another . . .

IN MEMORIAM

Nely Atefi

Edwin Kalousuk

GLOSSARY

ahso [grandmother]

ak'et'sech'ih [gravedigger]

Aklavik

Akureh neahnet'ih? [Are you here to visit or do you need something?]

alehlekeh [friends]

alla sho [barges]

alleh [spruce bough floor]

Babah Duweleh [The Able One]

Baghareh goded'zah [Anything extra creates a mess]

becheneh [dogsled]

Behchoko Fort Rae

beleh [wolf]

berreh [country food]

Bilagáana [White Man]

chaleh a racing sled with taller runners and handles for steering

d′se [muskrat]

dahk′o [a warehouse built on stilts]

daleleh [floats]

Dekanawidah [Great Peacemaker]

Déline [Where the Waters Flow] formerly Fort Franklin

Dene [People]

Dene bezieh golih [People with a kind heart]

Dene Bezieh Raseh [Strong Heart Man]

Denendeh [Dene Nation]

Desnedhe Che a traditional caribou crossing near Fort Reliance

Dettah [Burnt Point] near Yellowknife

Dineh Navajo

Dugha Indin place on Mackenzie River below Grandview

Duhogah River Mackenzie River

Duhoyieah gorigudih! [It's more beautiful in the islands!]

edst′ineh [crooked water; the crooked way] bad medicine

ehkoleh [non-interference]

ehseh [grandfather]

Farahezen [Black Rock Rim Around] a fishing camp.

Fieh Tehni-ah [Bear Rock Mountain]

Ga Doeh [Rabbit Island]

gah [Rabbit]

goba [morning light]

gohsheneh [to do things carefully, lovingly, and right the first time]

Gonihtl'ah [Start the fire]

Gwich'in a northern First Nation

Hinmatoowyalahq'it *[Thunder Rolling across the Mountains]*

hogan [traditional Dineh hut]

jawh [left] – dog team command

jee [right] – dog team command

K'afohun Camp [Willow Point] a fishing camp.

k'ats'ah [older willow]

k'ieh [willow]

K'ihnah Hihndareweh [Flies Around]

K'isho T'ineh [Big Willow People]

K'it'seleh T'ineh [Small Willow People]

K'ohoyieh [Under the Clouds] a fishing camp.

Kabami Tue Colville Lake

Kha-ehsoo [Goslings]

Koh Hehdien [Without Fire] an evil giant

kotweh [alcohol]

lebo lat'eh kolee a dish made of yeast, potatoes, and canned fruit

loogoolu [dog bells]

Lutsel K'e [snowdrift] a community on the south shore near the eastern end of Great Slave Lake

Mahsi [Thank you]

mehkoih [brush shelter]

Mola [White people]

Mola Neneh [White man's country]

Mola, k'ehnawh yawh ehkedehshih! [White people throwing each other around!]

muktuk [frozen whale skin and blubber]

Nats'ejee K'eh a treatment centre near Hay River

Ndilo Latham Island, Yellowknife

Nehwehsineh [Creator]

NoCh'o Marie-Adele Mountain's Dene name

Not'sin Nene [The spirit world]

Ohgosho [Big Eddy] a fishing camp

Ohk'ie Fiehk'la [Birds in Rock Crevice] a fishing camp.

Ohndah Dek'ieh Leline [Jackfish Creek]

ondieh [older brother]

Radelie Koe Fort Good Hope

Raidi Sho [big medicine]

rakegot'ineh [close relatives]

Rarei'eh [Wild White bushmen who were lost]

rayuka [northern lights]

Rehinht'lah [wake up]

Sa Ra-ahyile [midnight sun]

Sah Goneh [Bear Arms]

Sah [Bear]

Saho Diyineh [Bear spirit]

Sahtú [Great Bear Lake] – or a region including five communities in the Great Bear Lake region

Sahtúdé [Great Bear River]

Saulteaux a First Nation

se sieh [grandson]

Sedidileh hagoht'elih [not my business]

segot'ineh [relative]

Seh Leh Beyah [My Friend's Son]

Sek'e niyuh [breathe on me]

selaw [brother-in-law]

Selaw Bedew'ih [my brother-in-law's kindling]

Sheetao T'ineh [Mountain Dene]

Sheuyieh [Shares my name]

shingerih [old rotten wood]

sho t'serih [goosedown blanket]

siewh'a' a spitting can for chewing tobacco

Somba K'e [Where the money is] – Yellowknife

somba [money]

Suwehohinleni nest'abareh ehshuhe wohsi [If you don't listen, I will poke your ears with an awl!]

T'seku Dawedah [Woman Sitting Up There]

T'seku Nezhonih *[Good Woman]*

T'selih [Squirrel]

Tahsoh [Raven]

Tashunka Witko *[Crazy Horse]*

Thebacha Fort Smith

ts'iduwe [ancestors]

Tsigoindeh [the Talking Tree]

Tsiigehtchic fishing village north of Radelie Koe where the Arctic Red River meets the Duhogah

Tu Nedhe Great Slave Lake or region around Great Slave Lake

Tulita [Where the Waters Meet]

Wageh [Eagle]

Wakan Tanka [the Great Spirit]

Warih Duhgun [Rafter Poles Taken Down] a fishing camp.

Wasichu [people of European descent]

Wihst'edihdel [a legendary giant]

Wikwemikong near Little Current

Yamoga brother to Yamoria

Yamoria [One Who Walks the Universe] legendary hero, brother to Yamoga

NOTES

[1]   Laurence Rees, *Auschwitz: A New History* (New York: BBC Books, 2005), 204.

[2]   Geoffrey Bould, ed., *Conscience Be My Guide: An Anthology of Prison Writing* (London: Zed Books, 1992), 133.

[3]   Robert Weisbrot, *Freedom Bound: A History of America's Civil Rights Movement* (New York: W. W. Norton & Co. Inc., 1989).

[4]   Tom Holm, *Strong Hearts, Wounded Soldiers: Native American Veterans of the Vietnam War* (Austin, TX: University of Texas Press, 1985), 170.

[5]   John Neihardt, *Black Elk Speaks* (Richmond Hill, ON: Simon and Schuster, 1972), 218.

[6]   CBC News, "Mackenzie Valley pipeline: 37 years of negotiation" December 16, 2010. Accessed March 3, 2019. www.cbc.ca/news/business/mackenzie-valley-pipeline-37-years-of-negotiation-1.902366

[7]   David Kennedy and Lizabeth Cohen. *The American Pageant: A History of the American People, 16th Edition,* (Boston: Wadsworth Publishing/Cengage Learning, 2015).

[8]   Wiley Steve Thornton, *Genocide of the Mind: New Native American Writing,* ed. MariJo Moore, (New York: Nation Books, 2009), 31.

[9]   CBC Radio, "Former prosecutor in Leonard Peltier case calls for the activist's clemency," As It Happens, January 5, 2017. Accessed February 5, 2017. http://www.cbc.ca/radio/asithappens/as-it-happens-thursday-edition-1.3922729/former-prosecutor-in-leonard-peltier-case-calls-for-the-activist-s-clemency-1.3922732

[10]   Democracy Now. "Leonard Peltier Denied Clemency by Obama." January 18, 2017. Accessed February 5, 2017. www.democracynow.org/2017/1/18/breaking_leonard_peltier_denied_clemency_by

[11] Erich Friedrich and Renate Vanegas, *Hitler's Prisoners: Seven Cell Mates Tell Their Stories* (Dulles, VA: Brassey's, 1995), 78.

[12] CBC News "Stephen Harper's comments on missing, murdered aboriginal women show 'lack of respect'" December 19, 2014. Accessed March 10, 2019. https://www.cbc.ca/news/indigenous/ stephen-harper-s-comments-on-missing-murdered-aboriginal-women-show-lack-of-respect-1.2879154

SOURCES

Adams, Douglas. *So Long, and Thanks for All the Fish*. New York: Harmony Books, 1985.

———. *The Hitchhiker's Guide to the Universe*. New York: Harmony Books, 1979.

Alighieri, Dante. *The Divine Comedy (Inferno, Pugatorio, Paradiso)*. New York: Fall River Press, 2008.

Arendt, Hannah. *Eichmann in Jerusalem: A Report on the Banality of Evil*. New York: Penguin Books, 1963.

Atwood, Margaret. *Lady Oracle*. Toronto: McClelland and Stewart, 1976.

Bade, Patrick. *Auguste Renoir*. New York: Parkstone Press, 2003.

Baha'u'llah. *Baha'i Prayers: A Selection of Prayers*. Wilmette, IL: Baha'i Publishing Trust, 1982.

Bainton, Roland. *Here I Stand: The Life of Martin Luther*. New York: Penguin, 1995.

Baehr, Peter, ed. *The Portable Hannah Arendt*. New York: Penguin Books, 2000.

Benton-Banai, Edward. *The Mishomis Book: The Voice of the Ojibway*. Minneapolis, MN: University of Minnesota, 1988.

Bernstein, Carl, and Bob Woodward. *All the President's Men*. New York: Simon & Schuster, 1974.

Bhakivedanta Swami Pirabhupada, A. C. *Bhagavad-Gita*. Los Angeles: The Bhaktivdanta Book Trust, 1972.

Blondin, George. *When the World Was New*. Yellowknife, NT: Outcrop, The Northern Publishers, 1990.

Boorstin, Daniel, J. *The Creators: A History of Heroes of the Imagination*. New York: Vintage Books, 1993.

Bould, Geoffrey, ed. *Conscience Be My Guide: An Anthology of Prison Writing.* London: Zed Books, 1992

Brandes, Georg. *Michelangelo: His Life, His Times, His Era.* New York: Frederick Ungar Publishing, 1963.

Brown, Bern Will. *A Time in the Arctic.* Altona, Manitoba: Friesen Corporation, 2007.

———. *End-of-Earth People.* Toronto: Dundurn Press, 2014.

Brown, Dee. *Bury My Heart at Wounded Knee: An Indian History of the American West.* New York: Henry Holt and Company, 1970.

Bugliosi, Vincent. *Helter Skelter: The True Story of the Manson Murders.* New York: W. W. Norton & Co, 1994.

Burroughs, William. *Naked Lunch.* New York: Grove, 1994.

Capote, Truman. *In Cold Blood.* New York: Vintage, 2012.

Carlson, Richard. *Don't Sweat the Small Stuff ... and It's All Small Stuff.* New York: Hyperion, 1997.

Chaat Smith, Paul, and Robert Allen Warrior. *Like a Hurricane: Indian Movement from Alcatraz to Wounded Knee.* New York: The New Press, 1997.

Chalfant, William Y. *Cheyennes and Horse Soldiers: The 1857 Expedition and the Battle of Solomon's Fork.* Norman, OK: U of Oklahoma Press, 1989.

Chicago, July. *Holocaust Project: From Darkness to Light.* New York: Penguin, 1993.

Clark, Robert A., ed. *The Killing of Crazy Horse.* Lincoln, NE: University of Nebraska Press, 1976.

Cleaver, Eldridge. *Soul on Ice.* New York: Delta, 1968.

Cliche, Guylaine, and the Mohawk Traditional Council of Kahnawake. *Words of Peace in Native Land: Mohawk Culture, Values and Traditions.* Juniper Publishing, 2016

Clinton, Hillary. *Living History.* New York: Scribner, 2003.

Cogan, Jim, and William Clark. *Temples of Sound.* San Francisco, CA: Chronicle Books, 2003.

Cozzens, Peter. *The Earth is Weeping: The Epic Story of the Indian Wars for the American West*. New York: Vintage Books, 2017.

Cross, Charles R. *Room Full of Mirrors: A Biography of Jimi Hendrix*. New York: Hyperion, 2005.

D'Epiro, Peter, and Desmond Pinkowish. Sprezzatura: *50 Ways Italian Genius Shaped the World*. New York: Anchor Books, 2001.

Deloria Jr.,Vine. *Custer Died for Your Sins*. Norman, OK: U of Oklahoma Press, 1988.

Dixon, Andrew Abraham. *Michelangelo and the Sistine Chapel*. New York: MIF Books, 2009.

Dostoyevsky, Fyodor. *The House of the Dead*. Hertfordshire, UK: Wordsworth Editions, 2010.

Draper, Jason. *Prince: Chaos, Disorder, and Revolution*. New York: Backbeat Books, 2011.

Eisen, Max. By Chance *Alone: A Remarkable True Story of Courage and Survival at Auschwitz*. Toronto: HarperCollins, 2016.

Effeny, Alison. *Cassatt*. New York: Portland House, 1991.

Eigendbrod, Renate. T*raveling Knowledges; Positioning the Im/Migrant Reader of Aboriginal Literatures in Canada*. Winnipeg, Manitoba: University of Manitoba Press, 2005.

Fanon, Franz. *The Wretched of the Earth*. New York: Grove Press, 1963.

Frankl, Viktor E. *Man's Search for Meaning*. Boston: Beacon Press, 1959.

Freire, Paulo. *Pedagogy of the Oppressed*. New York: Continuum International Publishing, 1970.

Friedrich, Erich, and Renate Vanegas. *Hitler's Prisoners: Seven Cell Mates Tell Their Stories*. Dulles, VA: Brassey's, 1995.

Fritzsche, Peter. *Germans into Nazis*. Cambridge, MA: Harvard U Press, 1998.

Fumoleau, Rene. *As Long as This Land Shall Last: A History of Treaty 8 and 11, 1870–1939*. Toronto: McClelland and Stewart, 1973.

———. *Denendeh, A Celebration*. Toronto: McClelland and Stewart, 1984

——. *Way Down North: Dene Life – Dene Land*. Toronto: Novalis Publishing, 2010.

Gabankova, Maria. *Body broken, body redeemed*. Carlisle, UK: Piquant Editions, 2007.

Gayford, Martin. *Michelangelo: His Epic Life*. London: The Penguin Group, 2013.

Gilpin, Laura. *The Enduring Navajo*. Austin, TX: University of Texas Press, 1968.

Goldhagen, Daniel Jonah. *Hitler's Willing Executioners: Ordinary Germans and the Holocaust*. New York: Vintage Books, 1996.

Gordon, Robert, and Andrew Forge. *Monet*. New York: Abragale Press, 1983.

Gorman, Zonnie. *Growing Up with Heroes: The Code Talkers of World War II, a Daughter's Journey*. https://growingupwithheroes.com/.

Grandin College Yearbook. Fort Smith, NT, 1969.

Gregory, Dick. *Nigger: An Autobiography*. New York: Pocket Books, 1964.

Grinnel, George. *Blackfoot Lodge Tales: The Story of a Prairie People*. Lincoln, NE: Bison Books, 1962.

Hagan, William T. *Quanah Parker: Comanche Chief*. Norman, OK: University of Oklahoma Press, 1993.

Hale, Robert Beverly. *Drawing Lessons from the Great Masters*. New York: Watson-Guptill Publications, 1964.

Hart, Frederick. *Michelangelo*. New York: Harry N. Abrams, 1964.

Hammacher, A.M. *Vincent van Gogh: Genius and Disaster*. New York: Abradale Press/Harry N. Abrams, 1968.

Harry N. Abrams. *Renoir*. New York: Harry N. Abrams Publishers, 1985.

Hausman, Gerald. *Tunkashila: From the Birth of Turtle Island to the Blood of Wounded Knee*. New York: St. Martin's Press, 1993.

Heller, Joseph. *Catch-22*. New York: Simon & Schuster, 1961.

Helm, June. *The People of Denendeh*. Iowa City, IA: University of Iowa Press, 2000.

Herman, Judith. *Trauma and Recovery: The Aftermath of Violence – From Domestic Abuse to Political Terror.* New York: Basic Books, 1992.

Hesse, Hermann. *Siddhartha.* New York: MJF Books, 1951.

———. *The Glass Bead Game.* New York: Picador, 2002.

Hibbert, Christopher. *Florence: The Biography of a City.* New York: Penguin Books, 1993.

Hill, Dick, and Bart Kreps. *Inuvik in Pictures: 1958–2008.* Victoria, BC: Trafford Publishing, 2008.

Hill, Dick. *Inuvik: A History 1958–2008.* Victoria, BC: Trafford Publishing, 2008.

Hittman, Michael L. *Wovoka and the Ghost Dance.* Lincoln, NE: University of Nebraska Press, 1990.

Holm, Tom. *Strong Hearts, Wounded Soldiers: Native American Veterans of the Vietnam War.* Austin, TX: University of Texas Press, 1985.

Homer. *The Iliad.* Translated by Robert Fagles. New York: Penguin Books, 1990.

———. *The Odyssey.* Translated by Robert Fagles. New York: Penguin Books, 1996.

Hoss, Rudolph. *Death Dealer: The Memoirs of the SS Kommandant at Auschwitz.* New York: Da Capo Press, 1996.

House, Adrian. *Francis of Assisi: A Revolutionary Life.* Mahwah, NJ: Paulist Press, 2000.

Hurcomb, Fran. *Old Town: A Photographic Journey Through Yellowknife's Defining Neighbourhood.* Yellowknife, NT: Old Town Press, 2012.

Hunt, Irmgard A. *On Hitler's Mountain: Overcoming the Legacy of a Nazi Childhood.* New York: Harper Perennial, 2005.

Jenish, D'Arcy. *Indian Fall: The Last Great Days of the Plains Cree and the Blackfoot Confederacy.* Toronto: Penguin Books, 2000.

Jestaz, Bertrand. *Art of the Renaissance.* New York: Harry N. Abrams, 1984.

Johnson, Basil. *Ojibway Heritage.* Toronto: Emblem/McClelland & Stewart, 1976.

Kawano, Kenji. *Warriors: Navajo Code Talkers.* Flagstaff, AZ: Northland, 1990.

Kendall, Richard, ed. *Degas by Himself: Drawings, Prints, Paintings, Writings.* London: Macdonald & Co., 1987.

Kesey, Ken. *One Flew Over the Cuckoo's Nest.* New York: Signet, 1963.

Kidd, Bruce. *Tom Longboat.* Markham, ON: Fitzhenry & Whiteside, 2004.

King, Ross. *Michelangelo & the Pope's Ceiling.* New York: Walker & Company, 2003.

Kingsley, Bray M. *Crazy Horse.* Norman, OK: U of Oklahoma Press, 2006.

Kolson, Bren. *Myth of the Barrens.* Stony Plain, AB: Eschia Books, 2009.

Kovach, Margaret. *Indigenous Methodologies.* Toronto: University of Toronto Press, 2009.

Kresh, Shepard, III. "The Death of Barbue, a Kutchin Trading Chief." Arctic 35, no. 3 (September 1962) 429–437.

Krystof, Doris. *Modigliani.* Los Angeles: Taschen, 2006.

Kulchyski, Peter, Don McCaskill, and David Newhouse. *In the Words of Elders: Aboriginal Cultures in Transition.* Toronto: University of Toronto Press, 1999.

Lambert, Gilles. *Caravaggio (1517–1610): A Genius Beyond His Time.* Cologne, Germany: Taschen, 2007.

Lanzmann, Claude, dir. *Shoah.* 1985; IFC Films, 2010. DVD.

Laugrand, Frederic B., and Jarich G. Oosten. *Inuit Shamanism and Christianity: Transitions and Transformations in the Twentieth Century.* Montreal: McGill-Queen's University Press, 2010.

Lawrence, D.H. *Three Novels: Lady Chatterley's Lover; The Rainbow; Sons and Lovers.* New York: Barnes & Noble, 1993.

LeBor, A., and R. Boyes. *Seduced by Hitler: The Choices of a Nation and the Ethics of Survival.* Naperville, IL: Sourcebooks, 2000.

Legat, Alice. *Walking the Land, Feeding the Fire: Knowledge and Stewardship Among the Tlicho Dene.* Tucson, AZ: University of Arizona Press, 2012.

Levi, Primo. *The Drowned and the Saved.* New York: First Vintage International, 1988.

Lozzi Roma. *Rome its Origins to the Present Time*. Rome: Edizioni Lozzi Roma S. A. S., 2001.

Mailer, Norman. *The Executioner's Song*. New York: Little Brown & Co., 1979.

———. *Genius and Lust: Journey Through the Major Writings of Henry Miller*. New York: Grove Press, 1976.

Mails, Thomas E. *The Mystic Warriors of the Plains: The Culture, Arts, Crafts and Religion of the Plains Indians*. New York: Mallard Press, 1972.

Manson, Charles. *The Life and Times of Charles Manson*. New York: Simon & Schuster Paperbacks, 2013.

Manzione, Joseph. *I Am Looking to the North for My Life: Sitting Bull, 1876–1881*. Salt Lake City, UT: University of Utah Press, 1991.

Marquez, Gabriel Garcia. *Love in the Time of Cholera*. New York: Penguin Books, 1988.

———. *Of Love and Other Dreams*. New York: Penguin Books, 1994.

Massie, Robert K. *Nicholas and Alexandra: The Classic Account of the Fall of the Romanov Dynasty*. New York: Random House, 1967.

Mason, Nick. *Inside Out: A Personal History of Pink Floyd*. San Francisco: Chronicle Books, 2004.

Mathiessen, Peter. *In the Spirit of Crazy Horse*. New York: Penguin Group, 1983.

Matson, William B. *Crazy Horse: The Lakota Warrior's Life & Legacy*. Layton, UT: Gibbs-Smith, 2016.

Maysles, Albert and David, and Charlotte Zwerin, Dir. *Gimme Shelter*. 1970. Maysles Films.

McClain, Sally. *Navajo Weapon: The Navajo Code Talkers*. Tucson, AZ: Rio Nuevo Publishers, 1981.

McKeen, William. *Outlaw Journalist: The Life and Times of Hunter S. Thompson*. New York: W. W. Norton & Co., 2009.

Meili, Dianne. *Those Who Know: Profiles of Alberta's Aboriginal Elders*. Edmonton, AB: NeWest Press, 2012.

Metcalfe-Chenail, Danielle, ed. *In This Together: Fifteen Stories of Truth and Reconciliation*. Victoria, BC: Brindle & Glass Publishing, 2016.

Miller, Henry. *Tropic of Cancer*. New York: Grove Press, 1961.

Miller, J.R. *Shingwauk's Vision: A History of Native Residential Schools*. Toronto: University of Toronto Press, 1997.

Momaday, N. Scott. *House Made of Dawn*. New York: Harper Perennial, 1968.

———. *The Man Made of Words*. New York: St. Martin's Press, 1997.

Monti, Raffaele. *Michelangelo Buonarroti*. Firenze, Italia: Ministero per I Beni e le Attivia Culturali, 2000.

———. *Michelangelo Buonarotti, Readings and Itineraries*. Firenze, Italia: Sillabe, 2000

Montour, Patricia A., and Patricia D. McGuire. *First Voices: An Aboriginal Women's Reader*. Toronto: Inanna Publications, 2009.

Mooney, James. *The Ghost-Dance Religion and the Sioux Outbreak of 1890*. Chicago: University of Chicago Press, 1965.

Moorehead, Caroline. *A Train in Winter: An Extraordinary Story of Women, Friendship and Survival in Occupied France*. Toronto: Vintage Canada, 2012.

Moore, MariJo, ed. *Genocide of the Mind: New Native American Writing*. New York: Nation Books, 2003.

Moynahan, Brian. *Rasputin: The Saint Who Sinned*. New York: Random House, 1997.

Myles, Douglas. *Rasputin: Satyr, Saint, or Satan*. New York: McGraw-Hill Publishing, 1990.

Naifen, Steven, and Gregory White Smith. *Van Gogh: The Life*. New York: Random House, 2011.

Neeley, Bill. *The Last Comanche Chief: The Life and Times of Quanah Parker*. Washington, DC: John Wiley and Sons, 1995.

Neihardt, John. *Black Elk Speaks*. Richmond Hill, ON: Simon and Schuster, 1972.

Nez, Chester. *Code Talker: The First and Only Memoir by One of the Original Navajo Code Talkers in WWII*. New York: Berkley Books, 2011.

North, Dick. *The Mad Trapper of Rat River*. Guilford, CT: Lyons Press, 2003

Obamsawin, Alanis, dir. *Kanehsatake: 270 Years of Resistance*. National Film Board of Canada, 1993.

Oswald, Russell G. *Attica – My Story*. New York: Doubleday, 1972.

Pasternak, Judy. *Yellow Dirt: A Poisoned Land and the Betrayal of the Navajos*. New York: Free Press, 2011.

Peltier, Leonard. *Prison Writings: My Life Is My Sundance*. New York: St Martin's Griffon, 2000.

Philbrick, Nathaniel. *The Last Stand: Custer, Sitting Bull and the Battle of the Little Bighorn*. New York: Penguin Books, 2010.

Ponting, Rick. *Arduous Journey: Canadian Indians and Decolonization*. Toronto: McClelland and Stewart, 1986.

Powell, Peter, J. *Sweet Medicine: The Continuing Role of the Sacred Arrows, the Sun Dance, and the Sacred Buffalo Hat in Northern Cheyenne History*. Norman, OK: University of Oklahoma Press, 1969.

Powers, Thomas. *The Killing of Crazy Horse*. New York: Vintage Books, 2010.

Raffan, James. *Circling the Midnight Sun: Culture and Change in the Invisible Arctic*. Toronto: HarperCollins, 2014.

Rees, Laurence. *Auschwitz: A New History*. New York: BBC Books, 2005.

——. *Auschwitz: Inside the Nazi State*. New York: BBC Books, 2005.

Reitlinger, Gerald. *The Final Solution: The Attempt to Exterminate the Jews of Europe, 1939–1945*. Lanham, MD: Jason Aronson, 1987.

Rittner, Carol, and John K. Roth, eds. *Different Voices: Women and the Holocaust*. New York: Paragon House, 1991.

Rosenbaum, Ron. *Explaining Hitler: The Search for the Origins of His Evil*. New York: Random House, 1998.

Ross, Rupert. *Dancing with a Ghost: Exploring Aboriginal Reality*. Toronto: Penguin Canada, 1992.

Rudd, Mark. *My Life with the SDS and the Weathermen*. New York: William Morrow, 1973.

Rutherfurd, Edward. *Russka: The Novel of Russia*. New York: Ballantine Books, 1991.

Sainte-Marie, Buffy. "The Big Ones Get Away," *Coincidence and Other Likely Stories*. EMI, 1992.

Salinger, J. D. *Franny and Zooey*. Boston: Little Brown Books, 1955.

——. *The Catcher in the Rye*. Boston: Little Brown Books, 1991.

Savishinsky, Joel S. *The Trail of the Hare*. Yverdon, Switzerland: Gordon and Breach Science Publishers, 1974.

Scribner, Charles, III. *Bernini*. New York: Harry N. Abrams, 1991.

Selleck, Lee, and Francis Thompson. *Dying for Gold: The True Story of the Giant Mine Murders*. New York: HarperCollins, 1997.

Seuss, Dr. *The 500 Hats of Bartholomew Cubbins*. New York: Vanguard Press, 1938.

Shakespeare, William. *Hamlet*. New York: The University Society, 1901.

——. *King Lear*. New York: NAL Penguin, 1963.

——. *Macbeth: Coles Notes*. Toronto: Coles Publishing, 2003.

——. *Romeo and Juliet: Coles Notes*. Toronto: Coles Publishing, 2000.

——. *Twelfth Night: Coles Notes*. Toronto: Coles Publishing, 2000.

Shkilnyk, Anastasia. *A Poison Stronger Than Love*. New Haven, CT: Yale University Press, 1985

Siegel, Bill, and Sam Green, dir. *The Weather Underground*. New Video Group, 2003, DVD.

Simon & Garfunkel. "So Long, Frank Lloyd-Wright," by Paul Simon, *Bridge Over Troubled Water*, Columbia Records, 1970.

Sites, Kevin. *The Things They Cannot Say: Stories Soldiers Won't Tell You About What They've Seen, Done or Failed to Do in War*. New York: Harper/Perennial, 2013.

Smith, Linda Tuhiwai. *Decolonizing Methodologies: Research and Indigenous Peoples*. London: Zed Books, 1999.

Solzhenitsyn, Aleksandr. *In the First Circle*. New York: Harper/Perennial, 2009.

Steltenkamp, Michael F. *Nicholas Black Elk: Medicine Man, Missionary, Mystic*. Norman, OK: University of Oklahoma Press, 2009.

Stern, J. P. *Hitler: The Führer and the People*. Los Angeles: University of California Press, 1992

Stewart, Omer C. *The Peyote Religion*. Norman, OK: University of Oklahoma Press, 1908.

Stock, Dennis, and Lawrence Cunningham. *Saint Francis of Assisi*. New York: Harper & Row, 1981.

Storm, Hyemeyohsts. *Seven Arrows*. New York: Ballantine Books, 1972.

Thompson, Hunter S. *Fear and Loathing in Las Vegas*. New York: Vintage, 1971.

——. *Fear and Loathing on the Campaign Trail, '72*. New York: Simon and Schuster, 1972.

——. *The Curse of Lono*, New York: Bantam Books, 1983.

Tohe, Laura. *Code Talker Stories*. Tucson, AZ: Rio Nuevo Publishers, 2012.

Tolkien, J. R. R. *The Hobbit*. London: George Allen & Unwin, 1937

——. *The Fellowship of the Ring*. London: George Allen & Unwin, 1954.

——. *The Two Towers*. London: George Allen & Unwin, 1954.

——. *The Return of the King*. London: George Allen & Unwin, 1955.

Torczyner, Harry. *Magritte: The True Art of Painting*. New York: Abradale/Harry N. Abrams, 1979.

Underhill, Ruth M. *The Navajos*. Norman, OK: University of Oklahoma Press, 1956

Usher, Peter. Fur *Trading Posts of the Northwest Territories, 1870–1970*. Ottawa: Northern Science Research Group (Department of Northern Affairs & Northern Development), 1971.

Waite, Robert L. *The Psychopathic God*. New York: Da Capo Press, 1977.

Warren, Louis S. *God's Red Son: The Ghost Dance Religion and the Making of Modern America*. New York: Basic Books, 2017.

Weisbrot, Robert. *Freedom Bound: A History of America's Civil Rights Movement*. New York: W. W. Norton & Co., 1990.

Well, Stanley, and Gary Taylor, eds. *The Oxford Shakespeare, the Complete Works*. Oxford: Oxford University Press, 1988.

Weltfish, Gene. *The Lost Universe*. New York: Basic Books, 1965.

Williamson, Ray A. *Living the Sky: The Cosmos of the American Indian*. Boston: Houghton Mifflin Company, 1984.

Wilson, Shawn. *Research is Ceremony: Indigenous Research Methods*. Black Point, NS: Fernwood Press, 2008.

Wittkower, Rudolph. *Bernini: The Sculptor of the Roman Baroque*. New York: Phaidon Press, 1955.

Wolochatiuk, Tim, dir. Jonestown: *Paradise Lost*. Film Afrika World Wide. DVD. 2007.

X, Malcolm, and Alex Haley. *The Autobiography of Malcolm X*. New York: Grove Press, 1965.

Yarmolinsky, Avrahm. *The Portable Chekhov*. New York: The Viking Press, 1947.

Yogananda, Paramahansa. *Autobiography of a Yogi*. New York: The Philosophical Library, 1946.

Zappa, Frank, with Peter Occhiogrosso. *The Real Frank Zappa Book*. New York: Simon & Schuster, 1989.